"Sooner or later, every successful business realizes that customer experience is the experience that really matters. Brad's book lays out the road map for any leader who wants to make a difference for the customers they serve."
Seth Godin, author of *This Is Marketing*

"Brad's new book is perfect for new leaders as well as veterans who want to be sure they're current on best practices. The book is an easy read and provides tons of new ideas for packaging and delivering the Voice of the Customer upward, and the nature of the customer's needs and journey to the front line. I came away with five new ideas I can apply with my clients tomorrow."
John Goodman, author of *Customer Experience 3.0*

"I will use *Leading the Customer Experience* as a textbook for my teams by assigning reading, crafting study questions, then facilitating discussions on the assignments. It will allow us to further our goals of improving knowledge, enhancing the team dynamics and finding actionable strategies to incorporate into our business practices. The book is a low-cost, high-yield, must-have addition to any customer experience professional's library."
Debra Bentson, Senior Workforce Management Manager, Kaiser Permanente

"There are many books about the customer experience, but few as good as this one. Written by an accomplished practitioner with a depth of expertise, you'll learn everything you need to lead the customer experience if you read it and apply the lessons. Highly recommended."
Mark Sanborn, President, Sanborn & Associates, Inc.; author of *The Fred Factor* and *You Don't Need a Title to Be a Leader*

"*Leading the Customer Experience* is exactly what it says it is—a book designed for leaders focused on their companies' customer experience. If you're trying to figure out how to get your own company's CX efforts under way and operating on all cylinders, you'll find this book to be a very practical, organized and helpful tool. Use it!"
Don Peppers, author of *Customer Experience: What, How and Why Now*

"Brad is an industry expert and amazing at breaking down the keys to successful customer engagement, retention and expansion. He establishes a clear pathway towards effective customer experience that can be exercised at every stage of a company's maturation."
Hasan Ali, Founder and CEO, Air Tutors

"In this new book, Brad Cleveland provides insightful and powerful knowledge in a very clear format. I recommend it for students and experienced professionals."
Professor KJ Cheong, Chairman, CIRC, Korea

"Our city is going through an explosive growth period as many people look for the small town, outdoor recreational experience. It could be easy to lose focus on our customers: our citizens, visitors and business owners. Brad's book comes just in time to reemphasize our dedication to the customer experience. It will be a valuable tool in thinking about and implementing our strategic planning, our organizational structure and our continual evaluation of success."
Peter Hendricks, Mayor, Sun Valley, Idaho

"Brad's book is the work of an experienced and trusted consultant who clearly knows how to explore the many facets of customer experience. I enjoyed the case studies and many key recommendations in this well-crafted instructional manual accessible to all levels of professionals. The structure of ideas and approach of implementation are creating a thread of continuity that keeps you focused on strategic CX objectives. It's also a great source of immediate takeaways."
Pierre Marc Jasmin, MBA, Co-founder, Services Triad;
Board, SOCAP Canada Chapter

"Brad applied his vast, multi-industry experience and expertise to the intimately connected and burgeoning realm of customer experience. Today, the stakes for any company looking to survive, compete and grow in an ever-increasing customer expectations environment are higher than ever. By devouring and applying the concepts, strategies and tactics meticulously outlined in *Leading the Customer Experience*, CX leaders have a fighting chance of coming out on top."
Dominick J Keenaghan, President, INSIGHTS Middle East, Dubai

Leading the Customer Experience

How to Chart a Course and Deliver Outstanding Results

Brad Cleveland

KoganPage

First published in Great Britain and the United States in 2021 by Kogan Page Limited

2nd Floor, 45 Gee Street
London
EC1V 3RS
United Kingdom
www.koganpage.com

122 W 27th St, 10th Floor
New York, NY 10001
USA

4737/23 Ansari Road
Daryaganj
New Delhi 110002
India

Kogan Page books are printed on paper from sustainable forests.

ISBNs

Hardback   978 1 78966 689 2
Paperback   978 1 78966 687 8
Ebook   978 1 78966 688 5

Library of Congress Control Number

2021933819

British Library Cataloguing-in-Publication Data

A CIP record for this book is available from the British Library.

Typeset by Integra Software Services, Pondicherry
Print production managed by Jellyfish
Printed and bound by CPI Group (UK) Ltd, Croydon CR0 4YY

To my mom, Annie Cleveland

CONTENTS

08 Unleashing product and service innovation 169

PART FIVE
Build on the momentum

09 Rallying support for investments 191

10 Going from strength to strength 217

ABOUT THE AUTHOR

Brad Cleveland is known globally for his expertise in customer strategy and management. He has worked across 45 states and in 60 countries, and has appeared in media ranging from *The New York Times* to *The Washington Post* and NPR's *All Things Considered*. Brad's books and courses have been translated into twelve languages; he is also an instructor for LinkedIn Learning, with courses on customer management, strategy and leadership.

The organizations Brad has worked with include service leaders such as American Express, Apple, USAA, the University of California, and others. He has consulted or led workshops in over 70 percent of the companies with the top net promoter score (NPS) in their respective industries. Brad has also worked with the federal governments of Australia, Canada, and the United States.

Brad was founding partner and former CEO of the International Customer Management Institute, now part of London-based Informa plc. Today, he is a sought-after consultant and speaker.

He and his wife Kirsten have a grown daughter, Grace. They divide their time between Sun Valley, Idaho and San Diego, California.

To reach Brad:

Email: info@bradcleveland.com
Twitter: @bradcleveland
Website: www.bradcleveland.com
Blog: www.bradcleveland.com/blog
Office: +1-410-864-0212

FOREWORD

Finally!

Previously, those of us who are passionate practitioners of the customer experience had to choose between two types of books on our favorite subject.

As you probably know, one typically features folksy, anecdotal stories about the difference that CX can make to a business and its teams. The others are research-based tomes that attempt, through the prodigious use of statistics, to quantify the value that organizations acquire from investing in CX.

There's absolutely nothing wrong with either approach (in fact, I'm guilty of writing a few of the former… and I love digging into the gravity of the latter). However—until now—it was my opinion that no book captured both sides of the important impact an organization can realize by creating and delivering an extraordinary customer experience.

The anecdotal books are easily critiqued for not proving their case with enough evidence required for organizational investment and commitment. The other books frequently aren't presented in a manner that is accessible—and therefore applicable—to the busy executive or frontline manager.

Why do I say "finally"?

Because what Brad Cleveland has done is to deliver an engaging narrative based upon the exceptional depth of his own remarkable experiences. Plus, he reveals important research that provides the statistical verification required to prove his assertions on the customer experience. And he does so with a warm, engaging style that is easy to understand—combined with a detailed, step-by-step plan that every leader can execute to gain a competitive advantage through extraordinary customer experiences.

This is not just a book on the customer experience. It's also akin to a "user's manual" on how you can enhance the lifetime value of your customers while you expand the number of referrals your current customers provide. You'll want to read this book now. And I will wager you will pull it off the shelf and refer to it frequently as you execute your CX strategy.

Many years ago—before establishing my career as an author, speaker, and consultant on customer experiences—I was a globally syndicated movie reviewer seen on television stations around the world. Occasionally, but very rarely, I would announce that a film was a "must see." I would emphasize that anyone and everyone who liked movies should buy a ticket and view the film.

Now, I'm making a similar recommendation about Brad Cleveland's book. It is, quite simply, a "must read." Anyone and everyone in business who wants to curate customer loyalty and enlarge their earnings through the customer experience should read and apply what you are about to consume.

Scott McKain
CEO, The Distinction Institute
Author, *The Ultimate Customer Experience*®

ACKNOWLEDGEMENTS

So many have made this book possible. I am grateful beyond what words can adequately convey. (If I left anyone out, it is inadvertent and on me.)

Kathe Sweeney, Executive Editor at Kogan Page (the publisher), invited me to write this book and has been an inspiration from the start; our early conversation is recounted in the introduction. Eric Beckman, who produced the graphics, has an amazing eye for clean, effective design. David Levy, Nancy Wallace, Maria Canfield, Heather Wood, and my longtime colleague Debbie Harne all had a part in editing and proofing.

Nate Brown, an upcoming star and one of the brightest lights in customer experience, had enormous influence on the book. He's the friend I mention in Chapter 9 who owes me lunch at Jersey Mike's—but I owe him so much more for his insight and contributions. Rebecca Gibson, too, provided significant input; I've worked with Rebecca for years and she's helped us get across a lot of finish lines—always with better results than would have otherwise been possible.

I'm grateful to Kristen and Bob Allen, Jamie Baker, Matt Beckwith, Lori Bocklund, Laura Grimes, Jay Minnucci, Justin Robbins, Jeff Toister, and Alan Weiss, who each made important contributions. A special thank you to Lori for her feedback on one of the examples—I'm wiser for our discussion. Dave Whorton, an extraordinary leader and friend, reviewed an early draft. Micah Solomon, whose work in customer experience has been an inspiration for years, also provided encouragement. Lorey Pro graciously agreed to me telling the story that introduces Chapter 5. Scott Milrad, Content Manager at LinkedIn Learning, continues to open doors for me to deliver these principles to a worldwide audience as a LinkedIn Learning instructor.

Scott McKain, who wrote the foreword, has helped me become a better writer, speaker, consultant, and person. He reviewed every chapter, offering helpful comments along the way. I'm grateful to call him a friend.

I am so thankful for all who reviewed the pre-release copy and provided comments. I was intentional in who I asked—each has made an impact on me and my career. In alphabetical order:

Hasan Ali, Founder and CEO of Air Tutors, has built an incredible organization dedicated to helping students of all ages succeed.

Dr. Debra Bentson is a standout example in how she involves her team in learning and applying key principles.

Jeanne Bliss is a true pioneer in the customer experience profession; all (certainly including me) who seek her advice are wiser for it.

KJ Cheong is a friend, respected professor, and leader in Korea and far beyond.

Blair Clark, President of Canyon Bicycles USA, is leading the firm to hypergrowth in a crowded market because he knows and lives these principles.

Matt Clarke is one of the extraordinarily committed leaders who is driving customer-focused change within the government of Australia.

Jenny Dempsey's passion for all things customer experience is an inspiration to me and to so many.

Tara Gibb heads the International Customer Management Institute, ICMI (a company I helped establish), and it's a such a privilege to continue to work with her and ICMI's inspiring community.

Seth Godin has had enormous influence on me; I've benefited from his work for years and am honored to have his comments.

John Goodman is a friend and fellow author who provides advice that is wise and grounded.

Peter Hendricks is the mayor everyone deserves; he listens, cares and gets things done—a good combo for the city that is home to America's #1-rated ski resort (*SKI Magazine*, 2020).

Pierre Marc Jasmin is a charismatic leader who's positively influenced so many in our profession.

Dominick Keenaghan has led the way in the Middle East for years, and it's a privilege working with him.

Robert Pasin, CEO of Radio Flyer (the company that makes the iconic red wagons we all grew up with, and so much more), is one of the most caring and visionary leaders I know.

Don Peppers helped launch the CRM movement, and his work continues to be a guiding light; he's had influence on me throughout my career.

Mark Sanborn is the most inspirational author and speaker on leadership I know; I am so grateful for his input.

Anna Toikka and Odd Magnus Barstad are leaders with If, the insurance company that is leading the way in the Nordics through one of the most engaging, positive cultures I've seen.

Jeff Toister is a gifted speaker and author; he's also a friend who's provided indispensable advice to me over the years.

Three friends and I, who go back to childhood, try to get together at least once per year. Mike Farrell, Mike Mellenthin and Randy Mills saw a very early version of Chapter 1. I knew they'd call it like they saw it; I'm grateful for their encouragement, positive feedback, and enduring friendship.

Thank you, to my parents for their love and encouragement. My dad, Doug, was instrumental in kindling my interest in communications—the foundation of this book and my career. My mom, Annie, is an incredible mother—kind, gentle and wise. This book is dedicated to her. (For background, see Chapter 8.)

And finally, I am so grateful for my wife, Kirsten, and our daughter, Grace (now 18). Backstory: I read the draft version of this book to them on a road trip. Every word. Ten hours of reading. I sat in the back seat and read out loud, while Kirsten or Grace drove. They had helpful suggestions on clarity, spice, and usability; their overall assessment (and they are no pushovers): "It's great!" Whatever this book's eventual impact, however it might be received, that was the feedback that mattered to me most.

Introduction

There's the old expression that one started their career "on the ground floor." My career began *underneath* the ground floor. It's a perspective for which I remain grateful.

Let me explain...

In college, I got my first real job, part-time at a company that provided telecommunications and computer systems. As the lowest-ranking employee, I was tasked with installing communications cable. This meant inching my way through cramped, dusty crawl spaces. Greeted by the pitter-patter of small creatures just out of flashlight range, I squeezed past hot utility pipes, face-first into spider webs and other assorted debris.

It was dirty, hard work. I would occasionally get "coached" (which took the form of yelling and expletives) through lapses in quality. Install or secure a cable the wrong way (too close to utility pipes, loose connections, etc.) and it could fail months or years later. The message I heard through the swearing: the work I was doing *really mattered*.

It wasn't long before I was trusted with customer-facing duties, such as installing computer and phone terminals in offices and helping customers understand the basics of making calls or sending messages. On those days, I wore collared shirts and was coached to smile. "Your enthusiasm will help put them at ease, even get them excited about using the new system," one senior installer instructed. "And get rid of those fingerprints on that screen—I don't want to see even a hint of a smudge."

Some years after I had moved on, this company—top of the market for many years—was absorbed by a larger firm and eventually went out of business. As I understand it, the parent company produced glitchy products that distributors, including the one I'd worked for, never quite recovered from.

And that was another lesson learned about customer experience—yes, the products matter too.

In the three decades since, I've been in positions ranging from entry-level to CEO. I've found myself on both sides of the desk—as a consultant entrusted to advise leaders in other organizations, and as the leader ultimately responsible for the performance of organizations I've led. I've held leadership roles through global crises and in prosperous years, and have felt the weight of decisions that would impact employees, customers, business partners, and my own career.

In those early days spent crawling through tight spaces, I hoped to someday work my way up to the ground floor. I couldn't have fathomed then that my career would take me to 45 states and more than 60 countries (plus another five or so by Zoom). Nor did I foresee working with over 70 percent of the companies that, as of this writing, have the top net promoter score (NPS) in their industries. I walked through the doors that opened. I'm grateful for these experiences and the opportunities to learn so much from so many along the way.

With every year and experience, I realize how vitally important it is to make rapid learning a way of doing business. I've seen firsthand how various organizations are responding to challenges, opportunities, and evolving customer needs. I've noticed an unmistakable trait in the most effective leaders—humility. They know they don't have a perfect read on the future. They realize there are things they just don't know, and they listen actively and intently. They listen to customers, employees, peers, advisors, and their intuition. They are always seeking, always learning.

There's more change happening now than I've ever seen before, in virtually every part of the world and within almost every organization. Developments in artificial intelligence, data analytics, mobile technology, social connectivity, and others are ushering in rapid changes in products, services, and customer expectations. Customer needs and perspectives evolve by the day. As the Covid-19 crisis reminded us, anyone who is certain they know what is going to happen next month or next year is probably fooling themselves. And yet, as leaders, we have to anticipate and prepare for what's coming—we have to look ahead. We need an approach to leadership that is based on principles that work, come what may.

I'm writing this book because there's never been a greater need for a focus on customer experience. As we continue to work through unprecedented economic turbulence, there's never before been a time when it's more important for our efforts to bear fruit. Customer experience must be inviting and inclusive. It has to be based on principles that work, not cookie-cutter prescriptions that too often fail. And it has to work for your organization, your customers, your unique brand. It is principled leadership that leads to success, not catching the wave of the latest program or metrics.

Movements fade—bedrock principles live on

Let me make a prediction, one that may sound odd for the author of a new book on customer experience. I am convinced the term "customer experience" will fade. I've seen so many movements come and go over the past few decades. There was management by objectives (MBO), total quality management (TQM), and business process reengineering (BPR), to name a few. Customer relationship management (CRM), lean, six sigma, customer success, and others remain (for now) part of the mix.

Management movements can quickly become "so last year." Why does the focus change? Sometimes a global event creates a point of demarcation between the way things were and a new reality. Examples include 9/11, the financial crisis in 2008/2009, and the Covid-19 pandemic of 2020/2021. Disruptions that impact regions, industries, or specific companies can have similar effects. In any case, there's an innate hunger among true leaders to look ahead. We want to be on top of things and, more than that, to be visionary in a fast-changing world.

The names and labels may change. But the goals and principles of leading the customer experience will not go away. Yes, much of the world continues to work through the economic, political, societal, and technological upheaval ushered in by the Covid-19 pandemic and other developments. But *the bedrock principles we cover work in times of prosperity and struggle. They will not go out of style.* Learn them, implement and practice them, teach them to others, and you'll be ready to face whatever is ahead.

The world needs customer experience leaders

Customer experience leadership has never before been more important than it is right now. There are many reasons, but let me mention four that rise above all others—including one that may seem counterintuitive.

This is a unique journey

One reason effective leadership is so important—and it's huge—is that finding the right approach is a *unique journey* for every organization. If you could simply acquire "the answers" on what creates a great customer experience, leadership wouldn't be important. Truth is, generic or cookie-cutter approaches—the kind many seek through case studies or benchmarking efforts—just don't work.

In fact, others' stories can be as discouraging as they are inspiring. It's great (and important) to know about Amazon.com's powerful technology platform, the Emirates Group's exemplary service (limos for first-class flyers), or Zoom's success in scaling up (admittedly in fits and starts) as much of the world went online in early 2020. But I've witnessed too many organizations trying to emulate these successes without the same context or commitment to achieve them. "We want to be the Apple of home appliances," a manager at one manufacturer told me. Yet, I found little evidence they were taking steps to be more like Apple (assuming that made sense in the first place).

Other leaders throw up their hands in discouragement—"we'll never get there." Oh, you can—but not without shaping an approach to customer experience that works for *your* customers, *your* organization. You can and should learn from others. Let's together find answers that are right for you— not Amazon, Apple, or Emirates.

Customer expectations are evolving quickly

Your customers and their evolving needs are, of course, another reason customer experience leadership is so important. When customers see or experience innovation in products or services with any organization, they begin to expect improvements from others. They now know what's possible. Effective leadership is critical to ensure your organization stays one step ahead.

As a leader, you have to continually reassess and recalibrate what your customers need and expect. What does it mean to deliver a great customer experience? The answers evolve quickly. And the stakes are high. It's easy for customers to relay bad experiences to many others. But the connected world is a powerful friend when you consistently deliver great experiences.

Customer experience has an enormous (existential?) impact on your organization

The costs of bad customer experiences are staggering. Given a choice, customers will do business elsewhere—and many will tell others. The steep costs include damage to your organization's brand, the negative impact of employee dissatisfaction, and others. Get customer experience right or you might not survive.

The good news is, there's a powerful upside. Improvements that lead to better customer experiences don't just benefit customers—they deliver substantial returns to your organization. Better experiences come with more efficient operations, more engaged employees, and innovation in products and services that keep you viable (we'll be covering these benefits and costs throughout the book and specifically in Chapter 9).

The benefits of the customer experience movement have become widely acknowledged

Wait, what? Yep, it's ironic, but one of the biggest barriers to improving customer experience is how widespread and pervasive the customer experience movement has become. Most every organization is talking about customer experience. Most every organization believes they are employing its methods and principles. The movement, if measured by recognition, is wildly successful. But actual results can be a very different matter.

As customer experience ideas took the world by storm, hundreds of consultants and researchers flooded the market with books, training programs, and various methodologies. The space became cluttered, and I saw problems emerge. One is fragmented efforts within some organizations. I once discovered three different customer experience initiatives within the same insurance company—each with different methodologies and objectives. As you can imagine, the results were less than optimal.

Another problem is that customer experience initiatives have too often coalesced around teams that do not build broad-based efforts. Complex action plans, specific strategies, and arcane terminology take hold—all of which can have the effect of *excluding* rather than *including* others across the organization. That doesn't work either.

Effective leaders cut through the clutter. They make customer experience understandable and ensure all who are part of an organization know their role in it. They coordinate efforts and prevent initiatives from becoming siloed and exclusionary.

About this book

There are some things to know about this book before we get started. They will help you understand the structure and style:

It's conversational. When Kathe Sweeney, the Executive Editor at Kogan Page, first reached out to me about doing this project, she had a vision in mind: a book that makes customer experience understandable and accessible for leaders. There's a lot of information available, she said, but much is focused on specific topics or is deeply technical. "If you were to have coffee over the course of a week with an up-and-coming leader, what would that conversation look like? What stories would you tell, what practical guidance would you provide? Oh, and where are the landmines to avoid?" Make this book yours, she said, and make it conversational. From that first discussion, I've been excited about this project! (And I hope you and I can have coffee in person someday.)

It is designed to be helpful whatever your role. Maybe you're the senior leader with overall responsibility. You might be an entrepreneur with a startup company in need of a more robust approach. Perhaps you have leadership responsibility within a functional area such as marketing, product development, or customer service. Or maybe you're where I was when I began my career—I devoured everything I could read or listen to on these topics. If you have an interest in customer experience, this book is intended for you. I hope you find it helpful right where you are—and wherever you find yourself in the future.

It applies across industries and organizations. The principles we cover are applicable in any industry and any organization, from small companies to the largest enterprises. Yours can be in the private sector, government, or non-profit. Depending on your role, your customers might be internal, external, or both. You might be business-to-business (B2B) or business-to-consumer (B2C). Union or non-union. It doesn't matter—the principles of

FIGURE 0.1   Five major themes

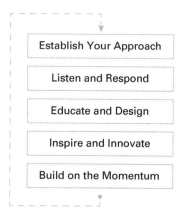

leading customer experience apply. You'll find a wide range of examples throughout the book.

It is designed to be an easy-to-use guide. The book covers five themes (see Figure 0.1), and there are two chapters for each theme. The chapters build on one another, and the topics we'll cover are interrelated. I encourage you to view each chapter as an important part of an overall approach. Within each chapter are key recommendations. They're summarized at the end of each chapter and collectively at the back of the book. While I don't advise you to try to implement them all at once, there will likely be some major initiatives you'll want to push along. The book will provide the detail to support them, and help you keep an overall inventory of where you are.

Ongoing pursuit

Organizations need leaders at all levels. I learned as much about the value of my work from those rough-around-the-edges supervisors I reported to in my first job as I have in any role since then. It's ultimately what happens day to day, and person to person, that makes a difference between success and failure.

I encourage you to view customer experience leadership as an ongoing pursuit. Understanding the needs and nuances of customers is ever-changing. But it's my hope and intent that this book will be a guide you can trust to identify relevant issues, and make the most of the opportunities you have.

I'm also providing additional resources at www.bradcleveland.com/resources. These include updated statistics, links to other customer experience sites, and more.

Thank you for joining me.

Let's get to work!

PART ONE

Establish your approach

01

Getting started

Customer experience lives or dies in the trenches. Come with me on a consulting project, and I'll show you an example.[1]

My assignment was to provide a series of workshops for a new and fast-growing company. Based in Toronto, they develop and provide business software packages. The company was (and is) committed to delivering outstanding customer experiences. Their innovative software products lead the industry, and they are committed to standing behind them with top-notch support.

The workshops they asked me to provide cover customer expectations and how they're evolving. They wanted to be sure they were staying ahead of the curve. Managers from marketing, technical support, IT, and others participated in the sessions. Beforehand, I spent a few days on an assessment, which included meeting and talking with employees and getting a sense of their culture. The deeper I looked, the more questions I began to run into.

For example, there were obvious inconsistencies in their support center—the area that provides customer service and technical support over phone, chat, and other channels. (Customer experience is far broader than customer service, but we'll get there.) Their director mentioned to me that she was grappling with a conundrum. Most technical support reps spent an average of 10 to 12 minutes with customers. One rep had an average handling time of over 20 minutes—double that of the others. "Is that normal?" she asked. "We want to ensure our customers have a good experience. But is there a limit to what that means?"

I spent some time that afternoon speaking with staff and listening to support calls. One employee had printed emails from customers tacked to his cubicle walls—dozens of them. "Thanks so much for the awesome service!" said one. "You helped us get unstuck—and then some," wrote another. Guess who had the long handling time? *Yep!*

"He's a bit of a braggart," whispered one of his peers to me. "I help twice as many customers in a day," said another. When I spoke to the rep in question, it was clear to me he *loved* his work and just wanted to deliver outstanding service. Their workload planners had run some "what if" scenarios. Should his handling time be the norm, they felt the expenses would threaten the viability of the business.

Back to the director's office that afternoon. "What should I do?" she asked. She had options. One would be to force the issue—set a ceiling. Exceed the threshold and you'd get a warning. But the rep with the long handling time would protest that he was the one providing the best service. He might quit. Even worse, he might stay and poison the environment, grumbling that the company doesn't live up to its promises. (You may recall working on a team with an unhappy employee—it can be so damaging to morale).

I had other questions. How did they know the average of 11 minutes was "right"? How would they know where to set a threshold? Perhaps 11 minutes was too long. Maybe it was too short. It was just a clock, an outcome. The fact that it was an average didn't necessarily mean it was a good target.

Their director ended up taking an approach that was very wise. She assembled a small team of several employees, including the rep with the long handling time. She put them in a conference room with a long table and provided them with index cards and markers. "Settle on the most common support call we get," she explained, "and write each step that you go through on a card; lay them out in order." She returned a couple of hours later to see cards neatly arranged across most of the table. There were branches here and there, reflecting the typical paths a support interaction can take.

"What did you discover?" she asked. One employee (who had a relatively short handling time) spoke up first. "I learned that I'm not taking some steps that could minimize the chance for a repeat contact. Good to know, and I'd like to make some adjustments."

The rep with the long handling time spoke next. "Well, I am clearly walking customers through features that others aren't. Sometimes they don't directly relate to the question, but our customers always appreciate the help. Many say, 'Wow, I had no idea the software could do that!'"

Now they were getting somewhere! After a robust discussion, this rep and his peers determined that he *was* going beyond technical support and providing, essentially, personalized training. But customers need this information, they all agreed.

Some months later, I returned to the support center. The enthusiasm was evident. The handling times of all employees had fallen into what they felt was a sensible range. The team had developed concrete quality standards to guide services. But I was the most excited about the strategy they'd put in place to improve customer experience. The teams were involved in initiatives that included:

- product improvements
- improvements to user guides and online resources
- marketing initiatives that better described benefits
- launching and facilitating a customer community that enabled customers to help each other

Support reps enjoyed lending some hours each month to these working groups across the company. The employee who once had the long handling time was involved in developing online videos and references for customers— and loving it. "We're working on things that help *all* of our customers, not just those who contact us for support!"

I've seen so many cases where the hero of this story would instead be the villain. Where stricter controls are established, support sticks to support, and outliers are coached into compliance. Where the creativity, humanity, and joy that once existed drains from the operation. Where great customer experiences begin to die.

Your organization might be very different than this one—different size, industry, or focus. And yet, there are characteristics of customer experience common to any organization. We'll turn to them next. But first, allow me to explain how the rest of the book is structured. Every major subheading in each chapter is a *recommendation*—a step I encourage you to implement as part of your customer experience initiative. Each chapter concludes with a

> " I've seen so many cases where the hero of this story would instead be the villain... Where the creativity, humanity, and joy that once existed drains from the operation. Where great customer experiences begin to die.

summary of the recommendations—five each. An overall summary of all 50 recommendations follows Chapter 10.

"*My goodness,*" you might be thinking, "*that's a lot!*" Yep, there's a lot to customer experience. And we're going to cover it step by step.

"*Is successful customer experience based on a formula?*" you might ask. "*Is this book like a cookbook?*"

No. If customer experiences were simply a matter of mixing the right ingredients in the right way, effective leadership wouldn't be in such high demand. You've got to make decisions that are right for your customers and your organization. And the answers for you will be different than for others. Cookbook, no. Guidebook, yes—one that can bring clarity and focus to your decisions and priorities.

Let me offer some friendly advice:

Don't try to implement all 50 recommendations by next Tuesday.

Don't get overwhelmed—this is a journey.

Do begin taking inventory of where your organization is vis-à-vis the recommendations.

Do begin moving some of the major recommendations along, beginning with those in this chapter.

Do build support and involve others.

Do track and celebrate progress along the way!

So, let's get to it...

Establish a broad and accurate understanding of customer experience

There you have it—the first recommendation. The first step in leading customer experience is to understand what customer experience really is... and to ensure your team understands it in the same way.

Most customer experience definitions refer to "touchpoints"—customer experience is the sum of all of the touchpoints customers have with your organization. While I don't disagree, I've found that description to be confusing to many. I think people get caught up on the meaning of touchpoint. It's easy enough to grasp when you think of a marketing piece or interaction in a store. But what about internet searches, passing comments

FIGURE 1.1   What is customer experience?

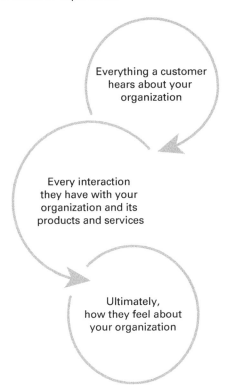

Everything a customer
hears about your
organization

Every interaction
they have with your
organization and its
products and services

Ultimately,
how they feel about
your organization

from friends, product reviews and many other factors? While they don't directly involve the organization, they do influence your perceptions of it.

So, I go a different route, simpler and with less explaining involved. I define customer experience (and I'll begin abbreviating it as CX) as:

- everything a prospect or customer hears about your organization;
- every interaction they have with your organization and its products and services;
- and, ultimately, how they feel about your organization.

Let's break this down a bit more, point by point.

Everything a prospect or customer hears about your organization. Some will come from your organization's marketing department. But much will also come from your employees, other customers, or other stakeholders (critics, reviewers, and others).

Every interaction they have with your organization and its products and services. This includes pre- and post-sales interactions, the support they receive, the ease of understanding and using products and services, and the products themselves.

How they feel about your organization. Ultimately, customers develop an overall feeling about your organization. It may be a sense of calm, confidence, or excitement. It could be one of stress or dread. In many cases, it's a combination.

Can you control everything a prospect hears about your organization? Of course not. But can you do such a good job that you create customer advocates who are inclined to say good things? Of course!

Can you control every interaction they have with you? Well, more so than some things—but stuff happens. Can you set up systems, processes, and training that ensure the vast majority of interactions go well? Hire employees who care about the work they do and the impact it has on customers? Shape a culture that supports good decisions? Yes!

I've found that, along with this definition, it's helpful to summarize three common characteristics of customer experience:

Customer experience is both far bigger—and much smaller—than many realize. In other words, customer experience is more than the product itself. It's more than customer service. It's more than your technology platform. It's all-encompassing. *It's big.*

But it's also the last interaction a customer had. Despite all of your effort—all of your processes, your work on products—just one interaction can leave customers with an indelible impression of your organization. I once found a human hair in a roasted chicken dish from what had been a favorite, frequented restaurant. Three decades later, I've never returned. In fact, every time I see a commercial, that experience comes to mind. Jan Carlzon is former CEO of Scandinavian Airways and author of *Moments of Truth*—a classic book that was a forerunner to many of today's works on customer experience.[2] He used to remind employees that customers will

> " *Despite all of your effort—all of your processes, your work on products—just one interaction can leave customers with an indelible impression of your organization.*

make inferences on the quality of maintenance based on the cleanliness of fold-down trays. Coffee stain from the last flight? *"Geez, I hope they're giving better attention to the engines."*

If you lead a team or a division but not the organization, don't think you can't make a difference. You can, right where you are. If you do lead the whole shootin' match—say, you're CEO or chief customer officer (CCO)—don't think your efforts are the end-all. You'll need customer experience to play out individual by individual, team to team.

Customer experience is often worse than leaders know. This trait is probably not universal—there may be exceptions. But unfortunately, it's very, very common, for several reasons.

One is that unhappy consumers may not complain to your organization. Yes, they may tell their friends and neighbors about a bad experience or fire off a negative comment on social media. But they might feel it will do little good to complain to the organization. Or they might expect doing so will be inconvenient, so they don't even try.

In his book *Customer Experience 3.0*, John Goodman refers to what he calls the iceberg effect.[3] His research reveals that many companies are aware of only a small percentage (often just 1 to 5 percent) of customers who encounter problems. So, for every 10 complaints, there are anywhere from 200 to 1,000 customers you don't hear from. With a 20 percent drop in customer loyalty commonly occurring when a problem isn't brought to the organization's attention, those 10 complaints could represent a loss of

FIGURE 1.2   The iceberg effect (courtesy John Goodman)

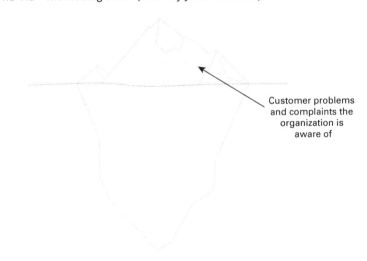

Customer problems and complaints the organization is aware of

anywhere from 40 to 200 customers. Suffice it to say, you might not be hearing the full story.

Another problem is surveys, which are a mixed bag across the business landscape. Some are working well—e.g., the quick and easy kind you take when hopping out of an Uber or Lyft. But many others aren't producing the objective input leaders need. One obvious challenge is that we're all over-surveyed. Even if your organization is sensible, your customers are getting a jillion surveys from others. They are exhausted. So, unless they are especially delighted or very upset, they simply ignore many surveys.

Survey begging is another problem. Each time I have a car serviced, the advisor makes it clear that their performance review is on the line. It works—I hesitate to share constructive feedback on other aspects of the experience, not wanting it to reflect on that person. And sometimes the questions are just way off. I recently endured a cumbersome process to fix an error with a credit monitoring service I've used for years. After many attempts and steps, I finally reached someone who could help, and she was superb. The survey question I received following the interaction: would you hire this person? *Yes! But the process to reach her… my goodness!* Where's *that* reflected in the survey?

Even with usable data, some organizations are not making use of the input they have. One problem is to over-generalize customer satisfaction scores. Your customer satisfaction might be reported as 92 percent, but lumping "somewhat satisfied" and "very satisfied" responses into the same bucket obscures problems.

We'll tackle these issues in later chapters, but suffice it to say, you may not have the full picture of your customers' experiences.

The returns on improving customer experience are better than many leaders realize. Now, here's some great news: improvements to customer experience do wonders! And they surpass what many leaders realize.

A part of what I'm talking about is the marketing benefit you get from customers who sing your praises. That can save a boatload of money in otherwise trying to reach prospects. But there's more to it than that. Lasting improvements to customer experience require you to improve underlying processes, technologies, and services. For example, the support center in the opening story helped the company improve training and reference resources for customers. They significantly reduced unnecessary service contacts and associated costs. And they contributed to innovation in the product itself.

So, customer experience can deliver big returns. But where do you begin? Let's turn to the framework that guides the rest of the book—and the approach I encourage you to take.

FIGURE 1.3   Leadership Framework, Chapter 1: Getting started

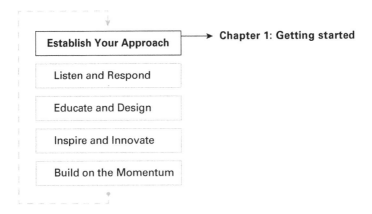

Use a proven framework to guide your leadership approach

Here is the simple, proven framework I use when advising organizations on customer experience. It forms the backbone of this book, and is built around five major themes, beginning with "establish your approach." Two chapters address each theme. Here's a sneak peek at what we'll cover.

Establish your approach. This includes establishing an understanding of what customer experience is, defining your vision and goals, and getting your team on board. Chapters include:

- Chapter 1: Getting started
- Chapter 2: Engaging your team

Listen and respond. While surveys—*effective* surveys, anyway—still have a place, we'll see how an overall approach to harnessing feedback, along with insights gained from customer service, employees, and other sources are all components of effective listening. The two chapters in this section are:

- Chapter 3: Harnessing the power of feedback
- Chapter 4: Boosting the value of customer service

Educate and design. Before you make deeper, longer-term improvements, you'll need to tell your customer's story in a way that compels change. You'll also need to shape processes and technologies that support and further customer experience. The chapters here include:

- Chapter 5: Telling your customer's story
- Chapter 6: Shaping processes and technology

Inspire and innovate. Cultures built on customer experience are proactive in every sense of the term. Ideally, everyone who is part of your organization is involved in anticipating customer needs and contributing to ongoing innovations in products and services. Chapters include:

- Chapter 7: Building a culture of customer advocacy
- Chapter 8: Unleashing product and service innovation

Build on the momentum. As you roll out changes, you'll measure progress, make adjustments where necessary, and celebrate accomplishments. The two concluding chapters are:

- Chapter 9: Rallying support for investments
- Chapter 10: Going from strength to strength

Pretty straightforward, right? Customer experience models can be mind-bogglingly complex. It shouldn't be that way. In fact, it *mustn't* be that way. Customer experience is a team sport, and (ideally) everyone in your organization should understand the role they play. Making lasting improvements involves hard work, but this framework can help you chart a clear course.

Build your core leadership team

The next recommendation is to build your core leadership team. By core, I mean those directly involved in guiding and managing your customer experience initiative. When it comes to execution, you need leaders who can put those ideas into action. Committed. Fearless. Visionary.

When you commit to transforming the customer's journey, you're challenging the status quo, the usual way of doing business. You're asking employees in almost every department to examine every facet of their work—and to remove barriers and obstacles to great customer experiences. It can disrupt how you've "always done things." It will ruffle some feathers!

That's why building the right core leadership team is one of the most pivotal steps. Unlike well-established departments with stable charters, many employees won't know what to expect from a CX leader or a CX team. And they might not know it yet, but many will be deeply affected by—and, hopefully, become an enthusiastic part of—the initiatives your CX team leads.

When building a customer experience team, there's the ideal... and there's the feasible. The ideal is the usual recommendations you'll hear from CX experts. The feasible? That's what you can do right now, right where you are, with what you have. Let's look at each.

> **"** *When building a customer experience team, there's the ideal... and there's the feasible. The ideal is the usual recommendations you'll hear from CX experts. The feasible? That's what you can do right now, right where you are, with what you have.*

CX team—the ideal

Customer experience calls for seismic shifts in your company culture—from the front lines to the board room. There's no room for individual lines of business or departments to opt out or pursue alternative strategies. Ideally, everyone must be on board. Here are some notes on the ideal team:

Start with a C-level customer experience champion. In a larger organization, change of this magnitude requires a C-level (top level of leadership) customer experience champion. This could be the chief executive officer (CEO), chief financial officer (CFO), chief marketing officer (CMO), or other. This person supports the sweeping changes (and budget) CX revolutions need. Customer experience champions (yes, ideally, you'll be able to cultivate more than one) lead the transition to a customer-centered culture, clarify collaboration expectations, and prioritize the resources needed to staff and fund CX initiatives. In a smaller organization, the owner, CEO, or someone with key decisions and budgetary responsibility could be the champion.

Add a strong customer experience leader. You'll need someone to lead the charge, and manage cross-functional activities, budgets, and timelines. In a growing organization, this might start with a CX manager who reports to the CX champion. In larger or more mature organizations, the structure may include a formal position, often a chief customer officer (CCO). In a smaller organization, the CX champion and CX leader may be the same person (perhaps you).

In any case, the CX leader will have key responsibilities: cultivating a unified focus on customers, establishing goals and metrics, building tools, and others. There's always more involved than what is on a job description. In her book, *Chief Customer Officer 2.0*, Jeanne Bliss adds an insightful qualifier: a successful CX leader "needs to be a sleuth, uncovering and navigating agendas and factors that slow down and can threaten the work, especially if some leaders question its connection to business growth."[4]

Build the rest of the team. With a CX champion and CX leader in place, you can build out the rest of your team. But who? How many? What will they do? That's up to you. According to a recent survey of organizations with over $500 million in revenue, most (65 percent of respondents) have a team that includes a dedicated senior leader and a formal CX department. Six to ten full-time employees is typical, but you could have fewer or more.[5] The numbers can be hard to come by, because many organizations incorporate CX responsibilities into existing job roles.

I have a file full of dozens of organization charts. There are no two alike. Most teams are established around two themes: areas that can bring quick wins, and ongoing responsibilities (creating journey maps, spearheading process improvements, and others). My recommendation: don't be concerned with defining the perfect structure just yet. Go at this organically. What do you need to get done? What's the most effective way to get there? In that sense, you'll want to go through the recommendations in the book, then circle back to this step.

CX team—the feasible

I recently listened to an audiobook that tells the story of John Houbolt, an engineer with NASA in the early 1960s.[6] This is a story that is only recently getting widespread attention. Houbolt was part of an all-out effort to reach the Moon by the end of the decade—the vision laid out by JFK in 1961. The prevailing wisdom in the early days of this effort was to build a rocket big enough to fly to the Moon, land, take off again and fly back to Earth. A second idea—somewhat more far-fetched—was to put a ship into Earth's orbit and use it as a platform to reach the Moon. Houbolt became an advocate for a third alternative, one that seemed preposterous to most: a lunar orbit rendezvous (LOR). This involved flying a ship to the Moon's orbit and then sending a small landing craft to the surface. This could theoretically save thousands of pounds of fuel. But it created an enormous challenge—two spacecraft traveling at thousands of miles per hour would have to rendezvous in the Moon's orbit before returning to Earth.

Houbolt fought a lonely battle in the early days of NASA, and was at first ridiculed by his peers. But other options would prove to be unworkable. He earned confidence as supporting evidence mounted. These were years NASA began to build and benefit from a more diverse employee base—stories recounted more recently in movies such as *Hidden Figures*. Houbolt's unwavering confidence in LOR—a solution he and his contemporaries worked forward and backward—enabled the crew of Apollo 11 to reach the Moon on July 20, 1969, then return safely to Earth. It was an extraordinary accomplishment. (When Houbolt died in 2014 aged 95, only some knew his story. With the rekindled focus on space, there's renewed interest in the accomplishments of these pioneers.)

I'm not going to suggest that a successful CX initiative is as difficult as going to the Moon and back. But it's not a walk in the park, either. And sometimes the least likely paths are those that get you there. I have seen, over and over, that successful CX initiatives don't always follow prevailing recommendations. Sometimes they can't. I've witnessed a national government change course and dramatically improve customer experience—an initiative that began with the vision and persistence of a few managers several layers

> 66 *I have seen, over and over, that successful CX initiatives don't always follow prevailing recommendations.*

down the organization chart. I've seen the supervisor of a contact center become manager, then VP, and now with cross-functional responsibility for improving customer experience. I've seen pockets of excellence in teams and departments become the catalysts that put their entire organizations on a better path.

If any of these descriptions fit you, my encouragement is to keep ahold of your vision. Make your case, push ahead, and don't give up. Do what you can with what you've got, then see what doors open.

Define and communicate your vision and goals

I recall sitting at the back of a conference room as an organization launched its customer experience initiative. Two presenters who were helping to drive the initiative presented a 75-minute overview. They covered, in 30 to 40 slides, the highpoints of plans. They used acronyms such as CX, NPS, and CSAT. They discussed surveys and response rates. They showed charts and graphs. And more charts and more graphs.

After the presentation wrapped up, attendees began filing out of the room. Being in the back, I was first out the door. Two people behind me were heading for a coffee station. "Did you get all of that?" one asked the other. "Not much," was the reply, "And we're up to our eyeballs in work; I hope this doesn't add much..." The conversation trailed away as they headed in the other direction.

> ❝ *The right metrics are important, for sure. But vision they aren't. Metrics don't win hearts and loyalties.*

Can you picture Richard Branson dreaming of a high NPS (net promoter score) when launching the Virgin Group? Did you ever hear Elon Musk touting CES (customer effort score) as the motivation behind new products? Or Mother Teresa discussing her work in terms of CSAT (customer satisfaction)? The right metrics are important, for sure. But vision they aren't. Metrics don't win hearts and loyalties.

Create a specific, compelling vision

A clear vision, well communicated and continually reinforced by you, is essential to engaging your employees, aligning objectives, and driving action. Vision can take many forms, including a vision statement, a mission statement, a set of values, or some overarching principles or standards. Don't worry about a specific formula or label for your vision.

I have colleagues who are huge fans of eyewear retailer Warby Parker (caution: CX reports take a toll on eyes). Warby Parker is renowned for exceptional customer experience design. Their mission is simple and compelling: "We believe that buying glasses should be easy and fun. It should leave you happy and good-looking, with money in your pocket."[7]

One coworker describes her recent experience this way:

When I arrive, there's no wait (easy) for a friendly sales advisor to provide expert recommendations (good-looking, happy). I'm not ready to buy yet, but my advisor informs me my favorites will be emailed to me, along with a virtual try-on app, in case I want to "try on" any more styles without coming to the store (easy). The app will even make suggestions (good-looking)! I stroll through the mall to a competitor and I'm thrilled with the price difference (money in your pocket). Maybe I'll buy two pairs—one for business, and one for weekends (fun)!

Here are some other examples of vision. USAA, the highly rated insurance and financial company, operates around four core values (summarized in just four words): Service. Loyalty. Honesty. Integrity.[8] Together, they are simple, clear and inspiring. And they pack a punch because at USAA they discuss and include them in any decision. That makes a real difference.

REI is a provider of outdoor equipment and services, and I love their mission, which also serves as their vision for customer experience: "We inspire, educate and outfit for a lifetime of outdoor adventure and stewardship."[9] As you might imagine, that gives their newest employees a good sense of what to do (and the inspiration to do it!).

And it's not just private companies having all the fun. Services Australia, the service arm of the federal government, is simplifying and improving services around this vision: "Make government services simple so people can get on with their lives."[10] It's a bold, ongoing initiative that is already showing strong results. I'm also seeing Service BC (British Columbia, Canada), the US Department of Veterans Affairs, and others within government strongly focus on shaping experiences that meet the evolving needs of their communities.

EXAMPLES OF VISION, MISSION, VALUES

Warby Parker mission

"We believe that buying glasses should be easy and fun. It should leave you happy and good-looking, with money in your pocket."

USAA core values

"Service, Loyalty, Honesty, Integrity."

REI core purpose

"We inspire, educate and outfit for a lifetime of outdoor adventure and stewardship."

Services Australia vision

"Make government services simple so people can get on with their lives."

How does Warby Parker, USAA, REI, Australia, or any successful organization know the experiences their customers want? They listen to and strive to understand them. They observe their behavior. And they build that insight into their vision, customer experience design and delivery, and success metrics. They inspire their employees to help make the vision a reality.

Identify high-level goals

With vision in hand, you're ready to develop the guideposts you'll use to make sure you and your team are headed in the right direction. Your goals describe what you hope to accomplish.

Business goals justify your CX initiative. In most organizations, CX investments are based on the belief (and backed by research) that organizations who adopt CX principles earn increased loyalty and improve their financial position. That's why the business key performance indicators (KPIs) used to measure the impact of a CX program will look familiar. They are most likely the metrics you use to measure organizational health now, based on your industry, maturity, and other factors. Examples include: decrease annual customer churn, increase revenue, boost customer lifetime value, improve market share, and others.

Customer experience goals are objectives you'll use to measure the success of your CX efforts. These may be department specific, and some may reflect what actually happens—wait times, average order value, and others. Some gauge perceptions—customer satisfaction scores or how easy they felt the experience was. And some will follow outcomes, such as repeat business, or cancellations. More organizations are also prominently including employee experience in their key goals (see Chapters 2 and 3).

We will explore goals, metrics and outcomes in more detail in coming chapters. For now, a compelling vision and a few high-level goals are what you need to get the wheels turning. Don't overwhelm your efforts with too many goals and metrics just yet. Walk before you run.

Avoid common pitfalls

"75% of customer experience initiatives fail!" That's a sensational headline. And one, even with a modest search of cases and literature, you'll see often (in fact, estimates go as high as 93 percent)[11]. My question is, if your focus on customer experience fails, what's the alternative? *Not* focusing on customer experience? That just doesn't make sense. Really, your organization has no choice but to ensure that you're focused on customer experience, and that it succeeds.

Now, there are some tough situations—and you might be part of one. Leaders in some organizations don't prioritize CX and won't invest in it. Their focus is on revenue, strategic acquisitions, or other priorities. Even more challenging, in my opinion, are those cases where CX is given lip service but provided little support. They say the right things but don't back it up. If you are reading this book, and part of such an organization, I understand. You are fighting the good fight! My encouragement is to hang in there. Continue to make your case. Ultimately, your focus on customer experience will prevail.

Even in the most favorable environments, customer experience can be misunderstood or underappreciated. I want to put my hand up here and make a few friendly recommendations. One is to set the right expectations. Often, the hardest part of a transformation as big as customer experience is simply deciding how to get started. That can be true whether you are a CEO who is spearheading an experience management initiative for 20,000 people, or a customer service team leader who is looking to kindle a flame in a team of four. My encouragement is to use the framework we cover in the book—but go into it with the right mindset. Establish the expectation that customer experience takes time—in fact, it doesn't have a finish line. It's an ongoing transformation that will shape who you are as an organization, and how you operate.

Also, the words you use when you talk about customer experience are important. It's not a program and shouldn't be called one. A program or project implies a short-term effort with a finish line. I use the term initiative, but depending on who you're talking to, even that can be misleading. Words such as transformation, movement, culture shift, and even revolution can help set realistic expectations with colleagues and employees.

Don't expect others to jump on board without a good reason to do so. An important part of launching this journey is to crystallize *why* customer experience transformation is so important. This can't be another run-of-the-mill project that employees can hunker down and wait out until the next initiative comes along.

> " *The words you use when you talk about customer experience are important. It's not a program and shouldn't be called one.*

And one more word to the wise: find allies to stand with you. The reality is, even a CEO can't do the work of customer experience alone. Think about other leaders around you who have a natural propensity toward customer experience, and get them on board as soon as possible.

Fortunately, it's quite easy to create a compelling case for CX. Organizations who are doing customer experience well are winning over customers and acquiring market share. Laggards are in danger of extinction. By setting clear expectations and establishing a strong roadmap, your chances of success are exponentially higher.

In time, you'll see the fruits of your efforts. Results will likely include improvements in revenue, market share, customer and employee engagement, new efficiencies, and others—the BIG things you're really after. In every case I've seen and every company I've worked with, the enthusiasm that customers have about your organization is the ultimate measure of how effective your approach is. That enthusiasm pays big dividends. (We'll explore benefits, costs, and investments in Chapter 9.)

Upward and onward

I am so excited for you as you embark on this transformation. Pursuing better customer experiences won't guarantee your customers will wear tattoos of your brand, as some Harley-Davidson customers do. But whether yours is a small firm, startup, government agency, non-profit, or multinational corporation, they will *feel* the alignment between their experiences and your vision and brand. Your products and service will resonate, and they'll tell others great things about your organization.

In Chapter 2, we'll look at employee engagement—an essential part of establishing your approach. Onward we go!

KEY RECOMMENDATIONS

- Establish a broad and accurate understanding of customer experience.
- Use a proven framework to guide your leadership approach.
- Build your core leadership team.
- Define and communicate your vision and goals.
- Avoid common pitfalls.

Notes

1 Cleveland, B (2020) Customer experience lives or dies in everyday decisions, *Forbes*, 18 March, www.forbes.com/sites/forbesbusinesscouncil/2020/03/18/customer-experience-lives-or-dies-in-everyday-decisions/#344faf9246d7 (archived at https://perma.cc/VYA5-GPGL)

2 Carlzon, J (1989) *Moments of Truth*, Harper Business, United States

3 Goodman, J (2014) *Customer Experience 3.0*, AMACOM, United States

4 Bliss, J (2015) *Chief Customer Officer 2.0: How to build your customer-driven growth engine*, Jossey-Bass, United States

5 Qualtrics XM Institute (2019) The State of Customer Experience Management, 2019, www.qualtrics.com/docs/xmi/XMI_StateOfCustomerExperienceManagement-2019.pdf (archived at https://perma.cc/6E8E-SP5W)

6 Zwillich, T (2019) *The Man Who Knew the Way to the Moon*, Audible Originals, United States

7 Warby Parker History, www.warbyparker.com/history (archived at https://perma.cc/ATZ2-VGC9)

8 USAA Code of Business Ethics and Conduct, www.usaa.com/inet/wc/about_usaa_code_ethics_corporate_governance?akredirect=true (archived at https://perma.cc/9JPK-MWAE)

9 Great Place to Work Institute (2009) REI—Working Together for a Better World, www.rei.com/pdf/jobs/2009-Best-Company-for-25-Years-REI-for-REI.pdf (archived at https://perma.cc/YK9L-D92G)

10 Digital Transformation Agency (2020) Services Australia Vision, www.youtube.com/watch?v=-NqxcNoT_kE (archived at https://perma.cc/G8VY-GNU5)

11 Thompson, B (2018) An inconvenient truth: 93% of customer experience initiatives are failing, *Customer Think*, 7 February, https://customerthink.com/an-inconvenient-truth-93-of-customer-experience-initiatives-are-failing/ (archived at https://perma.cc/HA62-6L8G)

02

Engaging your team

When my daughter, Grace, was 13, she bought a camera. She had saved for many months and was exploring models at a local camera store. When the owner of the store retired and wound down his business, she ended up going to Costco. Faced with a bewildering array of options, she settled on an all-inclusive package that featured lenses, memory and a carrying case.

She began using the camera with much excitement, and some pictures were great—but others were blurry or faded. I assumed it was a matter of learning the equipment. But over time, her enthusiasm began to wane and the camera stayed on a shelf. One weekend, some out-of-town family stayed with us, including cousin Kait, who is a professional photographer. "There's something wrong with the camera," she concluded. "Maybe the chipset or a lens fitting."

We took it back to Costco—long past the 90-day return threshold—and Grace explained to the person behind the service counter what happened. With a manager's okay, they agreed to an immediate replacement. Then the real magic happened. An employee in the camera area named Devon, who was just finishing her shift, stayed an extra 30+ minutes to help Grace unpack the new camera, ensure that it worked, and go over basic features. "You will LOVE this camera!" she said. "I have the same model."

The thing that struck me is that this was just one of thousands of interactions that day in a "big box" store. Yet, it could have a lifelong impact on a young person who was giving up on an interest. How do you create that level of engagement? And if Costco can do it, can you in what may be a very different organization, with very different circumstances?

In Chapter 1, we covered key steps required to get started in customer experience leadership. In this chapter, we turn to employee engagement. Engaging a team to support a mission is perhaps the ultimate mark of a

FIGURE 2.1   Leadership Framework, Chapter 2: Engaging your team

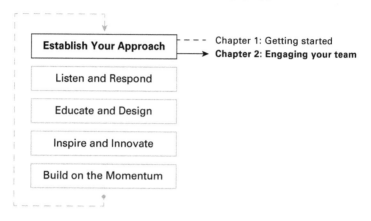

great leader. It sets you apart and propels your organization to achieve amazing results. And as many leaders have discovered, engaging your team is essential to customer experience leadership.

There's good news, too. There's no innate charisma or a certain leadership style you have to have. Instead, focus on the things that matter. Listen to and involve your employees. Get the dumb stuff—conflicting goals, misguided standards, and others—out of the way. Be authentic. Do these things, and it's very likely that employee engagement will move in the right direction. When that happens, you'll see the positive results in customer experience *and* employee experience.

Build on a foundation of employee engagement

The late Jack Welch, longtime CEO of industrial giant General Electric, led the organization to remarkable success. In an interview with the *Kansas City Business Journal* following his time at GE, he summarized the metrics he had focused on: "There are only three measurements that tell you nearly everything you need to know about your organization's overall performance: employee engagement, customer satisfaction, and cash flow."[1] He further emphasized employee engagement in a LinkedIn post: "It goes without saying that no company, small or large, can win over the long run without energized employees who believe in the mission and understand how to achieve it."[2] What was remarkable is that this advice came from someone who was often criticized for being brutally focused on the numbers and performance.

Everything I've seen over the years—in both the organizations I've led and others I've worked with as an outside advisor—corroborates the importance of employee experience. It is indeed the cornerstone of customer experience. When you peel back the layers of any customer-centric organization, you'll find a robust culture of honoring employees, encouraging their insight and ideas, and engaging them every step of the way.

> 66 When you peel back the layers of any customer-centric organization, you'll find a robust culture of honoring employees, encouraging their insight and ideas, and engaging them every step of the way.

Think about a customer's journey through your organization (a topic we'll cover more fully in Chapter 5). Basic steps might include learning about your products or services through marketing materials, your website or a sales rep; purchasing at a store, from a partner, or through your website; needing assistance, accessed through your mobile app, online resources, or contact center; and others. Every one of the products, services, technologies, and processes were selected, designed, implemented, or overseen by someone who works for your organization. Your best-laid plans for customer experience go nowhere without invested, dedicated employees.

Research bears out the connection between employee experience and business outcomes. Over the last two decades, the Gallup organization has, in a series of studies, identified the links between high employee engagement and healthy organizational outcomes—including better employee retention, higher customer satisfaction and loyalty, higher productivity, and better financial results.[3] As customer experience principles have become part of the business vernacular, numerous studies from other sources have added insight. Surveys from the Temkin Group, for example, find that employees who work for customer-centric companies are 30 percent more likely to be committed to their jobs.[4]

In short: if you're just beginning your customer experience journey, it's time to get comfortable with another "experience"—employee experience. Just as your customers desire products, services, and support that minimize frustrations and help them thrive, employees do too. Just as loyal customers say great things about your organization—especially when they feel an emotional connection to it—employees do too.

But what is employee engagement? It's a term most of us frequently hear and use, but what does it mean, exactly? We know it's not the same as employee satisfaction. An employee can be satisfied with their job for various reasons—geographical convenience, friendships, compensation—without really being engaged.

Here's how I define engagement: it is "the enthusiasm and emotional commitment an employee has to the organization and the work they do."

So how do you encourage engagement and grow it across your team and organization? The key driver, as it turns out, is purpose: Do your employees believe that their work matters? Do they feel they are making a difference?

> ❝ **Employee engagement:** *The enthusiasm or emotional commitment an employee has to the organization and the work they do*

Strengthen individual purpose across your organization

We all spend a high percentage of our waking hours working. For most of us, the primary reason is very practical: we require the means to buy the things we need and want. So, in a very real way, work is something we have to do. In that sense, it can carry a negative connotation. I *have* to go to the dentist. I *have* to get my car inspected. But we all know people, and hopefully you and I are among them, who LOVE the work they do. "I flunked retirement," as a friend of mine in his 70s put it when I asked him why he was going back to work. I'm pretty sure he's fortunate enough to not need the income. "I really missed being part of the action," he said.

In *Why We Work*, Barry Schwartz summarized three ways we can relate to work: work as a job, work as a career, or work as a calling.[5] Those who view work as a job mainly see it as a paycheck. They don't receive any kind of reward or fulfillment beyond salary and benefits. Those who view work as a career have a higher level of motivation—they want to get better at what they do, take on new responsibilities, and move up in the organization.

Those who view work as a calling are the most motivated—they understand how the work they do makes a positive difference for others.

The lost jobs and turbulence Covid-19 created likely shook these perspectives up—for a season. Many employees were happy to have, keep, or find work. But as we returned to a sense of normal, fulfillment once again emerged as fundamentally important. Work can and should be fulfilling, both professionally and personally. The underpinning of true employee engagement starts with a perspective: knowing that the work is important, that it is worthwhile. So, a secret to creating an engaging environment is to establish the connection between what your employees do and how it impacts others.

A different mindset

I've seen employee engagement do a 180-degree turnaround, time and again, with a change in perspective and approach. I remember, for example, the large consumer products company that had unusually high turnover in a customer service department. A new director brought me in to offer some advice. In our initial conversation, he relayed a silver lining to his challenge: "I could do about anything right now, and it could only get better."

Was he ever right. Customer feedback was awful, the culture was stifling, and employees jumped at any chance to move to other jobs. Of tens of thousands of employees in total, this department was second from the bottom in the annual company-wide survey of employee satisfaction. "So," I suggested, "Why not go big?"

As he would soon discover, his team would have answers. They just needed to be drawn out. He began an initial meeting by asking them about their value and purpose. One employee slouched in the back of a meeting

> ❝ I've seen employee engagement do a 180-degree turnaround, time and again, with a change in perspective and approach.

room responded this way: "We handle consumer gripes all day … how important can that be?" They decided to find out. How *could they* be more valuable to customers and the company?

Some simple analysis over the next few days revealed that 11 percent of customer contacts about a specific cleaning product were due to the cap being too hard to remove. Customers would force it off, too often shearing off the spray nozzle. The complaints all went something like this: "Hey, I just spent five bucks on this, and I can't even use it. And I have to get this job done!" The team related to the inconvenience and loss of money, but especially empathized with the hard work their customers were trying to complete—work stopped in its tracks by the company's faulty packaging.

They shared this data with their packaging supplier, who redesigned the caps. Those contacts went away, and many future customers benefited from a better product. That gave the team a glimpse of their potential—that small win began to breathe new life into the department. In the months that followed, the department became involved in marketing, systems improvement, and product development. A senior leader told me that team had become the "secret sauce" to the company's research and development. Fast-forward a year. Turnover was down to low single digits. Employees were excited and the department went from second lowest all the way to second highest in employee satisfaction. When they saw their true impact on customers, colleagues, and the success of the company, they began to understand their value and potential.

How engaged are your employees? For a quick assessment, the National Business Research Institute (NBRI) identified six traits of employees who are engaged.[6]

NBRI'S SIX TRAITS OF ENGAGEMENT

Engaged employees:

- believe in their organization
- have the desire to work to make things better
- understand the business context and big picture
- are respectful and helpful to colleagues
- are willing to go the extra mile
- stay up to date with developments in their industry

SOURCE National Business Research Institute (NBRI)

Consider your own team and organization in this context. What's going well? What barriers might be getting in the way? Later in this chapter I'll suggest essential metrics that help gauge and track employee experience. But begin making notes now of how things are going. I also encourage you to be an example. Understand and live your organization's mission. Make a habit of building that connection into conversations and decisions.

Ensure your culture supports customer experience objectives

What we're really getting at here is culture—one in which a focus on customer experience can thrive. Of course, the basics have to be in place: fair pay and benefits; a safe and inviting work environment; equal opportunities for anyone to advance; schedules that work well for employees and the organization. But just as engaging customer experiences don't happen by chance, the experiences that shape employee engagement don't just happen on their own. You'll need to help employees understand the power they have every day to make a difference.

One of my favorite commercials, which ran years ago now (it clearly made an impression on me) was from Home Depot. It reflected a time of turnaround for the building supply company, following a season of cost-

FIGURE 2.2   Cultural traits that support customer experience

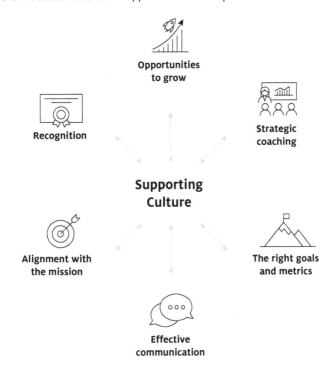

Opportunities
to grow

Recognition

Strategic
coaching

Supporting
Culture

Alignment with
the mission

The right goals
and metrics

Effective
communication

cutting and poor service that almost drove them to bankruptcy. The commercial depicts a confused and stressed dad getting advice from a knowledgeable representative on how to build a treehouse. The last scene shows the dad and his young son in sleeping bags, settling in for the night in the new treehouse. "Thanks Dad," his admiring son says.[7] It started as "just" an interaction in a building supply store. But who knew how important it was to *that* customer? Yes, it was just a commercial—a creation of marketing; and yet, it reflected a change in thinking at Home Depot, one that emphasized the role of each employee. Ultimately, this new perspective sparked a turnaround.

More than talk

What do successful organizations, those with the most engaged employees, have in common? I've observed some principles that, without fail, are at work—vision, values, communication, collaboration, and others. The key is to "live them"—not just give them lip service.

ALIGNMENT WITH THE MISSION

An important step to creating an engaging environment is to address the "whats" and "whys." Why does the organization exist? What are you trying to achieve? What's in it for customers, employees, shareholders and others?

One of the sectors I've worked with over the years is gas and electric utilities. An outsider might assume there would be more similarities than differences in company cultures. But I've noticed *vast* differences. A repairman in one company was effusive in how he described his role: "I keep the lights on for the families and businesses in my community." The description from a repairman in another organization: "I do what they say, whatever problem they send me to. No shortage of work here, man." Do you see a difference in perspective? Guess which company would struggle with fires, outages and untold loss to life and property? If you guessed the second company, you're right. And I'm sure not suggesting the problems were that employee's fault; he was just indicative of a lack of engagement in the culture.

As a leader, remember that it's what you do, *rather than what you say*, that really matters. There are countless organizations that codify their mission and values, but then encourage an entirely different set of behaviors through their policies and actions. Delivering great customer experiences may be the objective, but insufficient staffing resources or standards that stress volume-oriented production may send conflicting messages.

EFFECTIVE COMMUNICATION

You and I hear it all the time: communication is vital. It's true. Effective leaders at all levels, whether CEO or supervisor of a small team, are predisposed to keeping teams in the know. Good and bad, so nobody is second-guessing or wondering. When good communication is lacking the symptoms are predictable: conflicting objectives, unclear priorities, and low morale, to name a few.

What's not given as much attention is the question: *what* should you be communicating? I've observed organizations that communicate—a lot. But far too much of it is unnecessary or counterproductive: rules, policies, top-down cheerleading. What's a better focus?

Listening is a great place to start. Listening *is* communication. And it is essential. Remember the wise observation: we're born with two ears but just one mouth for a reason.

Another vital aspect of communication is recognition. What are you acknowledging and celebrating? What are you reinforcing? In study after study, participants say that personalized and sincere recognition—simply being recognized for doing a good job—is a powerful motivator.

CASE STUDY
Recognition requires preparation

Recognition depends on you knowing what's going on. I recall overhearing a conversation between two employees (I think they forgot an outside advisor was working away in that back cubicle they provided). Here's how it went (I've changed the names). Paul, a senior executive, decided to spend some time in the processing center. His intention was good—he wanted the team to know that he appreciated their efforts. And he knew it had been a busy few months for everyone. The problem was, he didn't prepare. Here's the discussion that transpired between Sarah and Jeff, two employees:

"So Paul was here today," Sarah said.

"Yeah, I saw him," Jeff responds. "It caused quite a stir. He doesn't come by that often."

"That's true. Did he say anything to you?"

"To me personally? No. Did he say anything to you? "

"Nope," replied Sarah. "I did hear his thank you to all of us."

Jeff laughs. "When he was standing in the aisle looking awkward? Yeah, I heard that too."

"I guess it was nice. It's good to know that he values the work we do."

"Sure, but..."

"But what?"

"It was so, I don't know, generic. It didn't feel as if it had much to do with us. Could he have said the same exact words to any department in the company? We've been pushing to the limits in processing, especially with the system issues we've been having. I'm sure he knows that? I think he does."

Sarah frowns, slightly. "Yeah, you're right about that. It would have been better if he had mentioned something specific. We've accomplished a lot in the last few months. But, you know what really bothered me?"

"Tell me."

"I saw him talking with Nicole for at least five minutes. She was animated. Glowing."

Jeff groans. "Well, that's not surprising. She knows how to play the game."

"But if he was going to single out one person for attention, it shouldn't have been her. There are so many people more worthy. Like Katie. Or Patrick. Their ideas to streamline processes really helped get us through the crunch."

Jeff pauses. "Agreed. I guess he didn't know."

Sarah is now a bit agitated. "But shouldn't he have known? Shouldn't he have talked to Laura first? She reports to him and could have prepared him. That would have made the visit more meaningful. And less annoying."

"Yes, that would have been good, for sure. We should do Laura a favor and tell her how we feel. She'll listen."

Sarah nods. "Ok, makes sense. I'll catch up with you tomorrow and we can talk to her. Have a good evening."

Moral of the story: recognition, even simple MBWA (management by walking around), requires that you have a basic understanding of what's happening. Epilogue to the story: Laura later talked to Paul. She committed to keep him better informed and, in doing so, conveyed the importance of having a basic grasp of what was going on. He took the advice, and now spends more time in the department. His encouragement and recognition are more specific and he's won the respect and loyalty of the team.

THE RIGHT GOALS AND METRICS

I remember visiting an organization and being given a list of team members ranked by their "productivity." The person at the bottom of the list was helping fewer customers and more of her cases were still open, waiting for resolution. Her manager was concerned. But as I looked further, the facts emerged. She was one of the team's most capable troubleshooters. The toughest customer problems were sent to her by her teammates. Those were the cases that needed more time and research.

Be very careful when setting goals and interpreting metrics. Beyond rote assembly lines, one of the biggest challenges in many organizations is that the work arrives randomly from moment to moment. That's true in a restaurant, a retail store, a contact center, a hospital's emergency department, and many other environments. Those delivering services don't control customer arrival rate, or the issues they need help with. So, if you're measuring success based on a production metric—e.g., how many customers are helped in a set amount of time—you may not be seeing the real picture.

Of course, even the most enlightened organizations set expectations. Getting things done—done right and on time—are not bygone ideas. You'll need to establish expectations that make sense and that employees buy into.

I once worked with a healthcare system that set up a resource center that patients could access 24/7 without the need to go to a physical facility. They incorporated the latest thinking and tools in telemedicine, and staffed the

> " Even the most enlightened organizations set expectations. Getting things done—done right and on time—are not bygone ideas.

center with doctors, nurses and physicians' assistants (PAs). All very cool and very advanced—other than the workflow and schedules, which were a mess. Few felt the need to adhere to what they saw as overly rigid schedules. The result was workload mismatches, missed appointments, and frustrated patients.

I was brought in with the unenviable task of making a case for better "schedule adherence" with the employees. I remember the first few minutes of the first workshop—looking out on a sea of faces, many with their arms folded. (Those are times, I've learned, that it's far better to listen than to talk.)

"Why are we here?" I asked. "What's going on?"

"So, you've seen our schedules, right?" one person asked. "They [referring to company leadership] seem to think we're some kind of assembly line. 'Start here, stop there. Take a break at 10:15.'"

It was a fair question, and I understood why he felt that way. "Let's kick that around a bit," I suggested. "What approach would make more sense?" We wrote a lot of comments and ideas on a white board. All the while, a central idea began to emerge—the importance of being available when needed.

The real turning point in the discussion came when a nurse near the back of the room stood up. She asked some questions of the group: How many have worked ER (the emergency room)? Every hand went up. How many know how to triage? Laughter with every hand up. "Look, every day, we're all making time-driven decisions in operating rooms and on hospital floors," she reasoned, "Not for our own comfort or convenience, but because that's when our patients and these situations need us, and when we need each other."

I saw heads nodding. She was right of course. Many of today's responsibilities are time driven. It doesn't matter if someone has the most incredible knowledge and expertise if they're not there when customers or colleagues need help. Her point helped to change the mindset. While schedules should not be overly rigid, they matter. Today, that organization is exemplary in their focus on customers, including a strong respect for workflow and schedules. Does your team understand the importance of timing?

Being in the right place at the right times is just an enabler. The other part of the equation is doing the right things—quality. Sensible and well-defined quality standards should provide necessary guidance for every employee to know what to do. In that context, they can and must be empowered to make decisions and take action (see discussion on quality standards, below).

Conflicting objectives are a killer to motivation and engagement. Ask your employees if there's ever a time they feel they have to choose between acting in the best interest of a customer and hitting a performance target. If so, revisit and revise your objectives so that they complement each other. The journey at Hershey is a good example of clarifying and focusing on what's most important.

CASE STUDY
From Metrics to Values at Hershey

There was a time we emphasized a lot of metrics at Hershey Entertainment & Resorts (where I served at that time as Manager, Training & Guest Experience). But we also were aware that a key element of employee engagement is making a connection between work and each employee's intrinsic values. So we came to the conclusion that we should put more focus on living out our values—we believed good results (including in our metrics) would follow.

These efforts led to a program called "Legacy Checks." Our intent was for our employees to live, breathe, and genuinely believe in our four core values—Own, Anticipate, Delight and Inspire. Rather than just posting values on a wall, we defined what it looked like to embody each value—with co-workers, customers, and in everyday work. We implemented an on-the-spot recognition program to reward people for demonstrating our values in their day-to-day work. This included a hand-written note, was tied to a monetary reward, and explicitly outlined the positive behavior and associated core value. Beyond the Legacy Checks, we used these values to guide the decisions that we made as leaders.

The end result: our employees authentically worked with the company's values as their guiding light, our leaders made decisions based on true business priorities, and we delivered exceptional experiences for our customers. We could see the positive results in both customer loyalty and employee engagement. And yes, in our metrics as well. In short, we focused on values rather than metrics. That made all the difference.[8]

Justin Robbins, JM Robbins & Associates

OPPORTUNITIES TO GROW

Lack of development opportunities is a serious demotivator, especially for younger generations. And it is so unnecessary in today's organizations. Building an organization focused on customer experience requires diverse skills and knowledge. Think about it—there's the products and services, the support you provide to them, internal and external communication, technology, processes, data analytics, and much more. Don't let your best employees get bored! Find ways to develop their skills and expand their responsibilities.

Good training is an important part of the answer. There are few things more stressful and frustrating than not knowing what to do. This is especially true for employees who directly interact with customers (if you've been there, you know what I mean!). Knowing how to approach any situation makes all the difference. Confidence is built through robust training and coaching (especially role-playing tough scenarios). When I recently asked an employee about her company's improved training, she said, "I went from dreading my day to looking forward to it; I love being a problem solver!"

STRATEGIC COACHING

Strategic coaching is also essential to employee engagement. By strategic, I mean ongoing, holistic and focused on developing the whole person. (Tactical coaching is limited in focus to specific skills or requirements.) Think of how athletes, from grade school to the pros, describe their most influential coaches. You're probably thinking of words like mentor or supporter. Or maybe a phrase, like "somebody who looks out for my best interest," or "wants me to be the best I can be."

When effective, coaching is something your employees want and look forward to. It begins by understanding that coaching is a relationship, NOT an event. The best coaches build relationships of trust, respect and account-ability. They help clarify goals, give honest and helpful feedback, and provide positive reinforcement. (Coaching doesn't become less important as an employee moves up the ladder. If anything, it increases. I've been a coach to senior-level executives and have in turn hired excellent coaches to work with me. Frankly, I'd feel lost without the perspectives they bring.)

The most common and, ultimately, most effective coaching is self-coaching. It's that self-talk each person has with themselves day by day, moment by moment. The leadership secret here is to approach training, coaching, and standards as opportunities to empower your employees to coach themselves. They must deeply understand the organization's mission and values. And they must be empowered to make good decisions on the fly. That's a strength that will then play out every moment of every day. And it's one of the strongest influences on employee engagement.

> ❝ *The most common and, ultimately, most effective coaching is self-coaching. It's that self-talk each person has with themselves day by day, moment by moment.*

Align quality standards with your customer experience vision

Dee Hock, founder and former CEO of the credit card system that became VISA International, once said, "Simple, clear purpose and principles give rise to complex and intelligent behavior. Complex rules and regulations give rise

FIGURE 2.3   Two types of standards: foundation and finesse

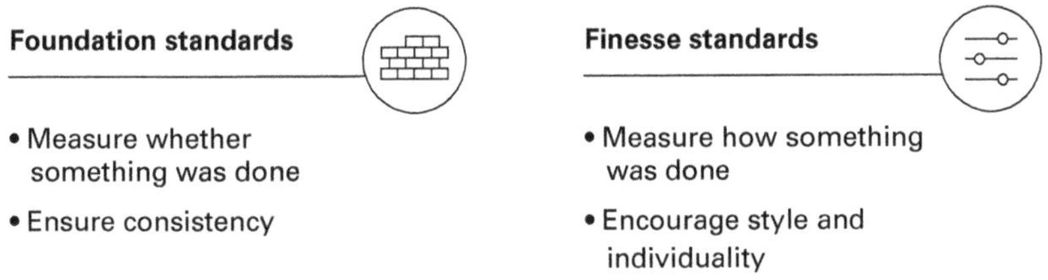

Foundation standards

- Measure whether something was done
- Ensure consistency

Finesse standards

- Measure how something was done
- Encourage style and individuality

to simple and stupid behavior."[9] You'll see more consistency and higher-quality customer experiences when your employees are equipped with simple, sensible standards aligned to your organization's vision.

First, what are quality standards? We've probably all used the term quality in a general sense: "I need some quality sports headphones," or, "Their team is very focused on quality." What we really mean is high quality, or exceptional quality. Quality is, simply, the attributes or characteristics of a product or service. So, to define what great quality means, you need a point of reference. That's where standards come in. And like other aspects of engaging your employees, *how* you approach quality standards is key.

Two types of standards

Aren't there a million and one things you could focus on when establishing quality standards? Sure! So how do you even get started? A helpful way to view quality standards is to think of them as either "foundation" or "finesse."

Foundation standards measure *whether* something was done. Be it testing a product, repairing downed powerlines, providing security at events, or any other aspect of customer experience, foundation standards ensure consistency. They're objective, consistent, and accomplished the same way by every person. They can be assessed with a simple yes or no. For example: The employee verifies required information. They enter data correctly. They go through authentication steps to verify the customer's identity. Consistency improves very quickly when you put foundation criteria in place. Foundation standards are essential to customer experience. But they are also vital to the employee's experience. They have to know what to do. Get the essentials down pat for various job roles.

Finesse standards measure *how* something is done. They allow for style and individuality and provide room for interpretation. For example, when working directly with customers, finesse standards might include listening carefully, probing appropriately for relevant input, and so forth. Think of high diving or figure skating in the Olympics. Finesse standards should provide clear guidance on what's expected, but performance happens in degrees. This is where much of the personality of your brand can shine through. Back them up with descriptions of the performance characteristics you're looking for. And make sure that everyone understands the standards the same way through training and coaching.

Every organization will have a mix of foundation and finesse standards across various job roles. I wouldn't worry too much about the ratio of each—it could be 60/40, 40/60 or half and half. The breakdown will vary and depends on the experiences you want for your customers. My encouragement is to get your employees involved in defining foundation and finesse standards. Ensure they are few, simple, and focused. It's inspiring (and confidence-building) to envision customer experience through clear quality standards. Knowing what to do—and having clear criteria to guide decisions—makes a big difference in employee engagement.

> ❝ It's inspiring (and confidence-building) to envision customer experience through clear quality standards.

Characteristics of effective standards

Effective quality standards—whether foundation or finesse—share several things in common:

1 **They flow from your vision**. The Walt Disney Company provides a great example of this. When Disneyland first opened, they described their vision, simply, as "We create happiness." They then developed a simple set of standards to guide "cast members."[10] Those same four standards are at work today: Safety, Courtesy, Show and Efficiency. Underneath each, Disney itemizes two or three key actions. Under show, for example, are the actions "I stay in character" and "I keep my area show-ready." They then describe more specific criteria and behaviors that support each action. You aren't likely to find gum wrappers littering the ground—that's not show ready. You won't find Cinderella smoking by the backstage

door—that's not in character. And a lengthy manual is not required (and certainly not recommended). Through this simple tiered approach, quality standards flow directly from Disney's vision.

2 **They are within the individual's control.** You want to make sure that the standards are within the team's or employee's control. You can't, for example, expect one person to keep customer wait times at the front counter to a minimum. That's a matter of forecasting and staffing decisions. You can expect employees to follow schedules, show up, and be available when customers or colleagues need them. You can expect them to rally available resources (calling help to the front counter or noting backlogs in production areas).

3 **They are easy to manage.** This means several things: your quality standards should be easy to understand and implement; they should be limited to a small, manageable number; and they must be concrete enough to be described and measured fairly. Disney's four standards can be memorized in the first morning of work. The actions and behaviors underneath each are built out and reinforced over time.

Have you established quality standards that support your customer experience vision? Do those you have need a rethink? This may be a significant opportunity. Quality standards are the bridge between day-to-day performance and your customer experience vision.

Initiate and encourage voice of the employee

The late Steve Jobs once famously stated, "It doesn't make sense to hire smart people and tell them what to do; we hire smart people so they can tell us what to do."[11] No one in your organization understands processes, products and customers more than your employees. Those closest to the work know it best.

Sources of employee feedback

The term "voice of employee" (VoE) may be relatively new, but the concept has been around for decades. Organizations have conducted HR surveys since the 1920s. Unfortunately, most were rolled out poorly, with ineffective questions and subpar analysis. The effort for many was another corporate "check box" but without much impact. Employee surveys have since evolved significantly.

A major push forward began in the 1990s, when many organizations gave this long-established process a fresh look. The focus then was on improving the nature of survey questions. Gallup introduced the Gallup 12—a dozen questions that get to the heart of employee engagement.[12] These questions were viewed by some as brazenly simple. One of them, for example, is "Do you have a best friend at work?" In fact, when first proposed, many of the questions seemed, as one leader put it to me, "not business-like." But the psychology undergirding them would be proven over time.

SOURCES OF EMPLOYEE FEEDBACK

- Annual/semi-annual survey
- Pulse survey
- Coaching conversations
- Organic conversations
- Stay interview
- Exit interview

A more recent development has come in the form of more frequent surveys. No matter how good the questions, it's tough to truly understand the hearts and minds of employees with a once-a-year survey. Let's look at some of today's popular sources of employee feedback.

PULSE SURVEYS

By adopting many of the same survey best practices used with customers (timely, relevant, correlated to a specific event), "pulse surveys" were born. An employee pulse survey is a short set of questions provided on a recurring basis (as often as every one or two weeks). Today's technology options make them easy to administer, and they provide timely insight on the employee experience. Pulse surveys became especially widespread as Covid-19 contributed to significant changes within many organizations.

Pulse surveys enable anonymous feedback and can quickly capture insight into strengths and problem areas. Response rates are high given how easy they are to complete. And they provide an easy-to-understand metric for measuring the employee experience. All told, the days of giant annual "HR surveys" are fading. Some organizations may continue yearly employee engagement surveys for trending and benchmarking purposes. But they are no longer a primary means by which leadership teams listen to employees.

COACHING CONVERSATIONS

A performance management process that enables communication and feedback between a manager and an employee is also essential. And it's not just the manager that should be providing coaching in these conversations. The employee also should be given the opportunity to provide insight into how their experience could be improved.

Here are a few tips from organizations getting the most of these conversations. They need to be routine and frequent, e.g., once a month. They should have structure, with preparation from both. Focus on two or three things going well and a key area or two to work on. To identify trends, the conversations should be documented (ideally, with the help of a performance management system) and brought together with customer survey data (a topic we'll cover in Chapter 3).

ORGANIC CONVERSATIONS

There's a well-worn assumption that employees don't quit a company, they quit a boss. However, research within specific organizations suggests that other factors also weigh heavily. Employees left "when their job wasn't enjoyable, their strengths weren't being used, and they weren't growing in their careers," conclude the authors of one study. "When you have a manager who cares about your happiness and your success, your career and your life, you end up with a better job, and it's hard to imagine working anywhere else."[13]

Organic conversations show you care—and they are essential to understanding the individuals who are part of your team. What work engages them? Where do they feel they can make the best contribution? What barriers are getting in the way? Sometimes the best way to listen and learn is to just be present. There's no substitute for unstructured and unplanned organic conversations. The most effective leaders have a good sense, an intuition, of when they need to be available for these opportunities.

STAY INTERVIEWS

Another tool to consider for deepening employee engagement is the "stay interview." Dick Finnegan, a retention expert who's authored many books and studies on the topic, defines a stay interview as "a structured discussion a leader conducts with each individual employee to learn the specific actions she must take to strengthen that employee's engagement and retention with the organization."[14] Stay interviews are, essentially, just focused conversations with a specific purpose and defined cadence. But I've found them to be informative and inspiring. And they underscore a key principle: retention is an important leadership responsibility. Exit interviews with employees who leave remain important—but (hopefully) represent just a small subset of employees.

Tracking employee experience

There are many ways to track employee experience, and I encourage you to establish a baseline that you can follow. Two common metrics include:

Employee engagement composite metric. A good pulse survey tool will collect data on key areas of the employee experience: peer-to-peer relationships, recognition, wellness, and others. It can then generate an overall employee engagement score. This metric is easy to understand. It should provide your team with the insight you need to isolate improvement opportunities. And it's simple—anyone can look at the number and get a good read on how employee experience is trending.

Employee net promoter score. Another popular KPI is employee net promoter score (eNPS). This is an internally focused mirror of the customer-facing net promoter score, or NPS (which we'll cover in Chapter 3). It asks, "How likely are you to recommend us as a place to work?" It is measured the same way as customer NPS, with detractors and promoters combined into an overall score. You can use it to establish a baseline and benchmark with other organizations. (One caution: I saw eNPS scores jump when Covid-19 ravaged the economy. Remember that variables such as financial incentives and overall employment opportunities can skew results.)

FIGURE 2.4   Employee engagement score

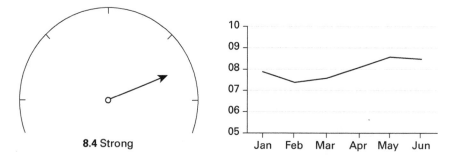

8.4 Strong

Ownership and action

Collecting and reporting employee experience insights is only the beginning. You must take meaningful action. This brings improvements and, just as importantly, demonstrates to employees that their input is highly valued.

Employee engagement requires a clear owner, and I've found this to be a hurdle for many organizations. Traditionally, the function of human resources (HR) has been somewhat of a "catch-all" for all things employee experience related. But unless you have a very strategic HR department, counting on them to own employee engagement initiatives will likely not work. These teams are generally not staffed beyond what is required to handle essential HR responsibilities. An alternative some organizations try is a volunteer committee. These working groups are often formed after employee survey results are released. I've seen some work well, but most aren't very effective; they often fizzle within several months.

So what's a workable approach? I believe it makes sense to incorporate employee experience into your customer experience transformation. Many of the principles are the same, and the two are strongly correlated. In fact, one of the primary reasons customer experience initiatives have failed in the past is because those leaders did not have ownership over employee experience. They

> ❝ I believe it makes sense to incorporate employee experience into your customer experience transformation. Many of the principles are the same, and the two are strongly correlated.

couldn't implement meaningful changes in areas outside their purview. Placing these two essential priorities—customer experience and employee experience—under one roof can help you push both initiatives. However you choose to structure ownership, the most important thing is to *do something*. Employees need to see that their perspectives matter through real action.

How will you know you're making progress? There are some tell-tale signs. For one, both survey results and employee retention will move in a positive direction. You'll see responses that reflect a customer-centric culture. Most (and ideally, all) employees—from senior leadership to new hires—will feel that they belong and are an important part of the culture. And, of course, you will be moving strongly towards your business and customer experience goals.

In Part Two, we'll turn directly to the theme of listening and responding to customers and employees. In Chapter 3 we look at how to harness the power of feedback. Then in Chapter 4, we'll explore how to boost the value of customer service—particularly in the strategic role it plays in listening and responding to customers.

KEY RECOMMENDATIONS

- Build on a foundation of employee experience.
- Strengthen individual purpose across your organization.
- Ensure your culture supports customer experience objectives.
- Align quality standards with your customer experience vision.
- Initiate and encourage voice of the employee.

Notes

1 Dornbrook, J (2015) Three questions with former GE CEO Jack Welch, *Kansas City Business Journal*, 30 April. www.bizjournals.com/kansascity/news/2015/04/30/jack-welch-leadership-analytics-advice.html (archived at https://perma.cc/VWV8-P89L)

2 Welch, J (2015) Three ways to take your company's pulse, *LinkedIn*, 5 May, www.linkedin.com/pulse/three-ways-take-your-companys-pulse-jack-welch/ (archived at https://perma.cc/5KUL-C5SH)

3 Harter, J (2020) 4 factors driving record-high employee engagement in U.S., *Gallup*, 4 February, www.gallup.com/workplace/284180/factors-driving-record-high-employee-engagement.aspx (archived at https://perma.cc/Y7GK-DGG7)

4 Qualtrics XM Institute (2017) Employee Engagement Benchmark Study, 2017, www.qualtrics.com/xm-institute/employee-engagement-benchmark-study-2017 (archived at https://perma.cc/4B64-8GP3)

5 Schwartz, B (2015) *Why We Work*, Simon & Schuster, United States

6 National Business Research Institute (2012) Employee Engagement + Customer Satisfaction = Financial Performance, www.nbrii.com/infographics/employee-engagement-customer-satisfaction-financial-performance/ (archived at https://perma.cc/B9YP-QS7B)

7 Home Depot (2002) Tree House (Online video) https://adland.tv/adnews/home-depot-tree-house-2002-30-usa (archived at https://perma.cc/SS32-VL94)

8 Cleveland, B (2019) *Contact Center Management on Fast Forward: Succeeding in a new era of customer experience*, ICMI Press, United States

9 Hock, D (nd) AZ Quotes, www.azquotes.com/quote/549118 (archived at https://perma.cc/ET84-JWK8)

10 Kober, J (nd) Disney's Four Keys To A Great Guest Experience, *Disney at Work*, http://disneyatwork.com/disneys-four-keys-to-a-great-guest-experience/ (archived at https://perma.cc/WE2N-T27Z)

11 Schwantes, M (2017) Steve Jobs once gave some brilliant management advice on hiring top people. Here it is in 2 sentences, *Inc.*, 17 October, www.inc.com/marcel-schwantes/this-classic-quote-from-steve-jobs-about-hiring-employees-describes-what-great-leadership-looks-like.html (archived at https://perma.cc/2VAC-F8A7)

12 Gallup Q12 Employee Engagement Survey, https://q12.gallup.com/public/en-us/Features (archived at https://perma.cc/EC9G-8B8B)

13 Goler, L, Gale, J, Harrington, B and Grant, A (2018) Why people really quit their jobs, *Harvard Business Review*, 11 January, https://hbr.org/2018/01/why-people-really-quit-their-jobs (archived at https://perma.cc/B3AG-N8J4)

14 The Finnegan Institute (nd) Stay Interview Certification Courses and Learning Modules, www.finneganinstitute.com/faq/#what-is-a-stay-interview (archived at https://perma.cc/GZG8-WVR8)

PART TWO

Listen and respond

03

Harnessing the power of feedback

I recently facilitated a meeting for executives of a large business-to-business company that provides human resources (HR) and payroll services. When compared to competitors, they excel in many ways—including size and market share. They've been a success story.

However, their leadership team sensed that not all was right, and they were seeing worrying downward trends in customer satisfaction scores. The cumulative scores were still good overall, but the trendline had flattened and was unmistakably moving in the wrong direction. More concerning were the "isolated" service delivery problems they were hearing about—they seemed to be more numerous. The meeting was an opportunity to discuss and, hopefully, get to the bottom of what was happening.

A key topic they (wisely) put on the agenda was metrics. They intended to take a fresh look at what they were measuring and what those indicators were telling them about customer experience. One of the attendees brought up social media, and we decided as a group to do a quick scan of their social presence.

My laptop was projecting to a screen in the front of the room, and as I toggled first to their Facebook page, I heard a collective gasp. Alongside marketing messages from the company, a frustrated customer had posted repeatedly about a simple password reset problem. His "updates" WERE IN ALL CAPS and he wrote a scathing summary of his experience. In it, he detailed his frustrations with their processes and inability to reach someone who could help. No one from the company had acknowledged or responded to the many posts.

We toggled over to Twitter, and what we saw there was even more disturbing. Dozens of customers were bantering about their poor experiences. There was no way their messages could be missed—most posts included the organization's Twitter address, along with hashtags such as #epicfail. The company, seemingly oblivious to the discussion dominating their feed, was posting breezy messages about community engagement. They came across as tone deaf.

An attendee in our workshop broke the stunned silence: "Well... that's awkward." This led to a rapid-fire discussion among the group. Why was the system locking him out? Why could he not get help through "normal" channels? Why was marketing not monitoring these posts? Why weren't those in customer service offering to help?

Over the next six months, this team rolled up their sleeves and got to work. They beefed up their ability to monitor and respond through social channels. They made systems improvements that reduced password problems. Perhaps most importantly, they improved the way they gauged customer experience—they dropped reports that don't add value, and added others they need. Customer satisfaction once again began moving in the right direction.

The key to all of these improvements was, first and foremost, knowing there was a problem. Feedback from customers and employees is like oxygen. You and your organization must have it to survive and thrive. It is essential to ensuring you're making the right decisions today, and that you're ready for tomorrow.

FIGURE 3.1   Leadership Framework, Chapter 3: Harnessing the power of feedback

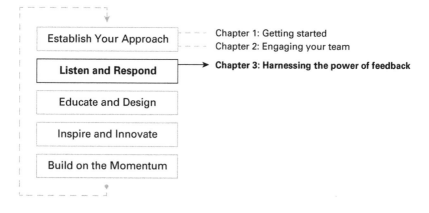

In Part Two, we turn to the theme of listening and responding. In this chapter we'll cover how to make the most of customer feedback—both real-time (as it happens) and with a longer timeframe in mind. We'll establish key performance indicators (KPIs). I'll provide a self-assessment tool that can help you gauge the efficacy of your feedback initiative. Then in Chapter 4, we'll explore how to boost the value of customer service and particularly the strategic role it plays in listening and responding to customers.

Practice seeing things from your customer's perspective

The most successful leaders are uneasy with depending on data alone to tell them what's happening. They take steps to put themselves in their customers' shoes. They want to deeply understand and experience the organization—and its products, employees and competitors—as customers do.

I agree. Get out there and see what's happening firsthand. Make it a habit. We'll outline a more formal approach for collecting and using data. But learn as much as you can, as quickly as you can, informally. Here are some suggestions for sources of insight. Each has a story to tell.

Direct input

One is direct input. The late Herb Kelleher, founder of Southwest Airlines, would often fly, talk with customers and employees and wander through airports. Howard Schultz, longtime CEO of Starbucks, spent significant time in stores, helping him make decisions such as investing in espresso machines that are shorter in height so that baristas can see over them and have eye contact with customers. And this responsibility applies to all levels of leaders.

Social posts — is this applicable to us?

Posts on social platforms provide an unruly, unvarnished and often very helpful source of insight. What are customers commenting on? Are the comments swayed to the positive or negative? What issues seem to encourage additional messages? You can use social listening tools for this if you'd like. There are many available, and they can help you pull in this information and gauge customer sentiment. But I'm referring here to simply peeking in now and then, getting a quick sense of what's happening and how your organization is responding.

Employee input

As discussed in Chapter 2, employees provide invaluable insight. As obvious as this is, many leaders don't take full advantage of this rich source of input. MBWA—management by walking around—will never lose its value. Employee surveys are also a necessity, and I make a point of looking through employee reviews of organizations on sites such as Glassdoor.com and Indeed.com. (Search for sites popular in your industry, region, or country— examples include JobAdvisor.com.au in Australia and Ratemyemployer.ca in Canada.)

Product and service reviews

Reviews such as those on Amazon, Tripadvisor, Yelp and numerous other sites provide valuable sources of insight. You'll see how customers describe your products and services, and their experiences with your brand. If available, it's a great idea to compare customer reviews with professional reviews from sources such as CNET or Consumer Reports. Culling through unfiltered input from customers can take some emotional toughness, but the most effective leaders do it as a habit.

Operational data

Operational data is another great source of information. For example, how are fulfillment times going? Contact rates for support? Internal quality metrics? There are many potential sources of information to mine. Yes, you'll want to capture and review this data as part of a formal process (see Chapter 6). But sometimes just following your intuition can reveal helpful insight.

> " Posts on social platforms provide an unruly, unvarnished and often very helpful source of insight.

Informal focus groups — How could we Incorporate this into our process?

While traditional focus groups take time and effort to set up, there are less formal alternatives. I recall having lunch with a senior VP of a retail company. As we were standing in line at a deli near their offices, a person behind us saw a logo on her briefcase. "Do you work there?" she asked.

"Yes."

"I am a customer. And a fan!"

"Thank you! How are things going?"

"Great, pretty much... um... I don't know if this is the place..."

"Tell me!"

"I'm not quite understanding the thinking behind changing some loyalty benefits. For example..."

The conversation turned into a friendly and informative three-minute "focus group" involving several people right there in the deli. While waiting in line! The VP thanked them for their insight and for being customers. As we walked to our seats, she said she was grateful for the longer-than-usual wait that day.

Doing the work

This one gets my top vote for best way to stay in the know. The late John C. Bogle, founder and former CEO of Vanguard (now the largest mutual fund company in the United States), helped handle customer calls in the contact center throughout his career. He often commented on how hard the job is. (On more than one occasion, customers with questions he struggled to answer asked to be transferred to his supervisor.) But what an example! What insights might happen should all of your executives spend some time doing (or at least observing) the work? (And consider making *Undercover Boss*, the Emmy Award–winning reality series, a must-watch.)[1]

Recommendations

As a leader, it's not practical to be directly involved in all of these sources all of the time. But finding ways to stay tuned in—beyond formal reports—makes a huge difference. And it sets the right example. Let me make a few simple recommendations:

- First, brainstorm and identify the many sources of insight that are available. That will probably trigger ideas on how you want to stay close to the action (we'll use these sources in a more formal approach to managing feedback, later in the chapter).

- Think about your schedule and how you can find time for this aspect of leadership. If it's not intentional, it's probably not going to happen.

- Be ready to work through any initial awkwardness. It's not easy, at first, to get out there and observe. And if you're brave enough to help handle the work—say in retail, the contact center, or operations—it takes time and practice. But it yields tremendous insight.

- Use good judgment in how you respond to what you see. Fixing issues in isolation is not the end goal; instead, you're getting a good sense of how well your organization is adjusting and responding.

Implement an effective tactical approach to managing feedback

Let's turn to more formal methods of listening and responding to customers. This area of management is often referred to simply as "managing customer feedback." But there's more to it than the label may suggest. It entails a number of interrelated activities.

I define managing customer feedback as "the process by which an organization collects, analyzes, and acts on customer feedback." This applies whether you're helping a specific customer, or whether you're referring to managing all of the feedback across the organization.

> ❝ **Managing customer feedback:** *The process by which an organization collects, analyzes, and acts on customer feedback*

If you do a search on managing customer feedback, you'll find different perspectives. But they tend to fall into one of two categories. One is tactical. This is when you act on feedback as it happens to solve problems or deliver personalized service. Let's say I'm a flight attendant working a flight. I find out in a casual conversation as you board that you and the debate team you're traveling with just won a national competition. I could make an announcement to the entire plane. Just imagine the memory you and your team will have of the applause from your fellow passengers!

Or maybe there's a problem. You post a note on Twitter: "So much for getting work done on this three-hour flight," which includes a photo of the tray table at your seat, broken and tilting. Our service team is able to respond with an apology (and perhaps a credit).

The other category of definitions is strategic. From this perspective, you collect and analyze feedback from many customers and look for recurring problems and opportunities. For example:

- The Australia Zoo uses customer feedback to shape custom visitor packages (such as the koala experience and the wombat encounter), which has boosted revenues per visit and repeat visits.

- Moen, a manufacturer of faucets and fixtures, uses customer feedback to guide the how-to videos they prepare for YouTube.

- Software company Intuit (maker of the popular financial tools TurboTax, Quickbooks and Mint) uses customer insight when designing accounting packages for specific types of businesses.

So, tactical or strategic? Which of the two definitions is correct? Both! Both are essential and closely related. Each of these organizations responds promptly to specific customers that need help. But feedback is especially powerful when linked to a strategic approach; they all have processes to collect, analyze and take action on a full range of input.

Let's look first at what it takes to respond to feedback as it happens—the tactical approach. There are five key steps that you'll want to ensure are in place.

The first is to identify feedback that requires you to respond as it is occurring. This can happen in a number of settings: in person; feedback through surveys (especially transactional surveys that may require immediate follow-up); posts on social media sites such as Twitter or LinkedIn; comments and ratings through sources such as Amazon, Yelp and Google; feedback through text, phone, chat, or other channels; and, potentially, many others. Not all feedback is response-worthy, nor is it all time-sensitive. I suggest brainstorming this with your team. When and how will your organization respond to feedback that requires a quick response?

Second, you'll need to set up tools that have essential functionality, including: pulling in feedback from all of the various sources; delivering it

FIGURE 3.2   Tactical approach to managing feedback

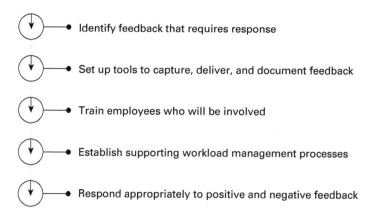

Identify feedback that requires response

Set up tools to capture, deliver, and document feedback

Train employees who will be involved

Establish supporting workload management processes

Respond appropriately to positive and negative feedback

to the person or team who will respond; and enabling you to document the feedback as part of your strategic approach. This doesn't have to require a large investment. For example, there are low-cost tools that monitor online posts from many sources and provide you with the means to engage. Investigate the technologies you already have, and the capabilities you will need (we'll explore tools in Chapter 6).

Third, you'll need to identify and train employees who will be involved. When service is delivered in person it will usually be those employees who are best positioned to respond. But what about feedback through surveys, posts on social sites and other sources? This might require a group you set up, or it could involve leveraging a customer service team (for example, your contact center). In a larger organization, this effort often begins in marketing, but I've often seen it quickly outgrow what marketing can handle from a resource perspective. So, a collaborative effort with marketing, customer service, and potentially other areas makes sense. Each person or team will need training in how to respond, and how to represent your brand consistently.

Next, responding to feedback in a timely manner requires that you have the right resources in place at the right time. So you'll need to establish a way to forecast the workload and ensure you've got the right people and technology capabilities available. And you'll need a process for monitoring and managing the work in real time so that issues don't fester. Finally, you'll need to assess how things are going and make adjustments as you go along.

Responding to positive or general feedback

As a customer, have you ever provided great feedback on products and services you love, but then never heard back? Or, worse, got a templated, automated response? It's a downer. Don't let that happen to your customers. The main recommendation here: show up! Get in the game and respond in a timely manner. I encourage you to establish response time standards—for example, 24 hours, end of the business day, within the hour, or whatever is appropriate for your brand and customers.

In responding to positive feedback, there are time-tested words that are always appropriate: "*Thank you!*" You can take things up another notch by being specific. If there is an opportunity to recognize an individual or team, be sure to do so. A friend of mine noticed an employee at Firehouse Subs hustling to get food out quickly and keep the restaurant in tip-top shape. He sent a simple tweet acknowledging the effort. Soon, he received this message:

> We saw that you tweeted a great note and wanted to let you know how great it was that our crew member, Dylan, received some special recognition. As a thank you for our support, we wanted to send you a box of Firehouse Subs items. We're hooking Dylan up with some swag as well.

My friend enjoys wearing the hat they included in a gift bag. He especially appreciates knowing that they did something to recognize Dylan. Celebrate the things that make your organization special and the customers who notice (for more ideas, see Chapter 7).

Responding to negative feedback

Elon Musk, the successful entrepreneur and CEO of Tesla, SpaceX and other companies, often highlights the importance of negative feedback: "You want to be extra rigorous about making the best possible thing you can. Find everything that's wrong with it and fix it. Seek negative feedback, particularly from friends."[2] Managing customer feedback inevitably involves handling negative feedback. And to Elon Musk's point, take steps to encourage it. You want to minimize the iceberg effect discussed in Chapter 1, by making it easy for customers to share feedback.

The first rule of the road is, as with positive feedback, *show up*. Imagine a customer walks into your office and says, "Hey, I have this problem," and no one even looks up from their work. That's how customers feel when they don't get any kind of reply. Negative feedback can be a ticking time bomb, so be sure to establish response time objectives.

Next, thank the customer for their feedback. Resist the urge to be defensive. When you demonstrate that you value the customer's time and opinion, it often changes the tone of the dialog dramatically. A friend who golfs told me he recently posted a mildly negative review of a course. It was genuine and pointed out things that could be improved. Instead of thanking him, the head pro insisted the poor experience was my friend's fault. That didn't go well. It led to more vehement feedback from him on other review sites. My friend went from passive detractor to genuinely ticked off and actively warning others to avoid that course. Remember, being "right" is far less important than disarming the situation.

If your organization messed up, acknowledge it in a sincere way. And use plain language. How often as a customer do you hear the words, "We regret any inconvenience this may have caused"? As writing coach and trainer Leslie O'Flahavan advises, "If you would never say something to a customer face-to-face, don't write it."[3] Instead, say something like, "Thanks for letting us know we let you down, and for giving us a chance to make it right."

The next step is to take ownership and resolve the issue—fix it! What would it take to earn back the trust and loyalty of the customer? This could take the form of a refund, a credit, a gift, or just resolving the problem. Customers will often tell you what it would take to make it right. Contrary to popular belief, most requests aren't unreasonable. If the customer is asking for the undoable, at least give some options; they often feel better just having some say. Some things shouldn't play out in a public forum, and you may need to move the discussion elsewhere. Finally, document what happened; problems tend to recur until a root cause is identified and resolved.

How you respond to negative feedback will, as much as anything, show the character of your organization. It's a tangible reflection of the commitment you make to be there for your customers. Let's now turn to the strategic approach for managing feedback.

> ❝ How you respond to negative feedback will, as much as anything, show the character of your organization.

Execute a voice of the customer strategy that fully leverages feedback

Whether your organization is a print shop with three employees, a government agency with 3,000, or a multinational company with 300,000, you need a strategy to fully leverage feedback. The process will be more involved for some organizations, but the basic steps are the same.

What is voice of the customer (VoC)?

I use the term voice of the customer (VoC) to describe this process. But is VoC really the same thing as a strategic approach to managing customer feedback? In some organizations, you bet. Their VoC program captures a wide range of feedback, analyzes it, identifies priorities, and ensures the organization is taking action. Some have all of the right components in place.

In other cases, though, VoC activities are far more limited. They may primarily revolve around surveys, but not include other sources of feedback. The VoC program may be too tightly controlled, with only limited involvement from the rest of the organization. In short, what some refer to as VoC might only be part of what is required.

I'm fine with whatever terms you and your organization prefer—managing feedback, VoC, or other. Just know that I am defining VoC in the broadest sense possible. I'm referring to a strategic approach that fully leverages customer feedback. Don't let terms, or what may be a stale, calcified VoC effort in your organization trip you up. You may need to clarify definitions and, most importantly, might need to reshape and upgrade your VoC program so that it is genuinely strategic.

The core steps in a strategic approach include identifying sources, collecting feedback, analyzing input, and taking action based on what you learn. You'll also need to establish and track key performance indicators that tell you how you're doing. And you'll want to assess and improve your feedback initiative, so that you continue to get more value from it. Let's take a look at each step.

Identifying sources

The first step is to identify the many sources of feedback. We got this rolling in the first section of the chapter. Now, you'll want to do a more thorough

FIGURE 3.3   Voice of the customer strategy

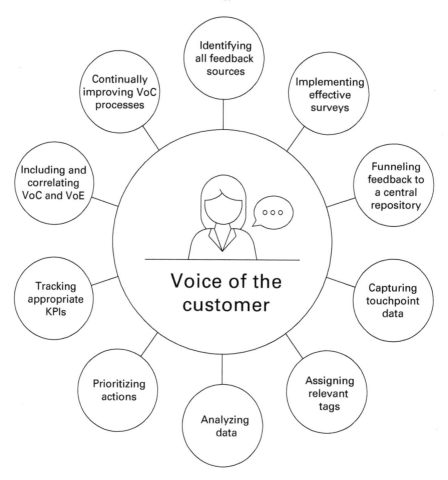

inventory with your team. Many organizations are not casting a wide enough net, so this may be an opportunity to get a step ahead of the pack.

Customer feedback is either structured or unstructured. Structured feedback comes in an organized manner, the result of directly soliciting input from customers. Surveys are the most obvious example. These can be short *transactional surveys* (such as when you're hopping out of the taxi or following an interaction with a service agent). Surveys can also be less frequent but more detailed *relationship surveys* that gauge how a customer feels overall about your brand. Beyond surveys, focus groups with customers can be a great way to gather insight. Welcome or exit interviews as customers come on board, or in those unfortunate cases where they cancel service, can provide helpful insight.

Unstructured feedback can come in many forms and tends to be impromptu. What are customers commenting on as they set up and use products? What are they saying when they post on social sites? Your employees are also close to the action. What do they hear? Someone in accounts payable learns why a customer is not paying an invoice. A support representative gets unsolicited insight on the competition. An executive just happened to sit next to a customer at last weekend's jazz in the park. Forums and reviews on Yelp, Amazon, Google and other sources can offer valuable, unfiltered input from customers.

You can see how many sources of feedback there are. I recommend putting a small team together to identify all potential sources. Build this inventory as new sources emerge. Don't settle for a limited or incomplete understanding of your customers.

GETTING SURVEYS RIGHT

There are two primary categories of surveys. A relationship survey (also called an enterprise survey) is the more comprehensive tool, generating feedback on all key elements that can impact customer satisfaction. Questions on a relationship survey are broad and cover issues such as product quality, ease of use, price, service, and others. They are sent at random to a small percentage of customers on a regular basis.

A transactional survey, as the name implies, is specific to an interaction or service. They are offered to a percentage of (or sometimes all) customers that completed a certain transaction. Transactions can be either self- or employee-assisted, and surveys can take place in any channel (app, text, chat, phone or other). They are designed to tie satisfaction to specific touchpoints.

Establishing this dual-survey feedback loop is important—but not enough to guarantee success. Design is key and while there's no perfect survey, the best share these traits:

- **Representative sample**. I recall an insurance company that had increasingly negative informal feedback from customers in social media posts and complaints to supervisors, yet positive survey scores. I discovered that surveys went only to those customers whose claims were paid in full—a classic case of an unrepresentative sample.

- **Free of bias**. Every part of a feedback process is at risk of bias—from the channel used to the scoring scale to the wording of the questions. A message imploring a customer to provide a high score takes the focus off the experience and puts it on repercussions for the employee or team (the colloquial term is survey begging—see Chapter 1).

- **Interpreted accurately.** I often see organizations point to high customer satisfaction scores that are either 1) not that great—e.g., an 86 percent satisfaction rate means 14 percent dissatisfaction, or 2) overly generalized— for example, they combine 4s and 5s in 5-point scales (or even 3s thru 5s), when research shows a vast difference in loyalty between the two.

While surveys are just a part of customer feedback available, they remain essential. But they are only effective if they are designed and deployed well.

Jay Minnucci, President, Service Agility

Collecting feedback

Once the many sources of customer feedback are identified, the next step is collection. Your feedback process should act as a funnel, catching data from all the various sources and bringing it into a centralized location.

Think about each source producing feedback that goes into a funnel, which directs it to a central repository. This could be a database that's part of your customer relationship management (CRM) system, a dedicated customer feedback system, a business intelligence tool, or perhaps something homegrown. I've seen many different approaches work. As you select the best technology alternatives, keep simplicity and flexibility top of mind.

INTEGRATING SOURCES

From a practical perspective, you may find that your organization has or requires many systems for capturing feedback. Silos with different owners is one of the common hurdles to a comprehensive approach to VoC. You may also find that there are many owners of the data, but no one with overall responsibility to pull it all together.

There are several leadership priorities here. One is to ensure that all feedback makes its way to a centralized repository—have your team thoroughly investigate options for technology and process integration. Temporary or manual workarounds may work for a time but be sure to include this requirement on your technology roadmap. Also, establish a single owner to oversee collection, technology and process support, and tagging. Then ensure that your overall CX initiative shepherds the actions that come out of the input. In the end, what you do with the data and analysis is what truly matters.

As you get feedback from various sources, it's helpful to be consistent in what you collect. Capturing data in a handful of key areas is particularly useful, including:

- **Touchpoint.** What was the touchpoint, or where was the customer in their journey? For example, this could be after a repair, or an interaction with customer service.

- **Objective.** What was the customer's objective? For example, they wanted to get their cable working again.

- **Experience.** What was the actual experience? The cable got repaired but it happened outside the promised window of time.

- **Emotional impact.** What was the emotional impact of this experience? The range you establish could be very satisfied to very unsatisfied, on a scale. I've seen alternatives such as very happy to very frustrated. What words best capture emotion in your setting?

These factors give you a solid foundation for comparing both structured and unstructured feedback. UL, a global company that provides product testing and certification, made a push to more completely capture the on-the-fly feedback their employees were hearing. They created a simple feedback form inside their CRM system. The link can be accessed quickly by any employee, anytime. For example, they can easily pull up the form from their phone and enter the customer's feedback. Nate Brown, who spearheaded the effort, said at the time, "This is a complete game-changer in how UL understands customers."[4]

Another example is an initiative at JetBlue Airways, the vision of Frankie Littleford, Vice President of Customer Support Experience, Operations and Recovery. The airline's founding mission is to "bring humanity back to air travel." Littleford believes this depends on an approach that builds relationships. The airline has been rolling out and perfecting a system that gathers information from all customer touchpoints into a single view. Interactions with a customer are shown in a single timeline. Artificial intelligence (AI) and machine learning are helping automate what were manual processes—finding and escalating high-priority issues, responding or routing the rest to the right teams for follow-up, and developing meaningful reports.[5]

Not all methods for collecting feedback have to be technology-enabled. Homeroom is a popular mac and cheese restaurant in Oakland, California. (Yes, it's a restaurant focused on mac and cheese and it's not to be missed if you're in the Bay Area. My favorites? The Aged White Cheddar Mac and the Jalapeño Popper Mac.) As her restaurant took off, founder Erin Wade encouraged employees to use simple index cards to share ideas, which they filled out by hand and turned in at the end of their shifts. In some cases, "no tech" can be a great starting point.

Analyzing input

This step is the fun part, where disparate data comes to life and begins telling stories. It's a bit like putting a snorkel mask on and jumping off a boat to explore a coral reef. What you discover is often amazing. A new world comes into focus.

It's important at this point to categorize the data so that you can make sense of it and see individual stories. Without organization, you'll have a

FIGURE 3.4 Collecting feedback into a centralized repository

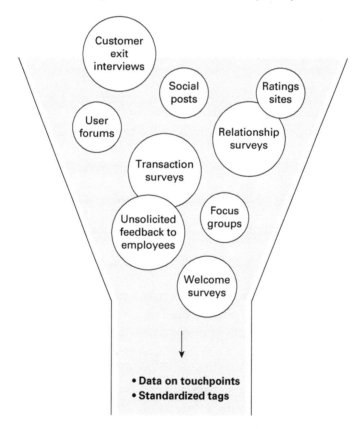

jumble of characters, plots, and themes. You already know from the collection step where the customers were in the journey, and what they were trying to accomplish. Now, you categorize the feedback "type" by assigning each a custom tag. This creates an additional layer of information that enables powerful sorting.

Common tags, say for a software company, would include price, new feature request, usability, bug, and others. Most organizations have a "catch all" tag for feedback that doesn't fit other categories. As you begin assigning feedback to relevant categories, my recommendation is to start out high-level and simple. You can later refine as you see ways in which more detail might be helpful.

Depending on the technology you have, your team may need to assign tags manually with some types of feedback. If you have a large database, you can harness tools such as text analytics to look for keywords customers are using. But some of this work may still be manual. Helpful AI, machine learning and cloud-based tools are progressing daily.

Analyzing feedback is not a perfect science and can in fact get a little messy. But keep a central objective in focus—informed conversations that bring about change. Emily Weiss, Founder and CEO of the fast-growing beauty company, Glossier, makes reviewing feedback a top priority. "Every customer has a microphone and she's reaching 50, 500, 5,000 or 500,000 of her nearest and dearest friends and is able to talk about her preferences,"

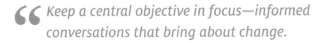

> ❝ *Keep a central objective in focus—informed conversations that bring about change.*

she said to a group of investors.[6] She then shared that she reads every comment that comes in. How feasible that will be as the company grows, only she knows. But I'm certain she'll find the time to stay close to these conversations.

Taking action

How does Emily Weiss weigh priorities when deciding on improvements the organization needs to make? I'm sure she has some great instincts—and a process to back them up. How about you and me? My encouragement is: don't wing it. Like Emily, use your instincts and back them up with an effective process. There are nine criteria central to a sound approach. Together, they can help you and your team make good decisions. They include:

Safety. It's been decades since Johnson & Johnson quickly recalled 31 million bottles of Tylenol following suspicions of product tampering. If you were old enough to care about following the news then, I bet you remember it. Though it cost millions of dollars, J&J earned trust that continues to this day.

Frequency. How often does the issue occur? If you fix the root cause, what's the potential impact? Many software programs wisely warn users when caps-lock is on as they are entering passwords. This simple solution has reduced a world of frustrations.

Magnitude. Let's say you are manager of airline operations, and there's one flight a day to a remote island. You might delay today's flight to the island—just a bit—so a couple on a late inbound flight can make the connection. Yes, it's a 20-minute inconvenience to other passengers—but a whole day's vacation for that couple (25 percent of their four-day itinerary).

Innovation. What kinds of things are on your customers' wish lists for your products and services? Example: as customers, we love notifications on status—e.g., delivery services (furniture, building supplies, et al.) that show we're the fourth stop, and the crew is just heading for stop #3.

Timing. Some issues can wait. Others need to be handled now, given the impact they have on the customer's perception and comfort level. For example, receiving an update on a claim is important but not necessarily urgent. However, a rejected payment that could result in an insurance policy lapse is time sensitive.

Customer segment. This consideration can be tricky—every customer is important. But most businesses prioritize their most loyal customers. In software subscriptions, you can often pay for the level of support you prefer; this helps companies and customers establish and understand expectations.

Prevention. A bedrock principle of effectively managing customer feedback is resolving problems before they happen or before they become larger. GM recently picked up in feedback that some Acadia owners saw a "shift to park" message after they had already shifted to park. GM launched a fast, effective effort to recall cars, repair the issue, and modify production.

Strategy. A biotech firm I worked with developed a strategy to differentiate from competitors through "white glove" 24/7 service. In an effort to improve access, they added chat capability to their website—and saw conversion rates immediately improve.

Brand impact. Brand protection and development is a key benefit of listening to customer feedback. For example, Patagonia is outspoken on environmental issues and examines feedback for opportunities to show support. Turner & Townsend, a UK-based professional services company, has a deep commitment to the Education Fund for children.[7] Only you, your employees, and your customers can identify and define your values. But if you want to be accountable and on point, build a good feedback system.

In the end, determining the best actions to take will involve analyzing a lot of data, seeking insight into what to fix or change, and assessing the customer experience and financial impact. Your data analytics person or team really earns their keep here. Companies that excel with this look for correlations, conduct experiments and, in general, listen to what the data is trying to say. As a leader, think about how your team is using this information to make decisions. Use the data—but don't discount your instincts, either. (We'll explore costs and benefits of improvements in Chapter 9).

Establish and track key performance indicators

Many successful leaders seek a single, overall metric—a key performance indicator (KPI)—that reflects the customer experience. The idea is to have an easy way for anyone to see how things are going. To use a sports metaphor, the actions your team takes represent what's happening on the field. The metric is the score. Having a way to keep score can be valuable—with some cautions in mind.

Measuring how people feel about something is never easy. There has never been, nor will there ever be, a perfect customer experience metric. That said, there are some good options to consider. I'll summarize them briefly here—a search on each will provide you with loads of additional detail and examples:

Customer satisfaction (CSAT). Customer satisfaction, or "see-sat" as its abbreviation is often pronounced, has been around for decades. Scores are based on variations of the survey question, how satisfied are you? Or, how would you rate your experience? CSAT is not a measure of customer loyalty, which is what we'd really love to know. In fact, only behavior can truly gauge loyalty. But a big advantage of CSAT is that it is very common, and you may already have years' worth of data that serves as a baseline. It's also in a structure that is very familiar to customers—we all frequently see and use 4- or 5-point scales, typical to these surveys.

Net promoter score (NPS). Introduced in 2003 by Fred Reichheld, net promoter score (NPS)® is based on the well-worn survey question, how likely is it that you will recommend us to others? Input is provided on a 10-point scale, with 10 being very likely to recommend. In calculating the score, 9s and 10s are considered to be promoters, 7s and 8s are neutral, and 6s and below are detractors. NPS is expressed as an absolute number between minus (–) 100 and plus (+) 100. It is the difference between the percentage of promoters and detractors. So if you have 65 percent promoters and 20 percent detractors, the NPS will be 45. A number like 45 sounds low to the uninitiated, but it's actually very good. Net promoter scores above 0 are considered good; I love to see scores above 50, which are excellent. Tesla, Amazon, Samsung and Starbucks are examples of organizations that scored above 50 in recent NPS benchmarks. Some critics question whether NPS is prescriptive enough in identifying improvement opportunities. But it's based on well-defined methodology and used by over two-thirds of Fortune 500 companies, so you can readily compare results with others.

Customer effort score (CES). Customer effort score (CES) was popularized by the excellent book, *The Effortless Experience.*[8] It's based on a characteristic of service that is very important to all of us as customers— was it easy to resolve a need or issue? Scores are based on the question, how easy was it to resolve your issue? Responses are captured on a seven-point scale—7 being very easy. While CES is a good option for customer service environments, it is limited in measuring overall perceptions of an organization. It's also not as widely adopted for benchmarking purposes. However, where it is a fit, CES is a powerful KPI. Research from Gartner that underpins the metric shows a strong correlation between resolution of a request, and loyalty.

Customer sentiment. Customer sentiment reflects to the extent possible what you really want to know—how customers feel about your products, services and organization. With analytics technologies, capturing customer sentiment is far easier today than even just a few years ago. You can include many touchpoints—a recorded service call, a written customer review, an email, a social post, and others—and quickly establish a customer sentiment score. Customer sentiment is not captured in a survey, but is analysis of feedback that results in a metric you can track. It requires a customer experience management platform that tags, organizes, scores, and reports on feedback. I find wide differences in how it's used, so it's not great for benchmarking. One big advantage, though (and it's a great one!): it does not require customers to fill out surveys. Customer sentiment is an emerging approach that many use alongside, but not as a replacement for, one of the traditional KPIs.

Customer lifetime value (CLV). Customer lifetime value (CLV) is not new to marketers. It's been around for decades. But it has more recently been rediscovered and is taking the CX world by storm. CLV is built on the principle that when you serve customers well, you boost their loyalty and, through repeat business, dramatically improve revenues and profitability. CLV makes some assumptions that not all executives are comfortable with—e.g., estimates of how long a customer will remain loyal, and the value of that loyalty (some feel the world is too unpredictable for long-term projections). Also, CLV takes some assembly. But it can be a powerful and, with reasonable assumptions, realistic representation of the value of customer experiences to customer loyalty and business returns. (We'll look more closely at CLV in Chapter 9.)

Which KPI should you use?

There are quite a few CX metrics from which you can choose. And you do have the option of using different metrics for different parts of the customer journey. However, it's generally best to establish one overall metric. Here are some tips: 1) choose the metric that most clearly correlates to actual customer behaviors, such as customer loyalty; 2) select a metric that encapsulates the larger customer journey; metrics that reflect only some touchpoints will fail to motivate your entire organization; 3) go with a metric that is simple to explain and understand.

Which KPI best reflects what we want to know

My choice? Well, it depends. If you're, say, a global consumer electronics provider, I like net promoter score; NPS works well for comparison and tracking competitive trends. For organizations (commercial and government) that are primarily focused on service, customer effort score is a great choice. And if you're already heavily using CSAT in surveys, that may be the way to go for an overall KPI. And the approach will be immediately relatable at more granular levels; for example, Lyft provides drivers with a weekly summary of overall ratings, along with scores in detailed areas that include navigation, safety, cleanliness, and friendliness.

Whichever route you go, let me add a few recommendations:

- **Ensure that overall scores are not the only thing senior executives look at.** Be sure to also follow customer behavior: Do they continue to buy? Do they try new products? What are they saying about you on social channels? Customers weren't dissatisfied with Kodak when they stopped buying film for their cameras; they just moved to digital alternatives (which, ironically, Kodak helped to invent).

- **Make sure you and others understand the sample behind scores.** For example, satisfaction scores in a customer service area can go down when you make improvements to products. The reason? Customer service will be handling only the most difficult issues that remain. Remember that you're not trying to produce scores. That's not the end game. You want results—better products, services and customer experiences.

- **Be aware of the limitations to any metric.** An overall metric does not inherently provide insight into what needs to change. Use the score as a tool to gauge status and progress, but make sure you're combining it with insights that drive action. We'll look at dashboards in Chapter 6, and explore ways to augment an overall KPI with supporting metrics that provide more specific direction.

Incorporating employee experience

Let's pick up with employee experience, a topic we introduced in Chapter 2. There, we looked at the need to initiate voice of the employee (VoE), methods for collecting data, and alternatives for establishing and tracking a metric. There's real power in comparing VoE and VoC trends. How strong is the correlation between VoC and VoE? Are there common themes—are employees pointing to the same frustrations as customers? As we discussed in Chapter 2, taking action and closing the loop is essential.

> **66** *How strong is the correlation between VoC and VoE findings? Are there common themes—are employees pointing to the same frustrations as customers?*

Assess and improve your feedback initiative

Every organization is getting feedback from customers and employees. But some use it far more effectively. Where does your organization stand? Here's an 11-point self-assessment that can give you a read on how mature your approach is, and where there may be opportunities for improvement.

- Your organization has a culture of actively and intentionally encouraging feedback and acting on it.

- Customer and employee feedback comes from a wide range of sources, which include surveys, interactions with customers, product reviews, social media posts, and others. ~ glassdoor?

- Employees understand how important customer feedback is, and they have the training and incentives necessary to encourage, document and act on it.

- You respond to time-sensitive customer feedback as it occurs.

- You have sufficient tools and systems for encouraging, analyzing and acting on customer feedback.

- You funnel customer feedback (even the things you've already responded to) into a central repository, where you can analyze it to identify deeper trends.

- There is a project owner accountable for ensuring that the organization is making the most of customer and employee feedback.

- You take action based on customer and employee feedback. You use it to identify improvement opportunities and to guide priorities.

- Your organization has a strategic process that includes collecting and analyzing feedback, acting on that feedback to make improvements, and assessing the results of these efforts.

- Your approach involves the broader organization and communicates back to them how feedback is being used.

- Your approach to managing customer feedback is an ongoing part of your overall approach to customer experience.

There is magic that takes place when you are intentional about listening to your customers and employees, then taking action on that insight. Jonathan Ive, Apple's former longtime Chief Design Officer, cautioned against listening only to the biggest, loudest voices. "What we've found is very often the very best ideas come from the quietest voices. Ideas are fragile."[9] Harnessing the power of feedback will enable you to hear all voices. And like anything, you get better at it with practice. Are you able to hear even those quieter voices?

KEY RECOMMENDATIONS

- Practice seeing things from your customer's perspective.
- Implement an effective tactical approach to managing feedback.
- Execute a voice of the customer strategy that fully leverages feedback.
- Establish the right key performance indicators.
- Assess and improve your feedback initiative.

Notes

1   *Undercover Boss*, CBS, 7 February 2010 to present.
2   Juma, N (2020) 50 Elon Musk quotes on success & the future of space, *Everyday Power*, 8 September. https://everydaypower.com/elon-musk-quotes/ (archived at https://perma.cc/V59R-YN6X)
3   O'Flahavan, L (2017) 5 Things you should stop writing to your customers right now, *ICMI*, 6 March. www.icmi.com/resources/2017/5-things-you-should-stop-writing-to-your-customers-right-now (archived at https://perma.cc/X7BQ-3SUQ)
4   Cleveland, B (2019) *Contact Center Management on Fast Forward: Succeeding in a new era of customer relationships*, ICMI Press, United States
5   Cleveland, B (2018) Managing Customer Feedback—as It Happens [blog] *The Edge of Service*, October/November 2018, www.bradcleveland.com/newsletter/oct-2018.php (archived at https://perma.cc/VHE7-CN77)
6   Loizos, C (2018) The beauty company Glossier just closed on a whopping $52 million in fresh funding, *TechCrunch*, 22 February, https://techcrunch.com/2018/02/22/the-beauty-company-glossier-just-closed-on-a-whopping-52-million-in-fresh-funding/ (archived at https://perma.cc/R78E-HZUA)
7   Parnell, L (2017) Action for Children: breaking down barriers to education [blog] *Turner & Townsend*, 4 May, www.turnerandtownsend.com/en/news/action-for-children-breaking-down-barriers-to-education/ (archived at https://perma.cc/69F5-553U)
8   Dixon, M, Toman, N and DeLisi, R (2013) *The Effortless Experience: Conquering the new battleground for customer loyalty*, Portfolio, United States
9   Ive, J (2017) Jony Ive's magical voice for Apple marketing, YouTube, www.youtube.com/watch?v=ydkvO6C9pTs&feature=emb_logo (archived at https://perma.cc/7AWY-NHNL)

04

Boosting the value
of customer service

Singapore is one of my favorite places. I love the food, enjoy the vibrant culture, and admire the world-leading innovation that's brought prosperity to so many who live there. Through my career, I've enjoyed a number of opportunities to participate in projects and conferences there.

My first visit (almost two decades ago now), however, brings back some uncomfortable memories. I was brought in to present to a conference of call center leaders. The theme: how a growing number of call centers were (and still are today) becoming valuable strategic assets. The best were (and are) directly involved in product and service innovation, based on insight picked up when serving customers. The discussion was interactive and it was inspiring to hear the progress being made by so many in the room.

There was a well-attended reception following the event. A journalist with *The Straits Times*, the main newspaper, asked if he could do a quick interview. I agreed and we headed to a corner of the reception area to talk. One of the questions he asked was, "How many call centers have reached this level of strategic value?" This was years ago, and many organizations were new to call centers. Far fewer had built them into strategic assets. My answer: "Our research shows that between 10 and 15 percent of call centers worldwide are leveraging this opportunity. This is a new and exciting development," I enthused.

At 4:30 the next morning, I was in the airport waiting for my flight back to the States. Groggy, I was flipping through a freshly delivered stack of newspapers. Then. There it was. My picture along with the journalist's article splashed across a page. My heart sank as I read the title: "85% of Singapore call centers not well managed, research finds."[1] In the stock picture, I'm smiling in suit and tie, looking like I'm smugly passing judgment on the entire city-state of Singapore. "NO!" I silently screamed to myself. "That's not what I said! That's not even close to what I mean!"

My new friends in Singapore had yet to wake up before my flight took off. Some 18 hours later when I landed in L.A. and turned my phone on, I thought it was going to melt down in my hand. "Why would you say that?" "Are we less advanced?" "I seem to recall you telling us Singapore was among the leaders." And the most heartbreaking to me: "I've been working for years to elevate the status of my center; this article is a setback."

I wrote many notes and apologies. And I sent a letter to the editor with clarifications that got good press. I even think most of my friends there understand what happened and have forgiven me. All is well that ends well. But I resolved at the time to be way more careful with the press. I also made a commitment to do everything in my power to be a voice for the strategic value of customer service.

The trend I was trying to explain to the journalist—boosting the strategic value of customer service—is alive and well and continues to develop today. Ignore it at your peril. It bothers me to sometimes see missed opportunities to serve customers well. It is especially painful, though, to see strategic value literally slip through our fingers. Along with customer feedback, customer service is our golden opportunity to listen (deeply, strategically) and respond.

In this chapter, I first encourage you to assess the current value of your organization's customer service. We'll then look at building services around

FIGURE 4.1   Leadership Framework, Chapter 4: Boosting the value of customer service

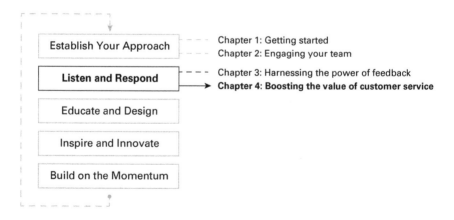

customer expectations, eliminating damaging (and all too common) service frustrations and shaping an effective customer access strategy. We'll conclude with a deeper dive into strategic value—an initiative that goes far beyond "customer service" and fuels customer experience.

Assess the current value of your organization's customer service

Truth be told, many organizations don't get nearly the return they could from their investments in customer service. Often, some misguided perspectives are at work. For example, service is just a necessary cost to be minimized. Or, service is important, but not a differentiator for us; being "okay" is good enough. Or, benchmarks (e.g., on customer satisfaction or costs of service) say we're right in the ballpark. Or most damaging: great service is expensive, right?

On that last point—if you think great service is expensive, just try not-so-great service for a while; you won't like the results. But here's the thing. I'm not overly concerned when I run into these views. I've seen how they can change—in many cases be completely turned around—with some sound analysis and the right business case.

Nope, the situations that worry me are those where the organization has largely bought into the need to provide good service. They are trying to do a good job. And yet, they haven't truly leveraged service to deliver on its potential. That's the worst case—big investments in time, money and energy without the big returns.[2]

Here's a simple framework for assessing the value of your organization's customer service. There are three levels on which effective service creates value. Thinking through each can be helpful in seeing the potential of customer service to shape better customer experiences.

Efficiency. The first level is efficiency. What do you picture when you think of customer service that is efficient? You may envision the right information being accessible at the right times to those delivering service. Or robust self-service capabilities. Or preventing repeat problems before they happen. Each is part of the answer.

Customer satisfaction and loyalty. A second level of value is contribution to customer loyalty. The principle is, if you were to measure customer satisfaction before and after a customer service encounter, effective service should translate into higher scores. In a classic study often cited in business

FIGURE 4.2   Three levels of customer service value

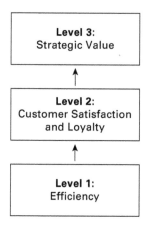

schools, Marriott found that 89 percent of customers who had no problems were likely to return, while 94 percent of customers who had problems that were resolved were likely to return.[3] When service is done right, it does maintain and even boost a customer's loyalty.

Strategic value. A third level of value is strategic. Strategic, meaning cross-functional, impacting the organization as a whole. Here, customer service contributes value to other functions. Every day, your customer-facing services have visibility on the organization's products, services and processes. Those insights can easily fall through your fingers. But when you're set up to capture and use them, they can help the entire organization improve and innovate.

Self-assessment—the strategic value of service

As you consider the strategic (cross-functional) value of customer service, rate yourself on these contributions. Customer service:

- Assists sales and marketing by providing insight on what customers want and expect. This includes identifying any mismatches between what was promised and what is delivered.

- Helps operational areas or manufacturing pinpoint and fix quality problems. This includes insight on products, processes, and user guides.

- Contributes to research and development (R&D). This includes sharing insight on customer requests, the organization's competitive strengths and weaknesses, and innovation opportunities.

- Identifies improvements needed in self-service capabilities, and is a part of designing and improving apps, websites, FAQs, how-to videos, and other resources.

- Serves as an early warning system for potential legal troubles, from product defects, security holes in an app or websites, inaccuracies in warranty statements, and others.

I love seeing organizations make the most of these opportunities. For example, the University of California's Retirement Administration Service Center (UC RASC) uses what they learn to shape retirement resources for their 130,000 members. Lutron—a global electronics company that makes lighting, temperature control, and other systems—harnesses customer interactions to help shape products, improve user guides and simplify connectivity (there's more detail on these examples later in the chapter).

Any organization of any size—from small bike shop to global IT company—can unlock the strategic value of customer service. It's a gold mine. But first things first. Before you can produce this third level of value, you'll need to build a strong foundation. That requires understanding customer expectations, and shaping an effective customer access strategy.

Develop services around evolving customer expectations

The experiences that customers have with any organization—not just yours or others in your industry—shape their perceptions. So you've got to continually revisit what good service means. For customer experience leaders, this can seem like a daunting challenge. Fortunately, it's not hit-or-miss guesswork. The International Customer Management Institute (ICMI) has identified 10 expectations customers have of customer service.[4] They include (in no specific order):

- be accessible (in the channels I prefer)
- treat me courteously
- be responsive to (and anticipate) what I need and want
- do what I ask, promptly
- provide well-trained and informed employees

- tell me what to expect
- meet your commitments and keep your promises
- do it right the first time
- follow up
- be socially responsible and ethical

What is changing, of course, is what these expectations mean. Accessibility is an example. For many organizations—even, say, a small retail store—customers assume that your services will be available from a convenient range of channels, which may include in-person, phone, self-service, mobile-friendly information, and any number of alternatives. They may initiate dialog through their smart watch or with voice command. Customers don't want to think about the channels or processes. They just want service to be understandable and easy.

Beyond these 10 expectations, there is another category of expectations that applies to service delivered in person, such as in a retail store or restaurant. It's called "tangibles," and refers to the aesthetics and functionality of the environment.[5] In other words, anything that impacts the customer's perception of the organization and service being delivered. These include:

- the facilities (comfort, appearance, functionality)
- employees' appearance (e.g., is there a dress code?)
- safety (e.g., masks during Covid-19 or a well-lit parking lot)
- amenities (e.g., Wi-Fi and water in waiting areas)
- design (e.g., how easy it is to get around a building or complex)
- other factors unique to your environment (e.g., daycare at a gym)

In fact, other customers can be considered one of the tangibles. Most restaurants require shoes and shirts, and some even ties or jackets. But for a snack bar at the beach, swimwear is fine.

You'll want to consider both categories—the 10 expectations of service and the tangibles. Then, regularly revisit customer expectations with your team as you shape your approach to service. I encourage you to be creative. For example, Andaz hotels, which is part of the Hyatt group, replaced the traditional lobby with a comfortable, open lounge; arriving guests are treated to a beverage as they are checked in by a host with a tablet. And here's one of my favorite examples: many dentists' offices, once dreaded by children, now feature greeters at the door, games, and a choice of flavors for cleanings. If your intent is to promote and encourage better health with these young customers, *why not make it fun?!*

Unfortunately, poor examples abound. Let me mention two—and my purpose is not to call them out here publicly, so I'm withholding names (I will send a copy of the book to them with a constructive note). One is a historic hotel in the San Diego area that I've stayed at many times over the years. It's one of my favorites, but they are, it seems, becoming complacent. The first thing you're greeted by these days is a long, slow-moving line in the crowded lobby, just to check in. It feels incongruent with the storied history of the property. We've sometimes made other arrangements just to avoid the hubbub—it's a process that begs for innovation.

Another example is a well-known manufacturer of windows and doors. The message on their homepage: Our goal is to exceed your expectations. One of my colleagues, part of the review team for this book, relayed to us an experience she's having with the company: "For two months, I've been trying to get help from them to replace rain strips on windows they provided. I've begged, I've pleaded. I've used a magnifying glass to painstakingly provide serial numbers. I finally got a quote by email for $1,400. Clearly, they're not interested in providing this help. I then found a little company called Swisco. Their website allows me to text pictures of what I need. Within five minutes, I was directed to a specific part number and tool to confirm measurements. I placed an order for $75 and can replace the weather stripping myself. What the manufacturer doesn't know is that we have a remodel in the works and there is no way we would consider using them again."

> ❝ *Like termites you can't see, poor experiences eat away at your brand and threaten your future.*

The hotel and the window manufacturer I mentioned have good brands and may be okay for a while. *Maybe.* One thing I'm sure of, though, is that they aren't aware of the damage they are doing. They are forcing good employees to field these frustrations and are squandering customer time and goodwill. Like termites you can't see, poor experiences eat away at your brand and threaten your future.

As you explore customers' expectations, let me make three recommendations. First, listen to your customers. Make the effort to get input from customers and employees firsthand. And make use of all forms of customer feedback to better understand expectations (see Chapter 3). Second, trust your instincts. If you prefer clean restrooms when you're on a road trip, if you would like to run a question by your insurance company on a Saturday morning (because you're busy the rest of the week), these may be obvious opportunities. Companies such as Wawa and GEICO have leveraged them into services that have fueled their brands. Third, and above all, make service easy and resolve issues quickly. Simplicity and speed are proving to be sure winners.

(There are resources at www.bradcleveland.com/resources that can help you and your team think through your customers' expectations.)

Eliminate the most damaging customer service frustrations

When my iPhone battery life began to diminish, I searched for "Apple support phone number." While Apple doesn't hide their phone number, I scrolled down the page to see what other options were available. It was a Monday morning, and I knew they would be busy. I navigated to the header—*Need service or support? Start your request online, and we'll find you a solution*—then selected my product and problem. I was then offered four options: bring the product into a store, send it in for repair (which I could schedule online), initiate a chat, or initiate a call. Current estimated wait times were provided for each channel. The automated tool issued me an "issue ID," and when I initiated a call, my product/problem selections were passed along to the rep.

Of course, with some behind-the-scenes knowledge, you know this intake method quickly resolves issues that don't need a live rep. It decreases misdirects by gathering critical information before the interaction is routed. I avoided the phone menu entirely since the automated system knew who I was and why I was calling. I was placed in the appropriate queue. The wait time estimate was provided, an acceptable five minutes. The rep who answered my call knew who I was, why I was calling, had my warranty information, and we jumped right into troubleshooting.

Why can't all companies do this? The principles that guide effortless customer experiences seem basic: don't make me wait, make it easy to access service, provide me with a knowledgeable and helpful service team member, create easy processes, and know who I am. The truth is, it's difficult to get customer service basics right, and many organizations don't. While customer service catastrophes still make headlines (remember Dave Carroll's hit song

United Breaks Guitars?[6]), run-of-the-mill customer service annoyances are still maddeningly common. And the consequences to businesses are dire. You've perhaps seen these or similar statistics: 88 percent of customers consider customer service when they contemplate a purchase, and 58 percent will stop doing business with a company after a poor service experience.[7]

For customer-focused companies who exist to provide effortless, pleasant, and sometimes dazzling customer experiences, this is their life's work. They know customer service is both a frequent customer touchpoint and a well-known source of dissatisfaction. As a result, resolving service frustrations is often among the first stops for any organization working to improve customer experiences. There are five universal frustrations that can point you in the right direction.

1. Don't make me wait

Waiting in line, waiting for a callback, waiting for a return to be processed, an order to be delivered, or an application to be approved. Customers don't like waiting. When left to wait too long, they're more likely to go somewhere else next time (if they can), tell their friends and family, and take it out on the employee who ends up helping them.

How long is too long? The answer can vary. Benchmarks provide useful data points but don't reflect your unique customers and the issues they are trying to resolve. An insurance company may find their customers are less wait-tolerant to file a claim, but more wait-tolerant to check on a payment. A medical center may find customers expect the contact center to be open before the day's first appointment at 5:00 am.

The great news is this information is available if you're willing to go to the trouble to get it. Survey customers about wait times. Correlate wait times with customer satisfaction data by customer type and service. Analyze the percentage of customers who abandon along with wait times. These steps will add up to a more complete picture. The bottom line: are your customers happy with the wait when they need help? In a customer-centric organization, this matters more than the length of the actual delay (see box below, the power of one).

I used to sympathize with organizations that grapple with busy Monday mornings or heavy seasonality. No more. Consider Balsam Hill, the world's largest provider of handcrafted artificial Christmas trees (the Vermont White Spruce is stunning). Mac Harman, founder and CEO, told me (and I'm resharing with his permission) that 60 percent of Balsam Hill's annual sales arrive in the five weeks from November 1 through the first week in December. That's no typo: *60 percent!!* How do they do it? A combination of five things: 1) all hands on deck, 2) business partners, 3) an incessant focus on preventing unnecessary customer service issues (better manuals, quality improvements, video and text FAQs), 4) chatbots, and 5) a secret ingredient that I can only guess at: Bailing wire and chewing gum? Magic? Co-sourcing with Santa? If Mac and his team can handle that kind of peak, the rest of us should be able to tackle those busy Monday mornings.

THE POWER OF ONE

Employees have an impact that goes far beyond the customers they directly help. Consider a group of 20 employees who are helping 100 customers over a 30-minute period of time. I produced a table of predictions based on the formula Erlang C. (Erlang C predicts staffing requirements when customer queues are involved—retail stores, contact centers, restaurants, or others. A search will locate web pages that provide Erlang C calculations, and most staffing software uses the formula. To access a simple Erlang C calculator, see www.bradcleveland.com/resources.)

FIGURE 4.3   Example of a customer queue

Average handling time: 5 minutes
Number of callers in half hour: 100

Employees	<= Number of customers waiting longer than x seconds =>											
	5	10	15	20	30	40	50	60	90	120	180	240
17	90	90	89	89	88	87	86	85	82	79	74	69
18	65	64	62	61	58	56	53	51	45	39	30	23
19	46	44	43	41	38	35	33	30	24	19	12	7
20	32	30	29	27	24	22	19	17	12	9	5	2
21	22	20	19	17	15	13	11	10	6	4	2	1
22	14	13	12	11	9	8	6	5	3	2	1	0
23	9	8	7	7	5	4	4	3	2	1	0	0
24	6	5	4	4	3	2	2	1	1	0	0	0

With 20 team members, 32 customers wait five seconds or longer. As things play out (just glance along that row from left to right), 30 customers are still waiting ten seconds or longer, 29 are still waiting 15 seconds or longer, and so forth. You can see that a couple of customers wait 240 seconds (4 minutes) or more.

What happens if you have only 17 employees? *Woah! Dozens of customers are waiting four minutes or longer.* Look at the results when you have just one more person who jumps in and helps out. You've seen that dynamic on expressways. When one car stalls on the side of the road, every lane can get backed up. And you've seen it in busy grocery stores; when they open one more checkout lane, all the lines shift around and everything moves more quickly.

Just remember, each employee has a significant positive impact on customer wait times—a ripple effect far beyond the customers they serve directly. Include this principle in training—knowing about it can put a new bounce in their step and pride in their work.

2. Make it easy for me to find help

Making it easy for customers to find help encompasses the entire customer journey, including customer communications, self-service, interactive voice response (IVR), and digital channels. Consider a recent problem you experienced. How easy was it to find the right place to direct your question—a dedicated Twitter profile, a phone number, an email address, a chat link? Was it a channel you prefer? Did you get to the right resource easily, or did you get transferred or moved to another channel? Did you feel confident you were in the right place?

Making it easy to find help takes thought and design. Those who design communications, phone menus, web pages, and mobile apps will need to anticipate when, why, and how customers will contact the organization. A solid customer access strategy, which we'll discuss in the next section, is an important tool.

3. Provide knowledgeable and friendly customer service staff

When things go wrong, your customers will turn to your employees for advice, support, and resolution. Customers will form an opinion of the company based on those they interact with. That is why hiring capable employees, training them well, giving them the tools they need, and empowering them to deliver good service is so important.

It is easy to obtain customers' perceptions of the helpfulness of your employees. Customer satisfaction scores, complaints, and employee observations can help you determine which customer service team members shine, and who needs additional training or coaching. Analysis of feedback and observations may also alert you to the need for improvements in recruiting and hiring, training and coaching, even goals and metrics, to support the service customers want.

4. Create customer-friendly policies and processes

Processes are at the core of service delivery. Processes largely determine how long customers wait, how easy it is for them to access help, and virtually every other aspect of service and support. Even the most dedicated customer service team members are crippled when they have to represent inconvenient policies or work within cumbersome processes. And we know the majority of escalated complaints are due to issues that needed multiple contacts to resolve or required the customer to navigate complicated processes.

As you map customer journeys (see Chapter 5), keep some goals in mind. You want customers to feel that getting to a positive resolution is easy and that you are there to support them. Gathering data on how well your processes are performing can take some digging. You may need to trace the customer over time, across multiple channels and departmental touchpoints. Technologies are getting far better. But in most cases, customer feedback and employee input will provide much of the information you need.

5. Know who I am

Consumers expect a seamless experience when they move from one service channel to another—for example, when opening a ticket in an online portal and then calling about it. When customers call multiple times about a single issue, they expect the representative to know who they are and what's happened so far. This means creating systems and methods to proactively identify customers. That will enable you to access their history, and track their journey through multiple contacts, touchpoints, and channels. From an experience perspective, your goal is for the customer to hear, "Hi Mr. Jones, I see you have an application started in our system. Are you calling about that today?"

Studies reveal these five frustrations as most common. But are they your customer's frustrations? And to what degree? I encourage you to use this list as a starting point, to fuel your own customer service pain point audit.

One more recommendation here: don't get discouraged. An experienced and influential practitioner who was part of the review team for the book shared these comments: "I'm feeling a little overwhelmed with this section. For one, there seems to be pressure from many to introduce new channels. But don't you have to do a good job with those you already have? Can't you direct customers to channels that will facilitate the help they need? Second, these five areas are presented as the basics. But they are hard, and I get discouraged. Is that just me?"

There's a lot of wisdom in his comments and I agree 100 percent. Don't get too clever before you get the basics in order. To use a sports metaphor, these five areas are "blocking and tackling" (the fundamentals). But blocking and tackling is not easy. That's why, whatever your sport, musical instrument, or craft, you worked on the fundamentals more than any other area. Over and over. That's why the greats stress them. They'll never be easy. This is an ongoing pursuit. Don't get discouraged and don't strive for perfection. Do keep working on them.

> **❝** *Don't get too clever before you get the basics in order... these five areas are "blocking and tackling" (the fundamentals). But blocking and tackling is not easy.*

Shape a cohesive customer access strategy

Whether you're a small startup, a national government, or a multinational corporation, you need a plan that defines how your organization will deliver customer service. In most organizations, the need for a plan becomes clear. Think about introducing a new product. How will you support it? What person or group will handle customer service issues? Will that impact resources and budgets? You get the idea—there are many decisions you and your team will need to make.

In customer service, the overall plan is your "customer access strategy" (it can also be referred to as a customer engagement strategy, or just service strategy). Let's look at what a customer access strategy is, and the components that make up an effective plan.

I define customer access strategy as "a framework—a set of standards, guidelines and processes—describing the means by which customers receive or are enabled to access the information, services and expertise they need."

> " **Customer access strategy:** *A framework—a set of standards, guidelines and processes—describing the means by which customers receive or are enabled to access the information, services and expertise they need*

An effective customer access strategy includes 10 components and my encouragement is to begin by identifying them and thinking about them together.

COMPONENTS OF A CUSTOMER ACCESS STRATEGY

- Customer segments
- Types of interactions
- Access alternatives
- Hours of operation
- Service level
- Routing
- People/technology
- Information
- Analysis/improvement
- Guidelines for deploying new services

First, consider **customer segments**. In a large organization, this is typically defined along with marketing, and it summarizes how customers are logically segmented. For example, insurance companies will identify segments by the policies needed, where customers are located, whether they are businesses or consumers, and so forth. Even the smallest organizations have segments to consider—your restaurant may encourage special celebrations, group functions, business meetings, or others.

Second, identify **types of interactions**. For example, placing orders, customer service, technical support, and others. Think through how each type of interaction could improve customer loyalty and build value. Some you'll work to eliminate (through improved products and services), some you'll want to automate through self-service, and some will best be served with the involvement of a person.

You'll then look at **access alternatives**. This step—where strategy really begins to get practical—identifies all of the possible communication channels (phone, chat, email, social media, text, video, app on smartphone or smartwatch, face-to-face, self-service, customer communities… the lot) along with corresponding telephone numbers, web addresses, email addresses, social media usernames, IVR menus, physical addresses, etc. Where more than one channel is involved in an interaction (say, when a customer begins in an app and has a conversation with a person) define as many possible combinations as you can.

Next, consider **hours of operation** and how they may vary for different types of interactions. Generally, self-service applications will always be available. Some employee-assisted services may be available 24/7, while others may have more limited hours. For example, customers can report emergencies such as downed power lines to their utility any time of day or night, with general customer service (billing inquiries, etc.) available during the day.

Next, **service level** defines the organization's objectives for speed of getting help. What are your goals to minimize how long customers will have to wait? Different objectives may be appropriate for different types of interactions, contact channels, and customer segments.

Next, you'll consider **routing**. This part of the plan covers how—by customer, type of interaction and access channel—each customer interaction is going to be routed and distributed to the right place. In other words, what person or what team is going to handle it?

The next component summarizes the **people and technology** resources required. This step transitions from "getting the customer to the right place at the right time" to "doing the right things." Which employees and which systems will come into play for each type of interaction?

The eighth component of your plan summarizes the **information** required. What information on customers, products and services will need to be accessible? What information should be captured during the service interaction? This is a logical place to summarize how the organization will comply with any privacy or reporting requirements.

In the next step, **analysis/improvement,** you'll define how the information captured will be used to better understand customers and to improve products and services. You may also want to summarize major performance objectives and how the value and contributions of customer service will be measured.

In the final step, **guidelines for deploying new services,** your plan should outline a framework for deploying new services, including technology architecture (corporate standards and technology migration plans) and investment guidelines (priorities for operational and capital expenditures). This step should also describe who will keep the customer access strategy current as services evolve, such as who has overall responsibility, how often the plan will be updated, and who has ownership of individual components.

You might be thinking, *whew,* there's a lot to it! To the contrary, though, it's a nightmare to not have a customer access strategy. A consultant who reviewed the book wrote: "This is so straightforward. If only everyone put thought into it. I'm working with a client that has thousands of contact points. There has been no impetus to provide any control or guidance. Anyone seems to be able to set up a Facebook page, LinkedIn group, or new phone number. Now they are grappling with how to provide service on all those fronts. It is a mess."

I've found without fail that the thought you put into your CAS will come back to you in both time and better decisions. Just recently, I've seen the benefits for a small catering company and a large government service operation with more than 10,000 employees. So just get started. Start simple and begin to build out these 10 components. You will soon see the benefits of having a common plan to work from. (There is a customer access strategy worksheet at www.bradcleveland.com/resources.)

What does a customer access strategy look like?

Customer access strategies are like business plans in that some are well documented and others exist only in pieces and in the heads of various managers. Too often, the latter is the case. But there are standout examples of plans that are effective and up to date.

A mobile phone company I have worked with has a well-organized customer access strategy, which lives on the organization's secure intranet. It consists of a cleanly designed home page, the centerpiece, which provides links to each of the individual components. The links access files (e.g., data-bases, documents) that make up the different parts of their plan, such as customer segments, access numbers and addresses, routing diagrams, customer service teams, hours of operation, service level objectives (and so forth). There are also links within these areas that allow you to logically move to others—but the home page will always get you back to the main directory.

The most impressive aspect of the plan is that it lists who is responsible for keeping the overall plan current, and the individuals who have ownership over various components, including marketing (customer segments) and IT/telecom (routing schematics). Each document has an "updated on ___" date notation. The plan is current, and they don't make major decisions without referring to it.

Your customer access strategy will be a guide that you can use to answer many important questions. For example, how should your customer service functions be organized? What kinds of skills and knowledge will your employees need? What system capabilities best support your strategy? Are your organization's overall strategy, customer access strategy, and the realities of budgets and resources in alignment?

Customers don't think of contact channels or departments. You don't hear a customer say, "I'm going to contact XYZ's customer service department." They simply say, "I'm going to contact XYZ." To them, customer service is the company. The best-led organizations know this, and they cultivate customer access strategies that enable their brands to shine through. (You'll find some additional examples and templates at www.bradcleveland.com/resources.)

> ❝ The best-led organizations cultivate customer access strategies that enable their brands to shine through.

CASE STUDY
"Playbook" at the University of California

Does a customer access strategy sound like something that would be nice to have? Actually, it's vital. Just ask anyone who's part of the University of California's Retirement Administration Service Center (UC RASC).

The University of California is the world's leading public research university system, with 10 campuses, five medical centers, three national labs and a network of researchers and educators. The RASC provides retirement administration services to professors, administrators and others who are part of the university's retirement plan—more than 130,000 active members, as well as thousands more who are inactive vested members or retiree health enrollees.

Ellen Lorenz, Director of UC RASC, shares, "The more we worked on our customer access strategy, the more excited we got about it. It has become a tool that all of us within the RASC use and reference. It gives the team a strategic view of why we do what we do—a view that doesn't get lost in day-to-day activities." Many RASC employees provided input into shaping the customer access strategy, which the team now refers to as the "Playbook."

The Playbook has brought many benefits: better focus on priorities, teams that are increasingly self-directed, and projects that come in on time and within budget. It even helps RASC employees envision and develop their careers. And the most exciting benefit? The University of California uses the RASC as an enticement to attract some of the best professors, doctors, researchers and specialized talent available in the global market.[8]

Make it yours!

What access channels should be opened up? What's the nature of the service you intend to provide? These decisions are yours to make. My advice: make your customer access strategy uniquely yours—do what's best for your customers and your organization. Here are some examples of how customer access strategies are playing out:

- Discover Card uses in-app messaging technology to enable customers to reach employees easily. Customers can respond to employees when they choose without having to start over on an issue. This is a big advantage over conventional chat, which requires customers to stay connected until a problem is resolved.

- Dyson, manufacturer of household appliances, prominently displays its website and toll-free number right on product handles—clearly visible to anyone who uses an appliance. While some organizations try to discourage contact by making information hard to find, Dyson sends the bold message that they are there to help.

- Intuit's Accounting Professional Division developed an active customer community where users help each other with questions. Intuit's contact center employees have become facilitators and a second level of support—problem solvers for issues requiring the company's involvement. The technology allows easy access to the community directly from software packages. (We'll discuss user community platforms in Chapter 6.)

- Barclays Bank, based in London, England, has been a pioneer in video banking, enabling customers to use their smart phone or tablet to chat "face to face" with a representative. The service is available 24 hours a day, 7 days a week, and supports a wide range of the bank's products and services.

- Many companies that provide technical support—Dell, Square, and others—have embraced co-browse capabilities, which enable the support rep to share the customer's screen and directly access the system to fix problems. These capabilities have significantly boosted quality and customer satisfaction, while reducing handling times.

These are just glimpses of approaches that came about thoughtfully. Observe the organizations you most enjoy doing business with, and you'll notice the best deliver services in ways that meet your needs and complement their brands.

Given the many ways to interact, a best practice is to create an easy-to-find online guide to access alternatives. Do a search on "how to contact [HSBC, KLM, Apple]" and you'll see good examples of the primary ways to reach the organization. And a word to the wise: organizations that make their contact information hard to find (usually in an attempt to minimize costs) are asking for trouble. A search will usually pull up other sources—blogs, customer communities, and sites that provide tips for reaching the organization. These can include contact numbers, advice on navigating difficult menus, or (when the company is perceived to be purposely hard to reach) direct contact numbers for administrative offices or executives.

Clearly, a customer access strategy is not something you throw together in an afternoon team brainstorm (though that can give the creative part a push!). It takes leadership, persistence, and participation from across the

> ❝ Organizations that make their contact information
> hard to find (usually in an attempt to minimize
> costs) are asking for trouble.

organization. But the payoffs are huge. From a customer's perspective, a good strategy will result in simplified access, more consistent services, and a high degree of convenience. From the organization's perspective, you are building a platform that enables you to boost the value of customer service.

Build the strategic value of customer service

Understanding customer expectations, eliminating service frustrations, and shaping an effective customer access strategy are important steps in building a strong foundation. But what about strategic value? How do you take your services to that level? A practical way to get started is to build a cross-functional team to analyze the reasons for customer service interactions. Graph the frequency of top drivers to discover trends, then act on what you're learning.

There are two essential categories of information. One comes from the interactions themselves: What are the drivers of customer service issues, the reasons customers need help? And what do you learn in the course of handling interactions? A second source of information comes from assessing the impact of improvements. For example, how many service calls are avoided as you improve self-service? How are customer reviews influenced by service improvements?

CASE STUDY
Lutron's "Insight Center"

Lutron, a global electronics company, is a major player in the Internet of Things (IoT) and connected home markets. Products include control systems for lighting, ceiling fans, shading and others, which can be controlled from smartphones, voice assistants (such as Alexa), and other devices.

Matt Dixon, advisor and co-author of *The Effortless Experience,* and Tim Donchez, Continuous Improvement Director at Lutron Electronics, recently presented a case study of Lutron's experience in harnessing strategic value. Lutron's contact centers handle complex interactions—they come from retail partners, distributors, electricians, architects, individual consumers and others. And they inherently involve products not only from Lutron, but from other companies as well. Tim shared an essential ingredient to success: "We hire great people, and we trust them to use their judgment to serve our customers."

Lutron records calls and uses analytics to better understand the content of those calls, but not with improving frontline performance as the objective. Instead, the goal is to mine the rich feedback customers provide on Lutron's products, brand, services, installation experiences and (as Matt puts it) "almost every other thing that leaders at Lutron need to make better products and deliver a better experience to their customers."

Tim points to numerous insights that have been gleaned through this approach. For example, a particularly vexing installation problem that drove a lot of calls was solved by addressing some confusing language in the installation instructions. In other examples, the contact center partnered with the engineering team on new product launches, and provided guidance to retail partners on products and services.

Tim summarizes the value of the contact center: "We've got a line of business partners out the door who want to get access to the data because it allows them to deliver products and experiences to our customers—to learn quickly what's working and what's not and then to act decisively."[9]

The real value in customer service is in being a set of antennae, the eyes and ears that can help you understand what's happening and to see ahead. Yes, service is necessary to help those customers. It always will be. But the real value is in helping ALL customers (and future customers) by being an engine of innovation. My encouragement is to revisit the self-assessment near the beginning of the chapter: How can you be proactive in helping the organization set and meet expectations? How can customer service be a partner in innovation and improvement across functional areas—marketing, operations, R&D, IT, and others?

Only a small percentage of organizations harness the strategic value of customer service. So as you develop this area, you'll be among the few and the best. And you'll be positioning customer service to strongly support your customer experience transformation.

KEY RECOMMENDATIONS

- Assess the current value of your organization's customer service.
- Develop services around evolving customer expectations.
- Eliminate the most damaging customer service frustrations.
- Shape a cohesive customer access strategy.
- Build the strategic value of customer service.

Notes

1 Poon, A (2004) Poor service standards: 85% of Singapore call centres mismanaged, *The Straits Times*, p A17, 12 October

2 Cleveland, B (2020) How to build a cross-functional team and improve your ROI on customer service, *Forbes*, 30 April, www.forbes.com/sites/ forbesbusinesscouncil/2020/04/30/how-to-build-a-cross-functional-team-and- improve-your-roi-on-customer-service/?sh=179f9005326e (archived at https:// perma.cc/A8ND-NZS9)

3 Kalb, I (2016), How customer complaints can improve business, *CBS News*, 23 June, www.cbsnews.com/news/how-customer-complaints-can-improve-business/ (archived at https://perma.cc/Q384-TU45)

4 Cleveland, B (2019) Customer Expectations Worksheet, Brad Cleveland Company LLC, www.bradcleveland.com/worksheets/Customer%20 Expectations%20Worksheet.pdf (archived at https://perma.cc/FUS2-L2ZA)

5 Ibid

6 Carroll, D (2009) United Breaks Guitars, posted 6 July, YouTube, www.youtube. com/watch?v=5YGc4zOqozo (archived at https://perma.cc/74RE-L7CA)

7 Microsoft Dynamics 365 (2020) Global state of customer service: the transformation of customer service from 2015 to present day, https://info. microsoft.com/ww-landing-global-state-of-customer-service.html (archived at https://perma.cc/UL2N-JCYC)

8 Cleveland, B (2019) *Contact Center Management on Fast Forward: Succeeding in a new era of customer relationships*, ICMI Press, United States

9 Ibid

PART THREE

Educate and design

05

Telling your customer's story

Josh Lewin, a sportscaster respected throughout the worlds of collegiate and professional sports, is a neighbor and friend of mine. He's currently a play-by-play announcer for the Boston Red Sox, as well as for the UCLA Bruins football and basketball teams. Along with many years of broadcasting, Josh has contributed an impressive repertoire of blogs, podcasts, and books.

When Covid forced shutdowns in early 2020, Josh and much of the rest of the announcing world found themselves with unexpected free time. To keep their skills sharp, a friendly competition emerged—announcing the mundane. Josh and other professional sportscasters announced mini-events such as pedestrians crossing a street, a microwave cooking lunch, even a palm tree swaying in the breeze. They then posted these short clips online (search for "Josh Lewin taquito" and enjoy an example).[1]

Josh can make even boring or lopsided games interesting. Heck, he can make a microwave cooking a taquito seem interesting. And it got me thinking. I'm no Josh, but I can tell a pretty interesting story if you press me. And so can you. Why, then, do we as leaders put up with what is often an appalling lack of attention to customer data? Do we (those of us leading customer experience) bear any responsibility here?

I'll admit, in my earlier years I put a lot of emphasis on logic and data. Just *prove* what you need to do—make your case and back it up with data. Boom, case closed. I've since discovered that it doesn't usually work like that. Josh wraps data in a compelling narrative. Similarly, there's a skill among customer experience teams and leaders that I've found to be surprisingly important—that of storyteller. Storytelling is an important part of "educate and design"—the next major theme in our framework.

This begins with developing... or maybe I should say, rediscovering... the art of telling a story. Rediscover because most of us were pretty good at it

FIGURE 5.1   Leadership Framework, Chapter 5: Telling your customer's story

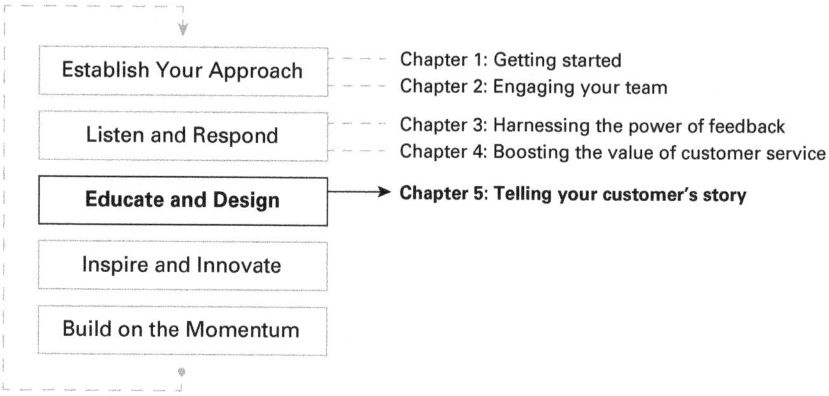

once. Recall a time when you were seven or eight years old. Circled up with friends, eyes wide, breathlessly describing a summer adventure or whispering about who likes who. You've got this.

Develop the art of telling your customer's story

In the Middle Ages, storytellers, often called troubadours, were honored members of royal courts. They were expected to know everything from noteworthy historical tales, to healing remedies, to court gossip. Few others had the ability to influence the thoughts and behaviors of people like the resident storyteller.

I've seen how successful customer experience leaders do much the same. Organizations and those who are part of them are, by nature, resistant to change. Without a compelling case or reason, they stay on course. Being a catalyst for change requires something different... something out of the norm... to stir them to action.

Enter a story—the customer's journey. It might be a narrative of our hero, the customer, overcoming obstacles and achieving unparalleled success. Or it could be a story of tragedy, one that leaves your colleagues longing for a happier ending. Until you show the impact that your organization has on the lives of your customers, it will be difficult to drive meaningful change. There are many tried and proven storytelling tools you can choose from, but regardless of the specific approach you use, compelling stories share some common elements.

Freytag's Pyramid

Any accomplished writer of movies or plays will know "Freytag's Pyramid" forwards and backwards. Gustav Freytag was a 19th-century German playwright who identified the components of effective stories. He didn't exactly invent them—they had been around for centuries and his work was largely based on his study of classics. But he gets the credit for identifying and communicating these components as part of a model that makes intuitive sense.

FIGURE 5.2   Freytag's Pyramid

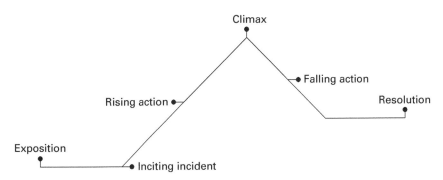

You can today find a plethora of well-researched and comprehensive resources (books, articles, courses, podcasts) on storytelling and presentations in business. (An example of a resource I recommend for those wanting a deeper dive is *The Leader's Guide to Storytelling* by Steve Denning.[2]) I encourage you to spend time with them as you feel the need and inclination. However, I still tend to cite and use Freytag's Pyramid due to its simplicity and familiarity. There's a good chance you had a writing or drama class where you learned the essential elements of Freytag's Pyramid:

Exposition (introduction): Here, the storyteller sets the stage, providing an introduction to the setting, characters, background and, of course, the hero.

Inciting incident: This is a trigger, something that happens that kicks the story into action.

Rising action: The action in the story builds.

Climax: This is the pinnacle of the story, the turning point for the hero.

Falling action: This is the action that happens following the turning point.

Resolution: This is traditionally referred to as the denouement, which means "the ending." The ending can be triumphant or tragic.

As you bring your audience on the customer journey, I encourage you to include these elements as part of the narrative. Let's say your company's main product is incident management software—a computer program that helps your customers track and fix problems with their technology systems (this is just an example—your organization might be very different). Here's how you might use Freytag's Pyramid to shape and tell a customer story.

Introduction: We were successful in sealing a deal with a new customer, which happens to be a well-known regional healthcare provider: XYZ Health Network. This is a win for our credibility in the market. XYZ is currently managing incidents with a competitor's aging application that is part home-grown and part off-the-shelf. They selected us because they had heard that our incident management system is reliable and that we back it up with great support.

One thing to remember, though. A critical must-do in bringing them onboard is that they *must have* the system live and working before March 1st. This is regulatory-driven and involves processing mandatory reports. Senior executives made it clear that missing this target would result in dire consequences for XYZ and their brand, and failure could put careers at risk. "Don't muck this up," as one executive put it.

Inciting incident: *Oh… no…!* We discovered—to our horror—that our February release broke a key piece of functionality in their application. It's just not working. All systems are customized somewhat, and there's always the risk that an update will cause a compatibility issue. That's why we have checks and balances. But as Murphy's law would have it, this marquee account is the one customer system having problems with the update.

Frankly, the problem is at least partially their fault; they didn't identify some of the parameters we needed to include in the design. We made it clear what was required on our end. But blame and finger pointing won't get us out of this or do either organization any good. The "go-live" date is compromised, and the customer's team—and ours—is in a state of panic.

Rising Action: Enter our own Sally Warton, a customer advocate extraordinaire (her official title is "relationship manager"). Sally springs into action. She organizes a cross-functional team consisting of members from development, support, and product management. This ad-hoc team, formed quickly for this purpose, gathers around a white board. "Failure is not an option," implores Sally, taking a cue from NASA director Gene Kranz as the *Apollo 13* disaster began to unfold. Will her efforts be enough?

Climax: The team, racing against time, identifies possible solutions, quickly discarding those that don't work or don't meet the timeframe. One promising workaround seems to fix the issue... but the system crashes in final testing. Time is running out. And then Tommy, one of our newest hires and fresh out of engineering school, has an idea for a patch that might just solve the immediate problem and buy the development team time to develop a permanent solution. The team works with XYZ to confirm and test the patch. It works! Yes, all is a "go!"

Falling action: XYZ's team was both thrilled and relieved by the creative solution. They said it was confirmation of their decision to choose us as their solution. "No 'big box' software company could have performed this miracle," said one of their IT managers.

We're doing a postmortem to identify exactly what happened with the February release. We can't expect acts of heroism to save the day next time. There's just too much on the line for our customers and our brand. We'll be following up with recommended improvements and a revised process for approving releases.

Resolution: XYZ got the system and the mandatory reports on time and within budget. With this solution working, they are strongly focused on helping their customers. And the crisis—well, only a few of us will really know how close we were to disaster. XYZ says our solution is saving them many hours of laborious report preparation. They have tremendous confidence in us and the tool, and have already been a willing reference for other prospects. Hats off to Sally, Tommy, and the rest of the team for turning what could have been a disaster into a win for our customer (and, of course, for our reputation)!

You get the point... be intentional in how you present your customers' narratives. It's one thing to report that updates are causing compatibly issues; it's another to wrap this data in stories that relay a richness in meaning and impact.

CASE STUDY
Clark Pest Control

When you think about the pest control industry, you probably don't envision customer-focused employees devoted to creating exceptional experiences. For most customers, it's a process you just have to get through—you hope it's as painless as possible, but brace yourself for whatever it takes.

Matt Beckwith, Director of Customer Experience at Clark Pest Control, is dramatically improving the experience. One of his secrets? Collecting and telling stories. Matt describes customers and their situations clearly and knowledgeably. Employees form an image of customers, their perspectives, and what success looks and feels like to them (and it goes far beyond simply getting rid of pests).

With hundreds of technicians in the field, there's no shortage of new stories. Some are filled with humor and compassion. "All the men and women that wear the Clark Pest Control uniform are the embodiment of our entire organization," Matt says. "They are often the only Clark team member that the customer will ever meet."

Through the power of these stories, employees learn how to treat customers. They view each home as a sacred place, that customer's refuge. They value their time above their own. And they know to be flexible when required to ensure the best possible outcome. Matt has made customer stories part of the fiber of the company's culture.[3]

Become a proficient educator

It's easy to give lip service to customer experience. Many executives will talk about it in generic terms, often giving the impression that it is some sort of transcendent reality. This can do more harm than good. It can turn customer experience into something ambiguous and meaningless. If you're reading this book (and have made it to Chapter 5) you know the truth—consistently great experiences require hard work, planning, and intentionality.

Telling the customer's story in a compelling fashion will answer the *why*. If it's going to stick, you now must offer the *how*. The best customer stories conclude with a call to action. This could include sharing knowledge across

> 66 Telling the customer's story in a compelling fashion will answer the why. If it's going to stick, you now must offer the how.

departments, reshaping misleading communication, urging employees to capture unstructured voice of customer input, or others.

Your job as educator is two-fold. First, you must bring the reality of the customer's journey to your organization in a way that can be easily understood by all. Second, you must educate and guide individual employees on the importance of their roles in that journey. The more relevant and specific you can make the call to action, the better. (Here's a tip: give employees a straightforward means to participate. It is not enough to educate on the customer journey or CX… you'll need to give them an opportunity to change a specific perspective or behavior.)

I've had a number of leaders tell me their approach has evolved. In their earlier days in customer experience, many would sound an alarm: "Hey, look at this voice of customer data. Look at all the ways we are failing them." That's understandable. As you listen to customers and begin identifying improvement opportunities, you'll be eager to jump in and begin fixing things.

The problem is, guilt and the stick (versus the carrot) rarely motivate others for long. In fact, they can be downright discouraging. Many leaders have learned that inspiration goes much further. They put more emphasis on celebrating the improvements and victories along the way. There is absolutely a place for identifying problems and needed improvements. But showing progress and staying positive makes all the difference.

So how do you get started? What are some ways you can include employees in the process and make the connections between what they do and what customers experience? There are some proven methods you can choose from. We'll look at a few of the most effective here, beginning with journey maps.

Harness the power of journey mapping

One of the most popular arrows in the quiver of a customer experience professional is the customer journey map. And for good reason… it's a straightforward, effective way to visually depict a customer's relationship with your organization. Journey maps are so popular that some equate customer experience management to journey mapping. Nope, a journey map is just a tool. But it can be a very powerful one.

There are countless ways to map a customer's journey, but the goal is the same: define a specific customer persona, and visually document their experience—the end-to-end journey. You'll show them moving along a series of "touchpoints." I'll summarize the basic steps involved, but make this process your own. Maps created in a vacuum tend to stay there. The more collaborative your team is in creating the map and describing their part in the story, the more meaningful it will be. You'll know you're successful when anyone in the organization, regardless of department or role, can understand the map, and see where and how they are part of the journey.

Step 1: Create customer personas

The journey mapping process begins by creating customer personas. The objective here is to identify a grouping of customers who share a relatively common journey. In other words, the key stages or "touchpoints" in their journey will be much the same. As a starting point, select the most common and straightforward customer group possible. The idea is that you will eventually have different personas and different maps associated with all of the various personas. But start simple; as your mapping skills increase, so can the range and depth of your maps.

You have full creative control to customize these personas to fit your customers and audience. Here are a few recommended data points to include:

- **Key objective:** What does success look like to this customer? Why did they engage with your product or service in the first place? Describe in one to two sentences.
- **Key objective KPI:** What is the one overarching measurement that will determine the degree to which success is accomplished?
- **Demographics:** Itemize some basic demographics, such as age range, geographic region, etc.
- **Challenges:** What keeps this person up at night? What do they find difficult or inconvenient in their work and/or personal worlds?

Let's say your organization provides management systems and training on health and safety. Alyssa, a customer, is an environmental health and safety manager. Her key objective is to ensure the health and safety of every employee. Her top priorities are training compliance and environmental improvements.

Step 2: Identify touchpoints

Now that you have a specific customer persona in mind, it's time to isolate each important interaction between your business and that individual.

FIGURE 5.3   Example customer persona

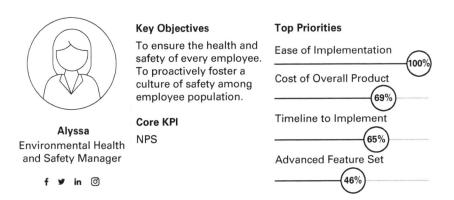

Customer Persona

Alyssa
Environmental Health
and Safety Manager

f ✗ in ⊙

Key Objectives

To ensure the health and safety of every employee. To proactively foster a culture of safety among employee population.

Core KPI

NPS

Top Priorities

Ease of Implementation
— 100%

Cost of Overall Product
— 69%

Timeline to Implement
— 65%

Advanced Feature Set
— 46%

This is written from the perspective of the customer, using their terminology wherever possible. Here, the map begins to take shape. Many organizations have found that simply isolating the touchpoints in a sequence can be a major eye-opener. This is not surprising as it represents a perspective shift for most—you are moving the focus off your business and forcing your group to think like the customer.

Naturally, every journey map is going to look different based on the types of interactions the customer has with your organization. That said, and to get you thinking, here is how a journey may progress:

- **Brand awareness.** The touchpoint at which the customer learns that you exist, and that you may have a solution to their problem. This step often coincides with needs awareness—the customer has a need and is now exploring possible solutions.

- **Pre-sales.** The stage at which the customer pursues additional information, receives a demo, and an account owner is introduced.

- **Sales.** The touchpoint at which a quote is provided, negotiations ensue, and the contract is executed.

- **Implementation.** The stage at which the customer is onboarded and begins to use the product or service.

- **Ongoing support.** The touchpoint at which invoicing or payment process begins; also, the customer may need assistance from customer support.

- **Renewal.** The stage at which the customer decides to renew the product or service and potentially expand the partnership.

Figure 5.4 shows an example of the customer journey map.

Step 3: Identify needs and expectations

In this step, you add important information about the customer and their needs and expectations. The more actual customer feedback data you have (see Chapter 3), the better. If you're early on in the process of collecting and managing customer feedback, making assumptions is okay. A "hypothesis map," as we call it, is far better than no map at all.

To a large degree, customer experience is based on understanding customer expectations, and helping identify and influence them throughout the journey. You'll want to capture customer expectations as accurately as possible at each touchpoint. Include a brief statement or set of bullets to outline the customer's core needs and expectations at each touchpoint.

Remember, as much as possible, to build the journey from the customer's perspective and in their vernacular. I've seen executives try to turn a customer journey map into an internal process map. Don't let that happen! Creating an internal "service blueprint," such as a customer access strategy (see Chapter 4) is essential. But it's not the same as a customer journey map. Politely guide your group back into the perspective of the customer.

FIGURE 5.4   Journey map, major touchpoints

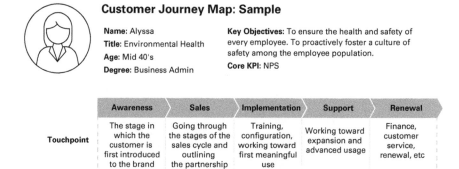

Figure 5.5 shows how your map might look at this point.

FIGURE 5.5   Journey map, expectations

Customer Journey Map: Sample

Name: Alyssa

Title: Environmental Health

Age: Mid 40's

Degree: Business Admin

Key Objectives: To ensure the health and safety of every employee. To proactively foster a culture of safety among the employee population.

Core KPI: NPS

	Awareness	Sales	Implementation	Support	Renewal
Touchpoint	The stage in which the customer is first introduced to the brand	Going through the stages of the sales cycle and outlining the partnership	Training, configuration, working toward first meaningful use	Working toward expansion and advanced usage	Finance, customer service, renewal, etc
Expectations	Timely turnaround from sales associate		Knowledgeable PM	Established POC for escalations	
	Clear website	Ease of use			Live answer phone
	Online demo	Proactive communication bi-weekly		Periodic recurring training	

Step 4: Identify pain points

The fourth and final step may be the most important. This is where you document potential friction points at each stage of the journey. You've captured the customer's needs and expectations. Now, these are areas where you sometimes or often fail to meet those expectations. This is where the journey map becomes much more than a hypothetical exercise. It's a strategic roadmap of how to improve the customer's experience.

Ideally, any employee can look at the map and find the areas of the journey where they play a significant role. By illustrating pain points at that stage, they understand their part in improving customer experience. And that is the power of an effective journey map. Not only does it illustrate the entire journey, it also provides enough tactical direction to drive behavior change.

There are many additional insights you can include on a customer journey map. For example, you could show a relevant key performance indicator (KPI) for each touchpoint (I've included a before and after net promoter score (NPS)). An online search will reveal many examples of journey maps. Some are far more extensive than the example provided here. You'll want to strike the right balance between detail and usability.

FIGURE 5.6   Journey map, pain points

Customer Journey Map: Sample

Name: Alyssa
Title: Environmental Health
Age: Mid 40's
Degree: Business Admin

Key Objectives: To ensure the health and safety of every employee. To proactively foster a culture of safety among the employee population.
Core KPI: NPS

	Awareness	Sales	Implementation	Support	Renewal
Touchpoint	The stage in which the customer is first introduced to the brand	Going through the stages of the sales cycle and outlining the partnership	Training, configuration, working toward first meaningful use	Working toward expansion and advanced usage	Finance, customer service, renewal, etc
Expectations	Timely turnaround from sales associate		Knowledgeable PM	Established POC for escalations	
	Clear website	Ease of use			Live answer phone
	Online demo	Proactive communication bi-weekly		Periodic recurring training	
Pain Points	Inconsistent brand voice across departments		Bugs in software lead to wasted time and lost data		
	Negative WOM	Sporadic and unclear communication		General lack of recurring communication	
	Lack of product knowledge from sales		Overwhelmed at go live and first stage		Sales turnover

NPS
(30%)

NPS
(75%)

Business-to-consumer example

Let's apply the journey mapping framework to a straightforward business-to-consumer (B2C) scenario. In this case, Sam is looking to purchase a piano for his daughter's music lessons. You can use a simple journey framework to depict this experience.

STEP 1: CREATE CUSTOMER PERSONAS

Persona description: Sam is a 38-year-old father and first-time purchaser looking to acquire a piano for his family's home.

- **Key objective:** To buy a piano that will meet the needs of a growing family, for under $3,500; have it delivered within two weeks.

- **Key objective KPI:** Sam will consider feature set, price, and timeliness of delivery. Customer sentiment and a mobile phone survey can help us measure these components.

- **Demographics:** Sam is a father of two. He's not a musician himself, but wants his children to be able to play. His salary is $70,000 and he has spent his whole life in the region.

- **Challenges:** Sam doesn't know much about pianos—and that's what is most intimidating. What's the difference between the $3,000 piano and the $8,000 model!? They look the same! Sam will need a basic education on piano features before feeling confident enough to make a decision.

STEP 2: IDENTIFY TOUCHPOINTS

Here, let's identify important interactions between your business (called Bream Brothers) and Sam. Here's how you might approach this:

- **Brand awareness:** Sam received a recommendation through his daughter's music teacher.

- **Online research:** Sam began to look at options and educate himself on the various features of different piano models.

- **In-store:** Sam arrives in the showroom for the first time to hear the various models for himself, and to ask questions.

- **Purchase:** Sam returns to the store to make his purchase and select a delivery date.

- **Delivery:** The piano is brought to Sam's home, moved to the desired location and tuned.

- **Post-sale support:** You engage with Sam after the sale, with the goals of ensuring satisfaction and elevating Sam to an ambassador for the brand.

STEP 3: IDENTIFY NEEDS AND EXPECTATIONS

As in Alyssa's B2B journey (the first example), the key to a positive customer journey for Sam is setting clear and achievable expectations at the right times. Let's look at the expectations Sam is forming:

- **Brand awareness:** Sam does not need a top-of-the-line piano. He wants the path of least resistance to a good, high-value option that will meet the needs of his daughter. Bream Brothers is known as being "beginner friendly" and has the best prices in town.

- **In store:** This is already an intimidating purchase for Sam. He needs a low-pressure, friendly engagement that will allow him to move forward with confidence. Bream Brothers' staff are not paid on commission, and are always thrilled to help people bring music into their homes.

- **Purchase:** Sam simply needs to be given the price he was promised, and to have the piano delivered by next week.

- **Delivery:** The family is very excited for the new piano, but they would be very frustrated if the delivery agents scratched the new wood floor in the living room. They expect the delivery to be on time and professional.

- **Post-sale support:** Sam has no idea when or how to tune a piano. He is hoping Bream Brothers can guide him on what needs to be done to keep the piano in tip-top shape for years to come.

STEP 4: IDENTIFY PAIN POINTS

Every journey has potential friction points. Understanding what yours look like can help to unify the organization on the best ways to improve customer experience. Here are some examples of friction points in Sam's journey:

- **Brand awareness:** The website is hard to find. People search for Brim Brothers or Bean Brothers, instead of Bream Brothers.

- **In-store:** Sam had to navigate past all the "high dollar" models. He became very overwhelmed before seeing the options that fit his price range near the back of the store.

- **Purchase:** Sam was not expecting a $200 delivery fee. This should have been communicated to him on the first visit as a valuable service that includes setup and tuning.

- **Delivery:** Delivery windows are too small, often resulting in representatives being 30 minutes late.

- **Post-sale support:** Failed to collect Sam's email address, prohibiting your team from sending proactive maintenance communications.

Journey mapping tips

I've been witness to many different journey map efforts. Here are some suggestions that may help you get the most from this effort:

Keep it simple. No map will be perfect, nor will any comprehensively cover every nuance and perspective. There is a trade-off between greater levels of detail and complexity that begins to diminish the map's effectiveness. My advice: keep it simple. Again, anyone should be able to read the map, understand the journey, and see their role in customer experience.

is this true for our map?

FIGURE 5.7   Journey map, consumer example

Bream Brothers Music: Customer Journey

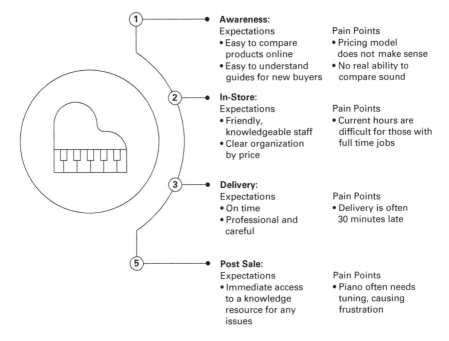

Awareness:

Expectations
- Easy to compare products online
- Easy to understand guides for new buyers

Pain Points
- Pricing model does not make sense
- No real ability to compare sound

In-Store:

Expectations
- Friendly, knowledgeable staff
- Clear organization by price

Pain Points
- Current hours are difficult for those with full time jobs

Delivery:

Expectations
- On time
- Professional and careful

Pain Points
- Delivery is often 30 minutes late

Post Sale:

Expectations
- Immediate access to a knowledge resource for any issues

Pain Points
- Piano often needs tuning, causing frustration

Stay focused on the customer. A common mistake is turning the journey map into an internal process map. Documenting and improving processes is an important separate effort (see Chapters 4 and 6), but don't intermingle the two.

Take action. A journey map is helpful in identifying pain points and improvement opportunities. But it has no effect unless you take action. I've seen robust analysis and beautiful maps in organizations that don't move on to taking action. It's only what you do that matters.

(There are links to additional journey mapping resources and examples at www.bradcleveland.com/resources)

Identify and leverage complementary tools

The customer journey map is a popular tool for telling the customer's story and educating colleagues on their roles in their journey. But there are plenty of other ways you can go about it. I've found that a journey map along with at least one complementary tool is an effective approach. Here are some other ways to relay the customer's story.

Voice of the customer (VoC) forum

Some organizations have built voice of the customer (VoC) forums into their cultures. A small, fast-growing software company in San Francisco is an example. The company provides a monthly "open house" forum focused on voice of the customer. All employees are invited, and the meetings have become an important part of the organization's culture. During the sessions, customer stories can take the form of recorded calls, screen capture sessions, or similar interactions. Moderators then open the session for input—which leads to robust discussion on how to improve existing products and services. Talk about getting employees engaged! This approach not only bridges the gap between employees and the customer, it also encourages collaboration and creativity across the entire business.

The customer room

Many organizations have transformed reception areas, hallways, conference rooms, and empty offices into "customer rooms." These are physical representations of the customer journey in visual storytelling format. Common features include pictures, videos, diagrams, journey maps and testimonials. They can even be made interactive with audio clips, simulations, and demonstrations. What better way to show employees you care than a mini-museum dedicated to customers!

I recently visited the headquarters of Radio Flyer, the Chicago-based toy makers best known for their iconic steel red wagons.[4] The company, founded in 1919, grew steadily for 70 years before facing an existential crisis in the 1990s—consumer tastes were changing, and competitors were coming out with more versatile plastic wagons. CEO Robert Pasin, grandson of the founder, oversaw an innovation-led turnaround that saved the company from bankruptcy and restored its global leadership. The lobby is a museum of the company's history and products that span a century. The innovation of today's product line—push trikes, scooters, fold-up wagons, a battery-powered ride-on Tesla for kids, to name a few—is testament to staying close to customers and their changing needs.

Graphic novel

Many organizations provide internal newsletters that are, at least in part, focused on customer experience topics. In a fun and clever twist, I'm aware of organizations that have created graphic novels that highlight customer experiences. For example, North Hills Veterinary Hospital in Rochester Hills, Michigan, displays a graphic novel on the walls of the lab. It illustrates everything from new puppy checks to end-of-life care. These publications can be both helpful and appealing, telling the customer's story in a way that is unique and engaging. And they serve as reminders of the importance of customer experience.

Customer charades

One format idea for workshops is "customer charades." Break your employees into small groups and either assign them a particular customer persona, or have them pick one out of a hat. Each group is then responsible for researching that persona. They then "become the customer." Bring the groups back together and have them "act out" their customers' journeys. If you want to take the exercise one step further, you can have them create simple journey maps.

The magic of this approach is in employees doing their own research, going through the process of personifying customers themselves. For many, this will have more impact than any type of top-down education you could provide. If your group is willing, you can video the performances and post some of the best for the broader organization.

Customers—in person

There will be times when you will not be able to fully simulate the customer's voice. Perhaps there is a challenging emotion at some point in the journey that is best seen to be understood. In these times, consider bringing a willing customer in to speak with your employees. I've found these sessions to be incredibly valuable and motivating in a way that no other format can provide. My encouragement: include all levels of the organization.

The key in any of these approaches is to get your employees involved. When they are part of personifying the voice of the customer, their understanding of customer experience will significantly deepen.

Keep your eyes on the prize—an engaged organization

Several years ago, I delivered a keynote to a healthcare industry conference. The audience was engaged, and the conversations during mid-morning break were vibrant. At the organizer's invitation, I stayed for the rest of the day to hear other speakers. All were knowledgeable and well prepared, and each shared important content.

As can happen at events, the presentations began to blend together as the day wore on. Slide after slide. There was a feeling of restlessness—even inattention—in the room. Then came the last speaker of the day, Lisa, who managed the customer-facing operation of a mid-sized biopharma company. As we began to prepare for yet another PowerPoint presentation, Lisa surprised us all. She sat on a stool at the edge of the stage. She had no clicker. She did not have notes. She simply told a story.

> **❝ She sat on a stool at the edge of the stage. She had no clicker. She did not have notes. She simply told a story.**

The story was that of a service failure, told through the lens of one customer's experience. The customer was the adult daughter of a man who was using a product manufactured by Lisa's company, an inhaler that delivered medicine to treat a chronic respiratory condition. The man was convinced the inhaler was not functioning properly, and that he was not receiving his prescribed dose of medicine. His daughter, Kristine, thought the inhaler was probably working as it should, but she wanted to be sure.

In a steady voice, Lisa shared Kristine's search for reassurance. The company website had FAQs about the inhaler, but none fully answered the question she had. The website directed people to check with their physician or pharmacist for additional information. It was a weekend, and Kristine didn't feel her concern was serious enough to have the doctor's emergency answering service contact him. She went to the pharmacy where her father had acquired the inhaler, but the pharmacist was off until the following day. The pharmacy technician on duty tried to be helpful, but couldn't provide a solid answer.

Lisa had our rapt attention. All of the side chatter, which had become louder as the day wore on, ceased. All stopped checking their phones. Every eye was on Lisa as she continued Kristine's story.

After visiting the pharmacy, Kristine re-checked the company's website and, after a bit of searching, found a toll-free number. When she called, she was presented with a half-dozen recorded self-serve options, none of which met her need. She knew the trick of pressing "O" to speak to a representative, but doing so took her to a "we are closed" message.

At this point in the story, Lisa paused for a few seconds. When she resumed, she said that the story had a happy ending. Kristine called the company on Monday morning, and was connected to a medical information specialist—a registered nurse—who conferenced in Kristine's father. The specialist listened to him carefully, asking clarifying questions along the way. She was able to assure both Kristine and her father that the inhaler was functioning correctly.

But Lisa was bothered by the fact that Kristine's journey was so circuitous, and that her own company had played a part in making it harder than it needed to be. She spent a few minutes talking—still without PowerPoint slides—about the changes she and other leaders made within their company to improve the customer experience, to make it easier for people like Kristine to get the answers they need.

The buzz in the room after Lisa finished was electric. It was good that she was the last speaker of the day, because no one would have wanted to follow her. By simply telling a story, she both exemplified the theme of the conference and showed the power of engaged leadership.

The best experience organizations in the world have a unique ability to turn all of their employees into customer ambassadors. That is the real goal—to educate and inspire your employees so well that they become an inherent part of customer experience. We'll pick up with that topic in Chapter 7.

KEY RECOMMENDATIONS

- Develop the art of telling your customer's story.
- Become a proficient educator.
- Harness the power of journey mapping.
- Identify and leverage complementary tools.
- Keep your eyes on the prize—an engaged organization.

Notes

1 Bolch, B (2020) Even with no games, something fun is Bruin with UCLA announcer Josh Lewin, *The Los Angeles Times*, 23 March, www.latimes.com/sports/ucla/story/2020-03-23/even-with-no-games-something-fun-is-bruin-with-ucla-announcer-josh-lewin, (archived at https://perma.cc/WW49-J4FZ)

2 Denning, S (2011) *The Leader's Guide to Storytelling: Mastering the art and discipline of business narrative*, revised and updated, Jossey-Bass, United States

3 Email interview with Matt Beckwith, 16 October, 2020.

4 This visit was through a tour made possible through the Tugboat Institute, a membership organization for CEOs and presidents of closely held, evergreen (non-public, non-venture capital-backed) companies.

06

Shaping processes and technology

Several years ago, travel and lots of great restaurants were beginning to take a physical toll on me. I had always thought of myself as being just a "few years" out of college. It dawned on me that more than a few had slipped by, and I needed to make some changes. I decided to do a reset on my health. After some investigation, I booked a visit to Canyon Ranch in Tucson, Arizona.

I've since learned that Canyon Ranch is an iconic health resource, and now I know why. The Canyon Ranch team put me through my paces—tests and advice on diet, cardio, strength, flexibility, my outlook—the works. I had an appointment one afternoon with a physical trainer named Lorey. We shared stories about our families, then she put me through a stress test on a treadmill. As we went through the results, she summarized the verdict: Not bad. Not great.

"Why are you here, Brad?" Lorey asked.

"Oh, you know, lose a few pounds, get in shape," I said.

"No, what's the bigger reason?"

"I want to stay active and be healthy as I get older. Good answer?"

"I want to mention something, and I hope you don't mind me telling you."

"Sure."

"My dad was your age when we lost him." She glanced towards the window with a faraway look. "I was young then." She continued softly and I strained to hear. "You know, every little girl wants a dad to walk her down the aisle."

FIGURE 6.1   Leadership Framework, Chapter 6: Shaping processes and technology

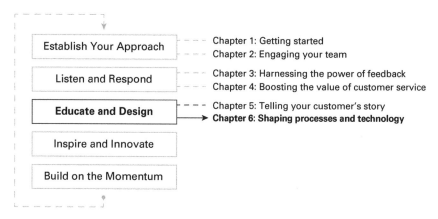

As I struggled to choke back tears, I knew in that instant that my outlook was forever changed. I was embarrassed at how casual and self-focused my answers had been. But I was so grateful to Lorey for her boldness. I thought of others who had experienced great loss. That afternoon, I became a man on a mission.

My new vision was to be in good health so that I have a better chance of being around for my family (and yes, being active and healthy). So I can, perhaps, someday walk my daughter down the aisle. Lorey helped establish key indicators, such as heart rate, weight, body mass index (BMI), and a few others. I needed some new technology—the right shoes and a heart rate monitor. She helped me understand how often I need to exercise, the bpm my heart needs to reach when doing intervals, the distance (if running or biking) required for effective "steady state" exercise, and others. It's all mapped out. While I don't know the future, I know I'm a little wiser and on a far better track.

A pursuit of customer experience aligns in many ways with a journey to better health. You must have a vision that is strong enough, inspiring enough, to propel the work it takes. You need goals, KPIs, and supporting metrics. You'll also need supporting processes and technology. We pick up with these topics here and in the chapters to follow. We'll look first at building your dashboards. We then turn to processes, technology, and change management—all necessary to propel you towards your vision.

Build your dashboards

To effectively lead the customer experience, you and your team will need dashboards. This is a good place in your journey to establish them. My advice, first and foremost: be absolutely clear on your vision. NPS (net promoter score), CSAT (customer satisfaction) or other indicators are not the equivalent of vision (see Chapter 1). They are important KPIs, but exciting vision they are not. Like my epiphany on health, your vision will point to the KPIs that make sense. Those KPIs will, in turn, lead you to supporting metrics.

The disciplines of customer experience and employee experience wouldn't exist without access to large amounts of data. That includes, increasingly, the insights generated by artificial intelligence (AI) and machine learning technologies. You can understand more about your customers and your employees through their behaviors, their direct feedback, and the results of their actions, than ever before. But the sheer number of different customer experiences across many touchpoints can lead even the most tenacious CX professionals to throw their hands up, wondering how to measure it all. Your dashboards will help you cut through clutter and tell a unified customer story.

Layered view

You'll most likely need department- and role-specific iterations of your dashboards. From a functional perspective, the marketing team will want to see customer experience in the context of response rates, conversions, and revenue. The digital team will need a view of page traffic and engagement. The contact center will need an eye on service levels, time to resolution and post-contact survey results. Senior leaders are interested in customer perceptions and outcome-related metrics, such as customer loyalty, repurchase rates, and customer lifetime value.

Dashboards are helpful when arranged in a three-layer cascade of detail:

The macro or strategic view: This view combines business (revenue, sales, market penetration), customer experience (customer satisfaction, net promoter score, customer effort score, customer churn or loyalty metrics), and employee experience (employee satisfaction, turnover). It should provide the ability to view data by product, department, or customer segment. This high-level view allows senior-level leaders to keep an eye on overall direction and to check in with managers on specific trends.

Example: *Your core CX team reviews last month's survey feedback on their macro view dashboard. They see CSAT is down noticeably for new customers. They notice that it's a trend that has been building since the last product release. There have been problems in the past with products launching before they were ready or with delayed documentation. It's a bit of a sore subject. The team asks the VP of Product to take a look.*

The mid or functional view: This view allows managers, analysts, and roles such as marketing, stores, and the contact center, to dive more deeply into relevant data. This enables them to connect the dots between their areas of responsibility and overall strategy.

The VP of Product sighs. She pulls up her dashboard, which also gives her access to voice of the customer (VoC) streams (complaints, escalations, post-call and NPS surveys). She then pulls up the post-call survey data and digs in. What she finds is interesting. When she drills into categorized results, she can see that more complaints were categorized as "feature-complaint." This is how the team categorizes feedback related to features that work as designed but that the customer doesn't like or doesn't understand. The reps in the contact center can help explain it— but by then it's already disrupted the customer's business. So, there's still dissatisfaction.

The micro or tactical view: This view is for specialized roles such as website managers, digital marketers, store or contact center supervisors, and product managers. It provides data down to the individual customer level.

The VP asks a voice of the customer (VoC) analyst to listen to a sample of poorly rated calls and document what he hears. The analyst goes to his VoC dashboard to filter for poorly rated calls tagged "feature-complaint." He also heads around the corner to the contact center, and checks with some reps. "What are you hearing about the last release?" After listening to calls and talking to reps, the analyst feels confident he found the gap. Many cloud customers were using the new release before the documentation was published. This created misunderstandings about the new features, especially with customers not yet familiar with the product. When the analyst validates this perspective with a team of reps, they emphatically agree. Communication for this release was late and lacking in critical detail.

The VP of Product presents these findings to the CX team, with a plan to improve future customers' experience. No product releases will be launched without complete documentation published several days ahead. Frontline

FIGURE 6.2   Dashboard layers

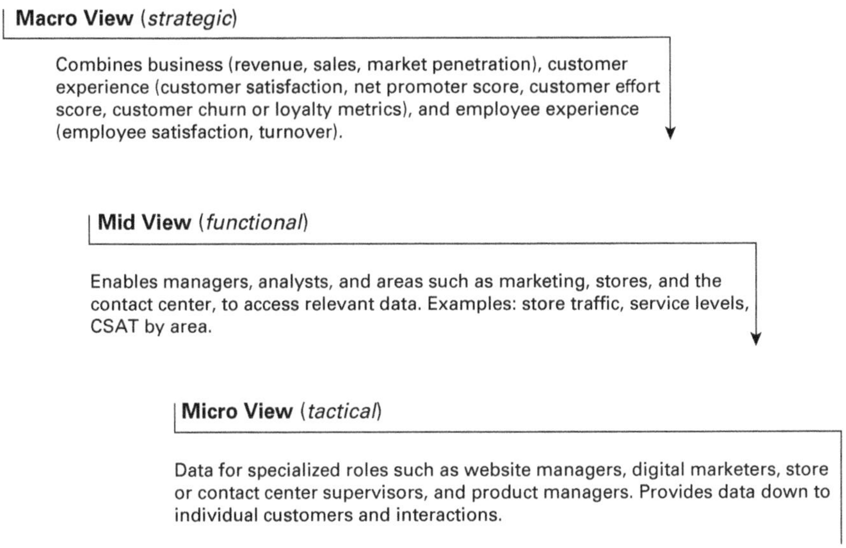

Macro View (*strategic*)

> Combines business (revenue, sales, market penetration), customer experience (customer satisfaction, net promoter score, customer effort score, customer churn or loyalty metrics), and employee experience (employee satisfaction, turnover).

Mid View (*functional*)

> Enables managers, analysts, and areas such as marketing, stores, and the contact center, to access relevant data. Examples: store traffic, service levels, CSAT by area.

Micro View (*tactical*)

> Data for specialized roles such as website managers, digital marketers, store or contact center supervisors, and product managers. Provides data down to individual customers and interactions.

reps will review the documentation ahead of the release to anticipate customers' (especially new customers') questions or concerns.

You get the gist here. This is one of a jillion ways to use a multi-layered, consolidated CX dashboard. And I'd point out the wise decision of the analyst to walk around the corner (or call or video conference) and have conversations with those closest to the issue. Dashboards are important tools. They don't replace firsthand experience, wisdom and intuition.

In terms of the dashboard itself, you can build or buy. You'll consider the expertise within your organization, budget, your organization's size, existing tools, and the scope of your customer experience initiatives. Some buy products and services à la carte and build their own dashboards. The preferred path for many is to buy a tool (cloud solutions and open platforms have made this much easier than it used to be). Also, be sure to thoroughly investigate tools that are already in use in your organization; there is likely something there to tap! Given the abundance of considerations, it's common to bring in outside help to inventory options and integrate the pieces into an overall approach. My advice: when it comes to building effective dashboards, do what it takes to get it right—don't skimp.

Design processes that support customer experience

I often hear executives comment that they wish their organizations had Amazon.com's technology capabilities. What they are really longing for is Amazon's processes. I believe it's safe to say that there are few technology capabilities Amazon has that others don't also have access to. In fact, Amazon builds tools for its own operation, then makes them available as products others can use (including even the smallest organizations). You can have Amazon's technology—but that's not enough!

> 66 *I often hear executives comment that they wish their organizations had Amazon.com's technology capabilities. What they are really longing for is Amazon's processes.*

The technology others have access to is available to you, and you can build powerful processes that make the most of it. But processes are something you have to earn. While Amazon was taking losses year after year, investing in better ways to do things, other organizations focused on the next quarter. The good news is, if you want to deliver better customer experiences, you can do so. There's no magician behind a curtain in any organization. It's a matter of resolve and focus.

Let's look first, generally, at why processes are such a big deal. Broadly speaking, customer experience management is part of the organization, an expansive process that includes many functions. More specifically, each part of customer experience management is a process. For example, an interaction during a sale or when a customer needs support is a process. In fact, any part of an interaction—say entering data—is a process. It involves a data system, a person or bot, and a set of actions. Now, consider any aspect of customer experience management you want to improve—let's say handling an order correctly—to meet expectations and avoid rework. Each of these variables has an impact. All are interrelated.

Thinking of processes this way highlights a principle that has long been at the heart of the quality movement: there is little use exhorting employees to improve customer experiences without making improvements to the processes they are part of. Through better processes, your organization will be equipped to deliver experiences that are consistent, effective and sustainable.

CX processes are cross-functional

A colleague of mine recently visited the contact center for a well-known health insurance company. While she was meeting with team members, she saw job aids referring to "building empathy" and delivering "apologies with heart." The quality assurance (QA) form measured employees on how well they helped customers manage their intense emotions over delayed claims. The training content emphasized how to explain complicated claims processes. When she met with the contact center director, she asked, "Why so much time and energy on training reps to manage customers who are disappointed... by you? Why not just fix the claim issue?"

He sighed. "It's not that easy. The claims department have their way of doing things. We've tried to meet with them over this issue a few times, but the message is clear—'stay on your side of the fence.' We do our best, but customers express frustration every day. We can't magically make customers okay with it."

This scenario—and I suspect you may have similar stories—is all too familiar in some organizations. In fact, according to PwC research, only 49 percent of consumers say companies they interact with provide a good customer experience.[1] Too often, there is a gap between what customers want and what is being delivered.

Customer-centric organizations spend proportionally more time designing processes and proportionally less time getting better at appeasing unhappy customers. They devote their attention to eliminating what makes customers unhappy in the first place. Of course, glitches will still happen, and the processes you use to resolve those issues are essential. Effective complaint resolution will always be part of your CX portfolio. But that shouldn't be the main focus.

The challenge? Without deliberate intervention, departments don't naturally work across functional lines. The marketing team focuses on messaging and response rates. The product management team is occupied with product design and development. Billing concentrates on revenue and collections, and the contact center on meeting service levels and creating positive customer interactions. Each team fixates on being the best they can be within the boundaries of their department.

This includes areas whose managers may not fully grasp the overall impact on customer experience. The legal department requires necessary "legalese" in customer documents. The compliance area demands stringent

FIGURE 6.3   Customer experience functions/processes

verification to protect customers and the organization. Every department can agree that designing processes and technology with the customer in mind makes sense. Even so, being customer-focused within a silo doesn't fix the most exasperating barriers to good experiences.

Great experiences happen by design through cross-department collaboration. They are shaped with a clear-eyed view of the customer as they traverse through the work done by marketing, product management, billing, and the contact center. That work must be coordinated and seamless for the trip to feel effortless, satisfying, and yes, sometimes even WOW. And to create that collaboration, your organization must have high-level sponsorship. Senior leaders must define a common vision and goals, and hold all accountable to pursue them (see the section "Define and communicate your vision and goals," Chapter 1).

Finding gaps and identifying priorities

The processes that impact your customers run through your organization like veins. This makes it challenging to prioritize the changes most likely to move the needle on your CX and business objectives. Let's use a healthcare insurance provider as an example.

Marketing sends direct mail pieces targeted at the desired customer, providing them with the website address (digital team) and a phone number (contact center). "Simple. Quick. Hassle-Free." That's what is promised. As teams map the journey from awareness (seeing an ad), to education (reading about it online), to enrollment (digital or contact center), they realize that while simple, quick, and hassle-free might describe the process once the application is accepted, it doesn't describe the "complete the application" step.

The application requires customers to provide their social security number, marital status, proof of prior coverage (where do you get that?), dependents and their social security numbers, past medical records, past and present prescription medications, and more. The web prevents customers from proceeding without complete entries and it does not save their information if they pause for too long mid-process. It becomes clear that "Simple. Quick. Hassle-Free" was what the marketing department *wanted* the customer to feel. However, the rest of the organization hasn't coordinated across departments—digital, user experience, contact center, legal—to deliver on this promise.

Once you start examining the customer journey in detail, it's easy to become overwhelmed by gaps to close. A simple way to prioritize opportunities is to first consider goal alignment and customer impact. Using the insurance provider as an example, if your primary goals are acquisition and revenue, resolving those gaps would lead to one set of priorities. Retaining existing customers would lead to another. Second, are there indications in customer feedback that completing the application is a customer pain point? If yes, then closing that gap is a priority. If there are higher customer pain points that align with "increase acquisition," that factors into your prioritization matrix.

Don't be overly alarmed at the gaps you may find when you start mapping customer journeys (discussed in Chapter 5). That is the point of mapping. It's why effective leadership is so important. This is a time to

> ❝ *Employees know your processes. They are aware of any gaps between what's promised and what's being delivered. And they understand the level of urgency and emotion around different customer pain points.*

leave egos and turf wars at the door. It's also why involving frontline employees is crucial. Employees know your processes. They are aware of any gaps between what's promised and what's being delivered. And they understand the level of urgency and emotion around different customer pain points.

Leverage the potential of technology

With a clear vision and sound processes, the right technology solutions tend to come into focus. As you look at ways to harness technology, some improvements will be incremental—small wins here and there—and others will be more sweeping. In some cases, you might even use technology to create new markets.

Automating existing processes

Here's an example of using technology to automate an existing process. Prior to the pandemic, things were humming along nicely for an IT company. One of their primary ongoing responsibilities was to support their clients—organizations using their IT services. They were staffed at the right levels and delivering on all goals. Clients and employees were happy. Covid-19 changed that overnight. When the crisis hit, a far greater number of their clients' employees were working from home and contacting the IT company directly (previously, they would start with their in-house IT resources who could provide basic support).

"We were going crazy under an avalanche of entry-level questions," shared the department manager. "My engineers were spending their days walking people through basic resolutions, such as how to reboot a router. We want to provide great support, but that's an expensive call for a router reboot!" He added, "If we followed the processes as they were written, we would tell callers, 'You need to call your IT department first.' But that's not a great experience for those individuals. They needed help. So, we spent time with clients and adjusted the process. Their IT departments were overwhelmed, so we decided to take on those entry-level questions since they were coming to us anyway."

The solution?

> Since we were already using an automated system to start new tickets, bots were a logical approach. We didn't want customers to feel like we were deflecting their issues—even though it would have been allowed by the terms of our contracts. Continuing to provide timely, responsive service was important to us. Bots allowed us to create a new ticketing process, where if a customer selected four of the most common entry-level ticket types, a chatbot would walk the caller through simple troubleshooting steps. If the issue was resolved, the bot would close out the ticket. If the customer needed further assistance, a ticket would be opened with a record of the attempted troubleshooting and a description of the issue.

> During the pilot, they had a user experience (UX) designer observe users and ask questions afterward. Our clients were 100 percent on board and are happy with the support this technology provides their IT teams and their frontline users. So much so, in fact, that their IT teams are considering implementing similar technology.

Designing the ideal customer processes should always—*always*—come before technology. In the example, the IT company started with a clear description of the desired experience: maintain high levels of service while reserving core team members for contacts that require expertise. When Covid-19 hit, they considered adding less-skilled team members to handle the contacts, but they decided the preference was for a more automated, scalable approach. The solution was successful on many levels; it provided a cost-effective way to meet customer needs and deepen connections with clients.

> 66 *The market is awash in technology solutions. If anything, it's crowded, confusing, and maybe a little overenthusiastic.*

The market is awash with technology solutions. If anything, it's crowded, confusing, and maybe a little overenthusiastic. Almost two-thirds of mature CX-driven companies still rely in part on "old school" methods, such as "talking directly to their customers, having the best talent on board, and doing market research," and "are less likely to seek out 'over-hyped' methods such as chatbots, predictive analytics, and augmented reality." More mature companies "don't get distracted by 'shiny' objects and stay focused on what they know will deliver results."[2]

> 66 Most companies known for delivering exceptional
> customer journeys do push the boundaries of
> technology to drive improved or different experiences.
> But they do so with a clear-eyed understanding of
> what they want those experiences to be.

Creating new processes

When automated teller machines (ATMs) were just beginning to appear, I was still very young. But I remember a neighbor commenting to my father, "No way would I trust a machine to give me the correct count. What if it's wrong? They'll think I pocketed the difference!" Some years later, I was the one pushing back. I enjoyed collecting CDs and resisted early efforts to purchase music in a digital-only format. No artwork? No liner notes? What would I put in my CD rack? (I've since changed my... um, tune on this.)

In standard CX and continuous improvement practices, you look for never-ending improvements on existing processes. Gap identified and closed, customer satisfied, journey saved. *Voilà*, all good. There are times, however, when it makes sense to look over the horizon and go big. Capitalize on the potential of new technologies to support entirely new experiences. Innovative companies—Apple, Netflix, Amazon, Tesla, Helly Hansen, and others—have done that by pushing the boundaries of emerging technology. They became astronomically successful by looking beyond what customers said they wanted (smaller phones, thicker insulation). They instead created distinctive markets.

Most companies known for delivering exceptional customer journeys do push the boundaries of technology to drive improved or different experiences.

But they do so with a clear-eyed vision of what they want those experiences to be. Eyewear retailer Warby Parker (introduced in Chapter 1) made their name with the in-home try-on experience; they then launched an app that leverages augmented reality (AR) to provide a realistic digital try-on experience.

Norwegian firm Helly Hansen, 145-year-old maker of ocean and ski gear, sees technology-driven customer experience as the path to the future. In an example, the company collaborated with a community of outdoor professionals to develop light, high-tech materials that store warmth regulated through ventilation zippers. They also recently became part of Toronto-based CTC, which kept HH headquarters in Norway and promised to allow their unique culture to continue—while bringing them into a global distribution and service network.[3]

Is it a contradiction to offer predictable, frictionless experiences—but also look to implement disruptive boundary-pushing experiences? No. But it does take leadership and good judgment. The alternative is to provide incrementally better experiences while staying in place. This leaves you vulnerable to competitors who are capitalizing on experiences AND innovation. To be successful, you likely need both.

There are two scenarios in which it makes sense to let technology drive customer-facing processes. The first is when you believe you can transform an existing process. Before speech recognition technologies, organizations were limited to touch-tone. You could make incremental improvements to phone menus, but it was still a pretty horrid experience. Relief arrived with conversation-based systems. Now customers can simply tell the system what they want. That, in turn, opens up a world of new opportunities. Once I tell the IVR I'm calling for "printer technical support," it can identify me by my phone number, verify my printer model and warranty information, ask me about the nature of my problem, and route my call to a support representative while presenting that I am already verified and qualified. Add in additional context for the rep—my customer history and custom troubleshooting steps—and imagine my perception of the organization when the rep says, "I can see you called about this issue yesterday. Were you able to install the upgrade you and Tom discussed? How did that work out?"

Services Australia, the service arm of the government, has made a successful push for customer authentication through voice biometrics. Automating the process reduces the time it takes to handle interactions. More importantly, it opens up many new opportunities. If the system knows who the customer is, it can deliver relevant information: "You can expect payment by 20 April."

Should additional assistance be needed, the system can deliver the customer's history to a service officer.

A second scenario in which it's appropriate to let the technology drive the process is to facilitate entirely new experiences. In the past, buying a used car was something many consumers dreaded. Along comes Carvana, an online-only used car retailer that has completely reimagined the process. As a customer, you begin by searching for cars that fit your needs and budget. If you click on a car, you get more details. Each detail page provides a photo gallery, a detailed report on the car's condition, and a guarantee that the car has not experienced an accident, fire, frame or flood damage. Click into delivery and pickup options, and you'll see how soon the car can be delivered. Selecting "Get Started" will initiate the buying process. When the car is delivered, you can take it for a test drive and then either send it back or complete the paperwork so it's yours.

Should Carvana rest on its laurels, there are other options. Shift, for example, will come to you, inspect your vehicle and make an offer on the spot. If you accept, they take the car, and the purchase price hits your account later that day. Shift COO Sean Foy, formerly of Amazon, said, "We don't want this to be a technology-heavy process for the buyer; we want to stay as frictionless as possible so that we can attract more and more people onto the site... it's really about removing friction from the product."[4] Foy alludes to the primary rule for leading with technology—it should be invisible to the customer, perform flawlessly, and enable seamless experiences. There's no formula or ratio that determines the right mix of incremental improvement and disruptive leaps. That requires leadership.

Important lessons

As you look for ways to leverage technology—whether incremental or disruptive—here are some important lessons:

Avoid applying technology solutions to broken processes. If customers complain they don't receive follow-up as promised, the most elegant fix may be to eliminate the need for follow-up. Empower employees to make the critical decision on the spot (perhaps with AI-enabled decision-making tools). Let go of or reshape processes that are cumbersome or broken.

Make sure your solutions work in the real world. You'll want to test that you're solving the right problems and not creating new ones. For example, you might find (as one organization did) that the new web application works great, but that some features aren't available in Safari. If Safari is the

Instead fix the process

preferred browser of Apple-evangelist customers, you might rethink rollout. In another example, the data you require your privacy-conscious customers to share to use the app makes them nervous. So much so that they're posting on Reddit today—a warning that's going viral. (These were both real-life examples of technology solutions that failed to hit the mark. The reason? Experience designers—developers, product managers, user experience designers—didn't anticipate the barriers.)

Coordinate with and incorporate digital transformation efforts. Many organizations have "digital transformation" initiatives underway. (Digital transformation broadly refers to harnessing digital technologies to improve efficiencies and create new or better experiences for customers and employees.) These efforts are not always coordinated with or part of customer experience initiatives. Ideally, digital transformation should be part of—a subset of—customer experience management. At the least, ensure that digital transformation and customer experience aren't on two different and uncoordinated tracks.

Don't fall for promises of magic. Millions of dollars are wasted each year on technologies that are never delivered, never implemented, sit idle, or (most commonly) simply fail to deliver promised results. While CX technology spending continues to break records, many organizations still struggle to provide satisfying experiences to their customers. Prioritize technology that supports your customer experience vision and goals. Pursue technologies that help you get closer to your customers, and to deliver experiences that are effective and simple.

Establish essential customer experience tools

Let's turn to a specific category of technology—the tools you'll use to manage customer experience. We'll first review the most critical CX technologies, those that are foundational to your CX initiatives. We'll then look at some "nice-to-have" capabilities.

Must-haves

CUSTOMER RELATIONSHIP MANAGEMENT (CRM) PLATFORM

I'm always amazed at the impact (both positive and negative) that customer relationship management (CRM) technologies can have. When there are multiple and disparate CRM systems, or when CRM capabilities are not properly maintained, the result can be a management and usability nightmare. But when the organization is united under one strong, well-curated CRM across marketing, sales and service functions, the tool becomes the lifeblood of day-to-day operations.

A key theme in CX is personalization—delivering unique experiences for specific customers that align with their characteristics. Your ability to capture customer profiles and preferences, history and status, and create appropriate experiences is dependent upon strong CRM capabilities.

Another fundamental benefit of CRM is to create a "one company" feel for the customer. "Omnichannel" capabilities are crucial in today's environment. There are few things more frustrating than trying to deal with an organization where departments operate like independent businesses, or where communication channels are disjointed. Lack of continuity and consistency will seriously diminish customer loyalty. A well-maintained CRM platform brings transparency to all customer interactions. It enables employees and systems to operate with a full picture and intelligently handle things that extend outside of their immediate purview.

KNOWLEDGE MANAGEMENT

Knowledge is the lifeblood of most organizations. And the theme of effort reduction is one of the most established tenets driving CX initiatives. Your ability to resolve issues quickly and easily almost always depends on real-time access to accurate information.

Enter knowledge management (KM). KM overlaps with CX both directly and indirectly. The direct overlap is in the areas of self-service and customer communication. With strong KM processes and a good tool in place, many issues that would have generated a support interaction can now be resolved by customers. Not only is this a better experience, it's also become an expectation. Customers don't want to have to reach out for information that should be immediately accessible through an app or website.

The indirect overlap involves employees' ability to access data. To facilitate a timely resolution for customers, employees need a reliable and immediate source of information. I still find cases where employees can't find basic information easily or without assistance. Organizations that focus on great customer experiences invariably also make knowledge management a priority.

There are some general paths to knowledge management you can take, though the distinction between them is blurry and fading. One is best-of-breed KM solutions, which are feature-rich and can be integrated with CRM

FIGURE 6.4   The value of information

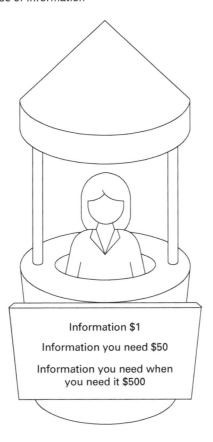

Information $1

Information you need $50

Information you need when
you need it $500

systems. Alternatively, KM features are inherently part of many CRM packages, but tend to have fewer features. Either could include both employee- and customer-facing capabilities. There are also many home-grown approaches (portals, collaboration platforms, and others). This remains a common approach, but is usually not as effective as KM capabilities that are integrated with or part of CRM systems.

Whatever the technology, your underlying processes are critical. When well-organized, well-curated, and universally accessible, the right information will have a powerful and positive impact on both the customer and the employee experience.

SOCIAL MEDIA MANAGEMENT PLATFORM

Engaging with customers through social media channels is a tangible example of how customer experience management is cross-functional. Marketing will often choose a tool, handle marketing-oriented messaging, and may handle some of the interactions with customers. But fielding the breadth and volume of customer interactions often requires more horsepower. Many organizations wisely equip their contact center or a team within customer service to help.

A social media management platform is critical. It should provide insight into how the brand is being represented and how customer sentiment is evolving; these insights will help highlight opportunities, gaps and priorities. To facilitate more effective engagement and service, it should also be integrated with your CRM and omnichannel routing tools.

Beyond the basics

The following are capabilities that I put in the category of "nice to have." You might view them as essential to your business, and I'd certainly support your intuition. Ultimately, the priority you assign to them is a matter of judgment.

CUSTOMER EXPERIENCE MANAGEMENT PLATFORM

Customer experience management (CXM) platforms are emerging, and not yet widespread. Those who do have CXM technology find that it becomes the heart of their voice of the customer program. My advice: if you don't yet have CXM, don't obsess about it, but do include it on your roadmap as you develop CX plans.

A capable CXM platform funnels all voice of the customer data into one system and, typically, uses AI and machine learning to organize, tag, show trends, establish scores, generate dashboards, illustrate return on investment (ROI), and even provide suggestions on next steps for CX improvement. With analytics capabilities, it can establish a customer sentiment score. Even a small organization can gain tremendous value from a neutral, automated approach available through CXM.

Many CXM platforms are also capable of facilitating "closed loop" processes based on triggers you configure. For example, when you receive a customer effort score of lower than 4 out of 7, you may want a supervisor to review the ticket and reach out to the customer. This can easily be set up to enable the communication to happen in real time within the right team— and with no effort from the core CX team.

CXM platforms are still fairly new, and improved functionality is emerging almost daily. Communities that track developments, such as CX Accelerator (www.CXAccelerator.com), are a good place to begin your research. While it may be possible to get by without a CXM platform, I don't advise doing so forever. Even small organizations can reap the benefits.

VOICE OF THE EMPLOYEE PULSE SURVEY TOOL

As discussed in Chapter 2, capturing the voice of your employees (VoE) is as important as your VoC program. A pulse survey tool enables employees to take a quick, mobile-optimized survey. They are easy to administer and are easy for employees to respond to; they can be used with some frequency (e.g., weekly if things are changing). They can enable anonymous text feedback, facilitate recognizing a coworker, and provide other goodies—all through a mobile app.

For customer experience leaders, this data is vital. When you want to understand why a customer experience problem exists, the first place to look will often be employee experience data. Chances are, once you resolve a hurdle for your employees, you'll also be resolving it for customers.

USER COMMUNITY PLATFORM

Customers can quickly develop a special affinity for a brand or product, and many will want to connect with others like them. "User communities" that bring customers together are becoming very popular. They aren't a fit for every organization, and you'll want to consider what might work for yours.

One option for building or facilitating a user community is to use existing social platforms—e.g., Facebook or LinkedIn. For example, Ecamm is a sophisticated software package that enables Mac users to control live streaming—ideal for vloggers, professors, and others who present remotely. It's a niche product that rapidly took off in 2020; users by the thousands gravitate to a simple Facebook site to ask questions and swap experiences.[5]

The other option is to use a tool to build your own community platform. As mentioned in Chapter 4, Intuit, maker of financial and tax software, has developed a robust community of users accessible directly from their software interface. If you want to know whether that new set of tires on your John Deere tractor should be expensed or amortized—someone in the community will know. Forums are moderated by Intuit employees, and content on the platform is archived and searchable. One fun feature is that users who post and reply are recognized by rankings—provide an answer that becomes an "accepted solution" and you'll be tagged as one of the elite.[6]

Excel in managing change and improvements

Customer experience transformation is characterized by continuous improvement and change. However, as a discipline, CX isn't defined by a single methodology that guides all activities. Far from it. Talk to 10 experienced practitioners and each will each share their own secret sauce—often with great conviction. (Tools and methods are CX geeks' equivalent of politics—don't be surprised by passionate debates.)

So let's simplify this discussion. There are three main categories of activities you'll need to address. (My goal is not to cover methodologies in detail, but to offer recommendations on how to approach this whole area from a leadership perspective.) The three areas are:

Change management. Customer experience initiatives involve guiding the organization through complex and never-ending change. Change management is largely focused on the people aspects of change. It centers around ensuring that employees understand, embrace and successfully adapt to changes. Prosci's ADKAR® Model and John Kotter's Leading Change Model are common approaches. And governance, which we cover in Chapter 8, is an important part of change management. Change management is distinct from and overarching to process improvement and project management.

Change management has always suffered from an identity crisis. IT professionals talk about change management in terms of rolling out new versions of software. Here, we're referring to the people side of change management. Both are necessary and should not be equated.

Process improvement. Your team will need effective methods to guide ongoing diagnosis and improvements to processes. In any CX initiative, process improvements are plentiful, diverse and ongoing. Examples include the ongoing adjustments and improvements to apps, websites, communication, forecasts, quality standards, reporting, knowledge management, and many others.

Bring on the alphabet soup—Lean, DMAIC, Six Sigma, Kaizen and others. Many tools that have been around for years remain indispensable: flow charts, cause and effect diagrams, statistical control charts and others. There's no need to reinvent the wheel. The key as leader is to ensure your team uses a methodology and tools that get things done. As your CX initiatives grow, your process improvement toolkit will expand. It's helpful for CX practitioners to be adaptable—your team is working across functions and often within activities that are already underway.

Project management. Your team will need an approach that keeps projects on track and within budget. Typical examples of CX projects include evaluating and implementing new technology, significant redesign of a cross-functional process, or creating a new CX-oriented workshop curriculum. In many organizations, larger projects are managed by dedicated project managers.

It is helpful to adopt a go-to approach for managing projects. Examples include Project Management Institute® standards and JPACE. The rigor in these methodologies can boost project success and reduce confusion and uncertainty. The one caveat is that one size does not fit all—you'll need to find a balance between too little and too much project management. There's managing and there's doing, and you'll want the right amount of both.

Recommendations

Here are some recommendations that relate to all three areas (change management, process improvement and project management):

- First, ensure your team uses methods that are appropriate to the task at hand. You may want to carve out time to get briefed by your team on the methods being considered. Get their help in making a good call.

- Find a balance between A) allowing anyone in any area to use any tool, and B) mandating a specific approach. A middle ground with a sensible mix of tools is where most land.

- Look for opportunities to develop expertise within your organization. You'll likely have individuals who have the golden combo—they are experienced with tools, understand projects and processes, and are good with people. Hang on to them! Get their help to deepen know-how across teams and activities.

- Different approaches often take root in different areas, and that's not necessarily a bad thing. Some tools are better suited to some activities (e.g., software development teams often use DevOps or agile). My encouragement is to be intentional when deciding if and where to allow different approaches.

- The proof is in the eating of the pudding. Hang on to methods that work, and make adjustments in those areas that chronically get stuck or go off track.

The overall message here is to not to reinvent the wheel. If you have a team of certified project managers, use them. If your organization has previously adopted lean methodologies, take advantage of that experience. When employees struggle to keep up with changes, settling on and using familiar tools can save time, boost confidence, and reserve mind-share for customer-focused work. And remember Nike's slogan ("Just do it!"); time spent ruminating over models is time you're not spending getting closer to your customers.

KEY RECOMMENDATIONS

- Build your dashboards.
- Design processes that support customer experience.
- Leverage the potential of technology.
- Establish essential customer experience tools.
- Excel in managing change and improvements.

Notes

1 PwC (2018) Experience is everything: here's how to get it right, www.pwc.com/us/en/advisory-services/publications/consumer-intelligence-series/pwc-consumer-intelligence-series-customer-experience.pdf (archived at https://perma.cc/M7NA-WATM)

2 Hotjar (2020) Customer Experience Trends and Stats, www.hotjar.com/customer-experience/trends-and-stats/ (archived at https://perma.cc/9XNY-G757)

3 European Business (2017) 140 Years of Innovation: Interview with Paul Stoneham, CEO at Helly Hansen, *European Business*, www.european-business.com/interviews/helly-hansen-as/140-years-of-innovation (archived at https://perma.cc/5KUK-V3AU)

4 Korosec, K (2019) Online used car startup Shift adds another $40M, snags COO in road to IPO, *TechCrunch*, 10 April, https://techcrunch.com/2019/04/10/online-used-car-startup-shift-adds-another-40m-snags-coo-in-road-to-ipo/ (archived at https://perma.cc/SKE8-ZAHQ)

5 Ecamm Live Community, Facebook

6 Nullar, L (2019) Community Rank Structure, *Intuit QuickBooks*, 30 November, https://quickbooks.intuit.com/learn-support/en-us/community-basics/community-rank-structure/00/421738 (archived at https://perma.cc/YE4N-ZL86)

PART FOUR

Inspire and innovate

07

Building a culture
of customer advocacy

I recall a consulting assessment for the service operation of a large utility in the UK. Their new director was concerned that customer ratings were moving in the wrong direction—even though internal metrics suggested things were fine. It didn't take long to find out why this was happening.

The company has a regulatory requirement to meet a service level objective of 80/30, among other service standards. (If you're not familiar with contact centers, that standard means that 80 percent or more of customer inquiries must reach company representatives within 30 seconds.) But I discovered that they had some tricks up their sleeves. If service levels began to drop, one of their "traffic controllers" would electronically place blocks of waiting customers into a holding pattern. This would allow customers just entering the queue to go right to agents. It immediately boosted the percentage of calls answered within 30 seconds. *Voilà*, target met!

As the queue abated and service levels improved (or so it appeared), they would release calls from the holding pattern and allow them to reach employees. In this way, this company could directly control their reported service level results, whatever their staffing levels. Never mind the abysmal wait times for customers unknowingly kept at the back of the line.

I pointed this practice out to their director when we met in her office later that afternoon. "That's cheating. There's really no other way to put it."

She agreed. "Yes, and I'm actually relieved to hear it. I've been here two months. I learned we've been doing that for years now." She continued, "Here's the problem, though. We don't have the resources we need. If I stop that practice, the reports will look much worse—and on my watch."

"Yes, but the reality IS much worse," I commented. "And you need to know what's really happening to lead effectively."

"And how do I explain the big drop in performance to our senior-level team?" she asked.

It was a good question. We talked through the possibilities. An important part of the answer, of course, would be to communicate the change in policy, why it was necessary, and why it would make things seem worse.

"And what's the worst thing that could happen?" she asked herself out loud. "If they listen and understand, great. I'll have the basis for getting the resources I need." She pondered further, "And if they don't listen... and they think I'm doing a bad job... they could fire me, worse case. Then again, this wouldn't be the place to build my career, would it?"

"That's right!" I loved the confidence. "Go for it. Make your case."

Fast-forward many months. I was working on another project, checking messages between meetings. I skimmed a press release that had just arrived, recognizing her name in the title. As I read further, I learned she had won a prestigious leadership award.

When I called her later that week with congratulations, she recounted what had happened.

"Our senior leadership team said they hadn't known what was happening before I joined the company. They were grateful I brought it to their attention. They were 100 percent supportive of me and the changes we needed to make." She continued, "There's more. I learned there were many other ways that we were glossing over performance problems. We had a lot

FIGURE 7.1   Leadership Framework, Chapter 7: Building a culture of customer advocacy

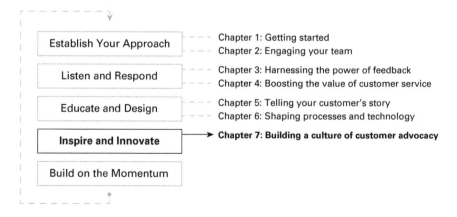

of work to do to rebuild our culture. We did the hard yards. Our team is now flourishing. And, of course, our customers are noting the difference."

"And you took the risk to get things moving in the right direction," I said, "And even won a well-deserved award. Congratulations!"

This utility is an example of an organization making a dramatic change, to a focus truly centered on customers. The next theme in our journey is to inspire and innovate. In this chapter, we'll look at how to build a culture of customer advocacy—within your team, division or, ideally, entire organization. We'll discuss principles and practices that ensure customers are the central focus. And we'll look at the exciting opportunity to encourage and engage with your brand advocates.

Establish a holistic definition of customer advocacy

In recent years, customer advocacy has been a hot topic in marketing and customer service circles. It's getting even more attention following the economic upheavals of 2020/2021. But if you do a search on the term, you'll find two very different definitions.

One is an **internal perspective**: focusing the organization on what's best for customers, creating great customer experiences, advocating for them, and helping them resolve problems. This is the prevailing view in customer service and operations circles.

The other is an **external perspective**: defining customer advocacy in terms of customers who advocate for you, spreading the word about your products, services and brand. This perspective is common among those in marketing and sales.

So, which of the two is correct? Both! I define customer advocacy this way: customer advocacy consists of the actions you take to focus the

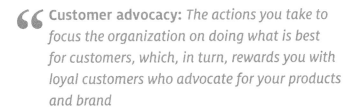

Customer advocacy: *The actions you take to focus the organization on doing what is best for customers, which, in turn, rewards you with loyal customers who advocate for your products and brand*

organization on doing what is best for customers, which, in turn, rewards you with loyal customers who advocate for your products and brand.

Market leaders have a holistic focus on both the internal and external aspects of customer advocacy. Of course, the main focus is on what you and your organization do. You won't have customers who promote your products and brand without identifying and meeting their needs, focusing on what is best for them. But it's increasingly expected (and powerful) to acknowledge and engage appropriately with customers who are fans and promoters.

How organizations approach customer advocacy can be broadly categorized into four quadrants:

Low internal focus, low external focus: the "unaware." These organizations are unaware of or simply ignore the principles of customer advocacy. This is unfortunate for them and for their customers.

High internal focus, low external focus: the "timid." These organizations do a great job of focusing on customer needs. But they miss opportunities to engage with customers who are brand promoters. They also miss opportunities to create additional brand promoters.

Low internal focus, high external focus: the "pretenders." These organizations see customer advocacy in terms of what customers who are brand promoters can do for them. But they haven't done the hard work to earn their loyalty.

FIGURE 7.2   Customer advocacy—internal and external

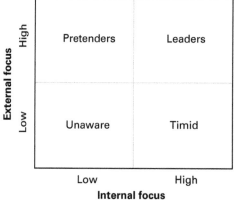

High internal focus, high external focus: the "leaders." These organizations work hard to understand customer needs, and focus on doing what is best for them; they earn a good reputation and brand promotion. They also acknowledge and engage appropriately with customers who are brand advocates.

Customer advocacy at work

Customer advocacy plays out in many different ways, small and big. Here are some examples:

- It can help guide individual interactions. A reservation agent mentions to the customer that, if they'd prefer, the afternoon flight would save $150.

- It can be the catalyst to more involved functional-level initiatives. This could, for example, lead to the decision to provide weekend hours in a customer service department. Or it might be the rationale behind establishing or improving a loyalty program that attracts repeat customers.

- It can also be the driver of dramatic change. When Charles Schwab returned to the financial firm bearing his name years after stepping away, he eliminated some areas of focus the company had invested heavily in. He simplified services and focused on services better aligned with customer needs. Schwab the company roared back and Schwab the person was nicknamed "the great emancipator" by some in the financial sector.[1]

I often get questions around definitions, especially related to what it means to do our part (the internal focus of doing a great job for customers). How is customer advocacy different than managing feedback (Chapter 3)? Or delivering customer service (Chapter 4)? Aren't these just examples of customer advocacy? Well, yes, partially. Do them well and you'll be advocating for customers for sure. Customer advocacy encompasses but *goes well beyond* the realms of managing customer feedback and delivering service.

Much of what we've discussed in the book so far is related to the past and present. What have customers said, and how do you use that feedback (Chapter 3)? What help and support do they need (Chapter 4)? What is their journey through your organization (Chapter 5)? How do you shape processes and technologies to support customer experience (Chapter 6)? Here, we look to the future. How do you build a culture that advocates for customers *before* any of this happens? How do you look ahead, and stay ahead of the game?

There's a scene in the movie *Jobs*, the biographical drama of Steve Jobs' life, where he is shown fiddling with a portable CD player. It's clumsy, heavy, and he struggles to get the CD loaded. The next scene shows him throwing the device into the trash. Of course, the rest of the story—the birth of the iPod, digital music, and how those features would find their way into the iPhone—is now history. Yes, that was vision and innovation, but it was also forward-thinking customer advocacy. Before those devices hit the market, customers weren't asking for them in feedback or service interactions.

My encouragement is to *not* view customer advocacy as a "project" or "initiative" of its own. That's not where we're going here. Picture it instead as an ingredient—it's the secret sauce to add a delightful complement to a recipe you already have. It should be part of, not a replacement for, all the other aspects of customer experience you have going: product development, marketing, communication, customer service, and others.

> ❝ My encouragement is to not *view customer advocacy as a "project" or "initiative" of its own. Picture it instead as an ingredient—it's the secret sauce to add a delightful complement to a recipe you already have.*

Customer advocacy makes your current CX initiatives work better. When established as part of your organization's culture, customer advocacy extends across the entire customer journey, from the first touchpoint and setting expectations, to problem solving and engagement well after the sale. Here are some examples of customer advocacy:

- When a UPS container misses a connection due to a snowstorm, operations managers know about it. Reports are immediately triggered and they look at alternative ways to get deliveries made on time. The system sends notices to customers that there has been an "exception" and what to expect.

- The person cleaning a room at Langham hotel, Chicago, notices that the toilet handle sticks after flushing. He can jiggle it to get it to work—but will the customer know to do that? He submits it for repair. Just one small part of many that add up to operations at the hotel being rated highest in the region.

- A tragic example of NOT advocating for customers was Boeing's approach to the 737 MAX aircraft. So many things had to go wrong to cause the Lion Air and Ethiopian Airlines accidents. The MCAS (maneuvering characteristics augmentation system) produced faulty readings. The planes went into auto correction. Pilots were not briefed on the MCAS system. Training manuals were insufficient. Certification of the aircraft glossed over these issues. Thinking ahead in any area would have avoided problems. Instead, 346 people lost their lives and Boeing is still working to regain trust. All of these areas—product design, manuals, training, certification processes, communication—all are part of customer experience.

How forward thinking is your culture? How embedded is customer advocacy into your organization's way of thinking? Improvement begins by acknowledging the importance of customer advocacy—and encouraging it in words and deeds. You'll also need to empower individuals and cultivate customer advocacy across functions—topics we turn to next.

Empower all employees to be customer advocates

The idea of empowering employees to be customer advocates sounds great to many leaders—in concept. But doing so is easier said than done if barriers are in place. These can include lack of training, misguided performance targets, limited decision-making authority and others. There are five components that are essential to turn developing employees into customer advocates. We've covered many in other parts of the book, so this is a place to take inventory and shore up those that need attention.

Philosophy. One is to have and reinforce a vision that defines what focusing on customers means. In Chapter 1, I mentioned USAA, the insurance and financial company consistently rated among top organizations for customer service. The company operates by the mantra, "We know what it means to serve."[2] That simple statement helps guide every decision. Wyndham's mission is another good example: "Make hotel travel available to all."[3]

Training and coaching. A second essential component is to instill a deep understanding of what customer advocacy is, and how it works, in your organization. This has to be practical for every employee and every job role. For example, address questions such as:

- What does it mean to put yourself in customers' shoes?
- How do you find the best solutions for them?
- To whom do you reach out when resources and assistance from other areas are required?

Training and coaching for every role and in every department should cover these issues. Many organizations focus on customer service areas. But this should apply to every area—operations, marketing, the warehouse, and yes, even areas many don't think of as customer-related such as accounting. Zappos has new employees go through a four-week onboarding process that includes learning about the company's history and values, taking phone calls and bonding with coworkers through games, activities and projects.[4] While that may not seem immediately feasible in your organization, you could do, say, short interactive workshops (they should emphasize involvement and practical application, not lecture). When done well, all enjoy and benefit from them.

Authority. Customer advocacy is about taking action to do what's best for customers. You can't expect employees to be effective unless they have the authority and means to make decisions. For years, Ritz-Carlton has given staff $2,000 of discretion, per employee and per guest, to resolve problems as the employee feels is appropriate. As a senior manager explains, "Sometimes the most delightful 'wow' moments happen in the blink of an eye. If employees are not empowered and need to cross layers of approval, these moments could be lost forever."[5]

Many executives are, at least initially, concerned with this level of empowerment. But I've seen the cost of adjustments go down and customer satisfaction go up when decisions are quick and happen through the employee directly involved. Employees appreciate the trust. They want to make good decisions that are right for customers and the organization. Because they happen on the spot, you are saving resources and aggravation by minimizing involvement of supervisors and managers to sign off on decisions. And customers notice—immediate decisions are impressive. The key is to have clear quality standards and values that lead to good decisions (see Chapter 2).

Goals and objectives. The right goals and objectives—ones that support and encourage customer advocacy—are also essential. When you establish metrics, you'll get what you measure (see discussion in Chapter 2).

Tools and processes. You'll also need supporting tools and processes. This does not necessarily mean you have to have the latest technology, but several capabilities are especially helpful. These include knowing the customer's history and preferences, the means to capture helpful information on customers and issues, and good communication tools for internal collaboration (see Chapter 6 for discussion on technologies).

Customer advocacy doesn't happen on its own. But if you've aligned these five components, you'll be strongly on track to developing employees into customer advocates.

WHAT IS EMPOWERMENT?

Customer-focused companies define empowerment differently than other organizations. It does not mean giving employees the authority to do whatever they want. That's a pretty scary thought for managers, who imagine employees recklessly giving away free products and services.

What empowerment really means is enabling people to provide an exceptional customer experience, and it has three critical components. The first is providing the necessary resources. A frontline employee can't make things right if products are defective, services aren't available, or they lack appropriate tools and equipment.

The second component is defining clear procedures. There needs to be a consistent way of doing things, whether it's producing a product, delivering a service, or solving a problem. This gets everyone on the same page and creates the consistency, reliability, and efficiency that customers want.

The final element is authority. Employees need some leeway to be able to deviate from standard policies and procedures when it truly makes sense to do so. You shouldn't need a manager's approval to quickly fix an obvious problem!

Jeff Toister, Author, The Service Culture Handbook

Develop customer advocacy within and across functions

One of the big payoffs in customer advocacy is in turning customers into brand advocates. That's a powerful outcome, but you have to earn it. Don't forget the real reason you have loyal customers in the first place: serve them well through well-designed products and services, and proactively solve problems for them. Equipping individual employees to be customer advocates is a start, but you ultimately need to get the entire organization on board.

You might be part or much of the way there already. I see organizations define and implement customer advocacy in very different ways. Here are some of the most common, and they represent increasing levels of effectiveness.

At a basic level, some organizations designate specific individuals to be customer advocates who work across functions. Much like patient advocates in a healthcare system, they help customers who have unique or urgent needs navigate the organization's departments and processes. And in a common variation, we've all had experiences where an employee went above and beyond to help. This is not the widespread cultural shift I'm pushing for, but it is a form of customer advocacy. It can be a way to get started quickly, with the goal of more widespread involvement in the future.

Other organizations have established customer advocacy teams or tiers within departments—operations, customer service, or others. In addition to helping customers resolve problems, the team works with the broader organization to identify and prioritize needed improvements to products, services and processes. In some cases, they have the title "customer advocates." This approach is one notch better.

Some organizations have established a central team that oversees customer advocacy across the organization's departments and functions. The head of the team may have a title such as customer advocacy officer. He or she will usually be part of, or report directly to, senior-level management. This sounds a lot like customer experience itself, right? Many customer experience tools and principles may be at work. In a variation, customer advocacy might be seen primarily as a marketing initiative, and in those cases, marketing drives the effort—again, often overlapping with other customer experience

FIGURE 7.3   Advocating for customers—levels of effectiveness

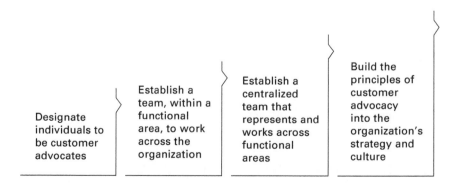

initiatives. If this all sounds confusing, it is. Stop the insanity! You'll (ideally) want to consolidate and unify these efforts under the umbrella of customer experience.

The best approach is to build the principles of customer advocacy into the organization's strategy and culture. There is no need to designate individuals, establish a team or launch an initiative. Customer advocacy works best as a set of values the entire company is on board with.

The all-in approach can be more challenging in larger organizations, but there are standout examples. Schneider Electric, headquartered in Rueil-Malmaison, France, has more than 135,000 employees. One of the ways they've worked the principles of customer advocacy into their culture is through an army of "customer advocates." These individuals are hand-selected across the business and put through intensive training. They become ambassadors equipped to spread CX strategy and principles within their functional groups.[6]

> ❝ The best approach is to build the principles of
> customer advocacy into the organization's strategy
> and culture.

Self-assessment

There are important aspects of equipping your organization to act within and across functions. The following is a self-assessment. Depending on where your organization is in this process, some may seem underdeveloped or out of reach, at least in the near term. Customer advocacy is not all or nothing, and you can begin to put it to use in any environment. But these are the things required to optimize an organization-wide approach.

- **Customer-focused vision.** You have a customer-focused vision. And you truly live it. An example I particularly like, noted in Chapter 1, is REI's mission: "To inspire, educate and outfit for a lifetime of outdoor adventure and stewardship."

- **Customer-focused strategy.** When implemented as an organization, customer advocacy means a different business model, one where you put your customers' interests at the center of decision making. Broadly speaking, product-focused organizations start with products and services and seek customers for them. A customer-focused organization begins with customers in mind and creates solutions for them. As Steve Jobs illustrated when he returned to Apple and turned the company around, this can mean a dramatic shift in priorities.

- **Support of senior leadership.** As you are probably already seeing, the support of senior-level leadership is key. Your leadership facilitates customer advocacy through cross-functional collaboration, establishing priorities, and reinforcing the goals of customer advocacy.

- **Customer-focused goals and metrics.** Wells Fargo ran into a world of trouble from goals and incentives they set around increasing the average number of accounts per client. It was later discovered that employees had opened millions of accounts on behalf of clients who didn't need or want them. In hindsight, better objectives would have centered around areas that boost loyalty, which would have organically led to more business with clients. (This is a culture change Wells Fargo is making—as a long-time customer I can see the difference.)

- **Cross-functional collaboration.** Cross-functional collaboration is essential to customer advocacy—and, more broadly, to customer experience. Look for processes that support collaboration, effective communication tools, and compatible objectives that roll up to an overall focus on customers.

- **Service level agreements (SLAs).** An important ingredient in collaboration is to establish expectations for internal response. You can get as formal and specific as needed. Internal SLAs underscore the importance of responsiveness and ensure that interdepartmental resources are anticipated and available as needed.

- **Engagement with promoters.** Customer advocacy is built on a cultural recognition of the enormous value of customers who are brand advocates. From a practical sense, this involves identifying them, highlighting their successes, and engaging with them as appropriate. This is often a function that resides within marketing. But you'll want to make sure it's a seamless aspect of your overall approach to customer experience. (We'll discuss this in the next section.)

Customer advocacy tends to flourish in organizations with all seven of these characteristics in place. In fact, it becomes a driving force. As Amazon.com founder Jeff Bezos put it, "We see our customers as invited guests to a party, and we are the hosts. It's our job every day to make every important aspect of the customer experience a little bit better."[7] At their heart, these steps are about alignment: aligning your mission, strategy, resources and focus around doing what's best for customers. Together, they create a powerful platform for taking action.

Acknowledge and empower brand advocates

—Staffas brand advocates

Customers are advocates for you when they positively promote your products and brand. Brand advocates, as they are often called, bring much value to your organization. For example:

- Research from Nielsen confirms what we all know intuitively: customer recommendations are far more believable than paid advertisements.[8]
- The most valued source of information about a product or service is people who have actually used the product or service.[9]
- According to Bain, loyalty leaders grow revenues 2.5 times as fast as their industry peers and deliver two to five times the shareholder returns over 10 years.[10]

And yet, studies also suggest that fewer than half of all companies know who their brand advocates are. Far fewer still recognize and engage with them. This is missing a huge opportunity.

Brand advocacy is often organic. A customer buys a coffee—Caffè Nero, Starbucks, Peet's or another favorite. It is warm in his hand, he walks around with the cup and it becomes, perhaps unconsciously, a bit of a status symbol: "I'm on the go, I've got my coffee." The brand, the logo, are seen by others. Hard Rock Cafe t-shirts and "Just Do It" baseball caps promote lifestyles and brands. Convenience chain Wawa owes its rapid growth to the experience they've created around customer input: plentiful gas pumps, an abundance of fresh food, clean facilities. Customers advocate for Wawas to locate in their neighborhoods. Wawa provides a "Submit a Site" page on the website.

Customer advocates are essential to many successful small businesses. Tourists visiting Boston seek out Mike's Pastry in the North End. Pizza lovers know that Pepe's Pizzeria in New Haven, Connecticut, is worth the line around the block. As a traveler, I deeply appreciate how often a resident will tell me, "Oh, you must try this restaurant," when they see me looking at a menu on a door. Or better yet, "If you want seafood, my recommendation is about two blocks down the street."

Customer advocacy creates your most powerful sales force. Also, advocates help you develop and enhance your products and services, make you aware of what competitors are doing, and can be the inspiration for some of your best innovation ideas. Advocacy is the secret ingredient to so many successful businesses, from small eateries to iconic brands. Once those customers give you a try, are satisfied, trust you, and become loyal, they get others excited.

How can you enable and make the most of this opportunity? It's helpful to differentiate passive and active promoters, then tailor your engagement appropriately. Let's look at each.

Acknowledge and encourage passive promoters

Research by BrightLocal finds that over 82 percent of consumers read reviews of local businesses before making purchase decisions. And a majority of consumers trust online reviews of a company's products and services as much as they do personal recommendations.[11] Many customers are willing to promote the brands and products they love. But not everyone is comfortable shouting from the rooftops.

So, customers who are advocates can be broadly categorized as passive and active. Typical characteristics of passive promoters include: they are willing to share (meaning, the product or service is sufficiently important to them); they write testimonials and reviews; they answer questions to reviews or on forums. In other words, passive advocates are open to conversation.

As a rule, it's beneficial to invite dialog. Effective shopping platforms encourage reviews and engagement. When a shopper has a question, the platform should enable others to provide answers. This simple, effective approach helps set expectations and provide relevant information. For example, Tripadvisor connects travelers through the review process. A father planning a surprise trip to San Diego for his family recently asked another reviewer about the details of a basketball court: "Are there basketballs available? Do we need to bring our own?" That led to other questions about dining options and fun things to do in the area. This was customer-to-customer dialog. The hotel received the booking. And the reviewer who helped this customer received a thank you from the hotel, which is turning her into a more active advocate.

It's important to note that not all negative reviews are bad. A low review of a resort with the comment that there's no nightlife activity on the property might be exactly what another traveler is looking for! Don't be afraid of bad reviews. Don't edit them and don't delete them, and consider a genuine, gracious response.

How do you get customers to write reviews? The best approach is to simply ask them. One study found that more than two-thirds of customers will respond to a personal request for a review. The manager of Alce 101, a new farm-to-table restaurant in Solana Beach, California, recently asked me if I'd be willing to write a review (I was raving about the ranch fresh corn chowder). *(Shrug) Sure!*

I bought a pair of ping pong paddles recently from Rivon. An employee named Sorin followed up with an email with links to videos, an ebook and other goodies. He followed up a week later with another email: "How would you rate your purchase so far? Would you be willing to post a picture or video of your winning game?" Between you and me, I haven't even taken the darn things out of the package yet, but I feel like I'm part of a new community.

Passive advocates are having an increasingly important impact on many organizations. They are influential. Their engagement is visible but not intrusive to other customers, and it's believable. You further customer advocacy as you encourage dialog (positive and negative) and engage where that makes sense.

> ❝ *Passive advocates are having an increasingly important impact on many organizations... Their engagement is visible but not intrusive to other customers, and it's believable.*

Recognize and reward active promoters

Active promoters are comparably more demonstrative and outgoing than passive promoters. There are four primary traits found in active advocates: They are eager sharers. They converse with you and appreciate and expect recognition in return. They convince others to try your products or brand. And they will try new or other products from your organization based on your reputation. Active advocates appreciate being part of the action.

There are degrees of how "active" your active advocates are, and they need and expect corresponding levels of engagement from you. As you think through the many possible alternatives for engaging with both passive and active advocates, I encourage you to develop what some refer to as a brand advocate pyramid. Begin with four levels that represent degrees of brand advocacy: new customers, passive advocates, active advocates, and influencers. There are no hard and fast definitions for the categories, but noting a distinction and tailoring your activities for each will put you on a good path.

At the base level, there are the many new customers, some of whom are passive advocates; here, simple connections and recognition go a long way. At the top of the pyramid are those active advocates, much fewer in number,

> ❝ There are degrees of how "active" your active advocates are, and they need and expect corresponding levels of engagement from you.

who are truly influencers. For them, a much more involved level of engagement makes sense, such as VIP or inner circle programs. (You might even consider hiring them. DirecTV found a lead engineer through the thoughtful blogs—both complimentary and critical—that he was posting.)

It's inspiring and helpful to observe organizations that do a great job of engagement. One is LEGO. The mere mention of the company takes many of us back to childhood. Loyal customers save LEGO sets for their kids and grandkids. A big reason the brand remains viable and known across generations is because of how they engage. They have design contests, robotics challenges, and introduce new products around fun stories on social platforms (Facebook and others). They keep advocates engaged and ensure they are part of the company's direction. In fact, input from customers is what drives the development of new kits. (For other examples of engagement, go to YouTube and search for GoPro, Glossier, Red Bull, or Patagonia. See how these organizations engage with customer communities, earning tens of millions of views.)

In a business-to-business example, Google Business Solutions features customer advocates in commercials. They promote their small businesses while showing how Google helped. LexisNexis, a legal and risk management services company, provides opportunities for customers and prospects to connect and exchange ideas. According to executives, these sessions have dramatically reduced sales cycle time and improved sales.

FIGURE 7.4   Brand advocate pyramid

Influencers:
VIP status and inner
circle opportunities

Active brand advocates:
Acknowledgement, active
engagement, rewards

Passive brand advocates:
Acknowledgement and
simple connections

New customers:
Welcome, thank you, introduction
to resources

Your unique brand

When I was growing up, I used to love watching the American sitcom *Happy Days*. (I'd occasionally get in trouble, and knew it was really bad if I got grounded from seeing one of the shows.) I recently had the opportunity at a conference to meet and introduce a childhood hero—Henry Winkler ("the Fonz"). Since *Happy Days*, he's been executive producer of a number of hit series, appeared in numerous movies, and recently won an Emmy for his role in the HBO series, *Barry*.

However you're familiar with Henry Winkler, he brings uniqueness and authenticity to everything he does. As we talked backstage, we shared stories of how things change for all of us, and how new challenges and opportunities come along. He reminded me of advice that my mother used to give me—"just be yourself." It was sound advice then, and it still is. I believe it's good advice for organizations, too.

Motorcycle company Harley-Davidson has incredibly loyal customers. Riders join clubs and wear Harley clothes, and some even have Harley tattoos. Many CEOs and chief marketing officers point to Harley as the holy grail of customer loyalty. They wonder aloud what they can do to be more like Harley. The answer: don't be more like Harley. Be more like you. Connect with your customers in your own way to build excitement that is unique to your brand.

Build brand reputation and momentum

I recall a new restaurant with great food and impeccable service that quickly built a following. Referrals spread rapidly, reviews were positive, and before long, the wait to get in became longer. To customers, this was just confirmation that the restaurant was a great choice. But over time, the food became less predictable, the service less consistent. They became complacent. And the word of mouth that was working for them began to work against them. In less than two years, they were out of business.

Sadly, businesses lose advocates daily. Often, this stems more from neglect than from anything you *do*. There are important principles for maintaining trust and keeping the momentum going. They may and should feel somewhat repetitive to the themes we discussed in building relationships with passive and active brand advocates. That's the point here—keep it going!

- **Keep treating the relationship with respect.** Advocates expect continued excellence in services and products. When something goes wrong, they expect you to make it a priority and fix it. And they expect you can do this without them needing to make a big effort.

- **Continue to express appreciation.** A colleague of mine works with Independence Blue Cross, and often stays at the Sonesta hotel in Philadelphia, near their main offices. I remember her commenting that she was traveling and working over a birthday. She later recounted this story: "I arrived at my hotel room the evening of my birthday. There were banners on the TV and over my bed. The employees had all signed a card for me, and there was a birthday cake for me to enjoy. Imagine my surprise and delight!"

- **Ensure you remain accessible.** Open up a range of channels so that customers can engage in ways that they choose. Promoters like to stay connected, so it's important to maintain a thoughtful presence through social media. Take steps to promote hashtags and facilitate connections. I know of a college student who posted a picture on Instagram in her new Vineyard Vines sweatshirt. "Love it—just in time for spring," she commented and included their hashtag. The company immediately "liked" her post—simple but loyalty-building.

- **Continue to actively listen.** Advocates like to know that their ideas and experiences are important to you. So, check in with them. Get to know their needs and ask them what else they would like. 4th Street Boutique in Rochester, Michigan is an example of a small company that engages with promoters in fun ways. The owner encourages customers to model clothes;

she publishes photos of real customers on Instagram. Followers know what's new, and can dialog on styles and trends. Many posts have a "save it in my size" comment. They feel like they are recognized and part of the fun.

• **Show your support.** Recognize the things your promoters are doing. Congratulate them on their accomplishments, awards, accolades. A LinkedIn post from a brand to congratulate someone for a promotion is deeply appreciated, and it shows you care. E-commerce and retail company L.L. Bean featured a story about Tyler Armstrong, a teenager with the goal to climb the world's Seven Summits. As he works towards his goal, he's raising money for muscular dystrophy research. It's a great story and a perfect complement to L.L. Bean's reputation for quality gear and great service.[12]

• **Be present.** While I don't gravitate to Woody Allen for advice, I believe he got it right when he said 80 percent of success is just showing up. The Boston Marathon is sponsored by large, iconic brands such as Adidas, but also by smaller, local organizations such as the Dana-Farber Cancer Institute. Even the smallest businesses can support advocates by sponsoring community events, promoting concerts, or hosting a table at a business fair.

Your brand advocates trust you. They want that trust to continue. Keep your end of the bargain and you'll be powerfully furthering customer experience.

KEY RECOMMENDATIONS

• Establish a holistic definition of customer advocacy.

• Empower all employees to be customer advocates.

• Develop customer advocacy within and across functions.

• Acknowledge and empower brand advocates.

• Build brand reputation and momentum.

Notes

1 Razeghi, A (2019) Business According to Chuck: The leadership of Charles Schwab, American Management Association, 5 April, www.amanet.org/articles/business-according-to-chuck-the-leadership-of-charles-schwab/ (archived at https://perma.cc/T8MZ-LNE5)

2 www.usaajobs.com/military (archived at https://perma.cc/YXF7-GTW2)

3 Wyndham Hotels & Resorts (2020) Our Awards, https://corporate. wyndhamhotels.com/about-us/our-awards/ (archived at https://perma.cc/ JKR8-BXFK)

4 Christoffersen, T (2020) Memorable onboarding for new hires, the Zappos way, *Zappos*, 28 January, www.zappos.com/about/stories/memorable-onboarding-new-hires (archived at https://perma.cc/66CA-GGSA)

5 Thompson, S (2018) Delivering remarkable experiences is how you win more customers, *Entrepreneur*, 7 June, www.entrepreneur.com/article/313859 (archived at https://perma.cc/A2GH-DKHF)

6 Brown, N (2019) Developing a customer-centric culture, *ICMI*, 12 August, www.icmi.com/resources/2019/developing-a-customer-centric-culture (archived at https://perma.cc/4KWN-QM7P)

7 Goodreads (nd) Jeff Bezos Quotes, www.goodreads.com/quotes/794527-we-see-our-customers-as-invited-guests-to-a-party (archived at https://perma.cc/ VK3D-B4RE)

8 McCaskill, A (2015) Recommendations from friends remain most credible form of advertising; branded websites are the second-highest form, *Nielsen*, 28 September, www.nielsen.com/us/en/press-releases/2015/recommendations-from-friends-remain-most-credible-form-of-advertising/ (archived at https:// perma.cc/C2FZ-LS4S)

9 Baer, J and Lemin, D (2018) Chatter Matters: The 2018 Word of Mouth Report, www.kmosek.com/wp-content/uploads/chatter-matters-research-fall2018.pdf (archived at https://perma.cc/HBK5-VQMV)

10 Markey, R (2019) Are you undervaluing your customers? *Bain and Company*, 16 December, www.bain.com/insights/are-you-undervaluing-your-customers-hbr/ (archived at https://perma.cc/6R2K-D6RL)

11 BrightLocal (2019) Local Consumer Review Survey, www.brightlocal.com/ research/local-consumer-review-survey/ (archived at https://perma.cc/6KAL-M39E)

12 LL Bean Trailblazers: People who inspire us, L.L. Bean

08

Unleashing product
and service innovation

I was first to arrive at the conference room of a new client, and had time to meander the perimeter, coffee in hand. I read their vision and mission, which was posted on one of the walls, and then moved to another to scan history and pictures. Others soon arrived. Each, I learned, had different roles related to customer experience. This was a meeting to kick off a project that would assess the operation and lead to recommendations on opportunities and priorities.

As the dozen or so attendees filed in, we found seats and went through the usual introductions and pleasantries. The senior VP responsible for the project then put a thick report on the table. It was a whopper, bound in a massive three-ring binder. Glances around the room suggested all were familiar with it, and the countenance of the group seemed to drop. "This is one of the reasons you're here," said the VP, looking my way. "Our company paid a lot for this advice, and implementing it has been..."

"Interesting," said someone to her left, to nervous chuckles.

"Trying," offered another, to nods.

"Character building," smiled another, which brought some laughs and helped break a palpable tension.

The report was produced by a consulting firm hired to conduct a strategic assessment encompassing all of the organization's major functions. It provided dozens (I do mean dozens and dozens) of recommendations related to customer experience, purportedly based on "best in class" practices translated into improvement targets. Issues addressed included quality standards, metrics, budget allocations, and many others.

The organization's goal was to improve processes, close gaps, and *innovate*. But the team noted two significant underlying problems. One was that the recommendations were presented in relative isolation. Like moving the dial on a soundboard, the team had discovered that a change in one area would impact others (often moving them in the wrong direction). The second was the lack of an overall roadmap for implementing the recommendations. They were at their wits' end trying to make it all work.

Let me suggest two more problems: first, this kind of benchmarking will never be a good way to innovate. By nature, you're looking to others for a baseline. Someone is already fishing that part of the river. The other problem (and you may have already screamed it out by now): is it even a good idea to emulate others when so many customer experience initiatives supposedly fall short? When surveys show that most customers are not overwhelmingly thrilled? When your organization is unique?

There's a better way forward. In this chapter, we'll look at important principles that drive innovation. Among them: ignore the critics; look for ways to turn products into services and vice versa; and go after waste with a vengeance. We'll also look at governance—yes, it's critical to innovation. But first, let's turn to recommendations on how to tap the enormous creative potential of your employees.

Strive for universal participation in product and service innovation

I once had a chance to meet and talk with the late W. Edwards Deming. Dr. Deming was one of the world's preeminent quality gurus, and author of the

FIGURE 8.1   Leadership Framework, Chapter 8: Unleashing product and service innovation

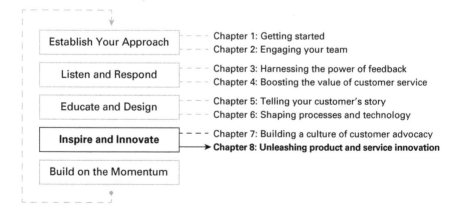

bellwether book, *Out of the Crisis*.[1] This was years ago, and I was young and eager to learn. He lamented the fear he found among employees in many organizations. (One of Deming's famous 14 points for total quality management was to "drive out fear.") I nodded in agreement, but I had little experience to relate to what he was saying. To be candid, it seemed a bit dramatic.

I'm not proud that it took me three decades to fully grasp what he was saying. Countless studies, focus groups and conversations later, I get it. Many employees see innovation as risky. Innovation is a cool word. But at its heart is change—doing things differently.

> 66 *Many employees see innovation as risky.*
> *Innovation is a cool word. But at its heart is*
> *change—doing things differently.*

In some cases, it's shot down subtly. Mention a new idea, and your manager might respond with a question: "Isn't billing due in three days?" Or an unconvincing, "Sounds good, we'll have to take a look." A colleague might chuckle, "We've never done it THAT way." In many cases, the organization's top leadership is 100 percent behind innovation—but they are unaware of how it plays out with managers, supervisors and employees in the ranks.

Innovation, the late Peter Drucker points out in his landmark book, *The Discipline of Innovation*, is the "effort to create purposeful, focused change in an enterprise's economic or social potential." He adds that it's different than other disciplines. You hire accountants for accounting, marketers for marketing, and lawyers for your legal department. But where are your innovators? Your employees! Innovation comes not from genius or exceptional talent, Drucker says, but from a "conscious, purposeful search for innovative opportunities."[2]

Many organizations follow the "you get what you reward" school of thought. To boost innovation, they offer incentives—stock options, cash, or a percentage of the idea's value. In his book, *Drive*, researcher Daniel Pink warns that rewards don't always work the way we think they do: "People use rewards expecting to gain the benefit of increasing another person's motivation and behavior, but in so doing, they often incur the unintentional and hidden cost of undermining that person's intrinsic motivation toward the activity."[3]

According to Pink, many employees value "autonomy" over extrinsic benefits. In this context, autonomy is the freedom for an employee to work on a project of their own choice or approach their work independently. Companies known for a healthy innovation pipeline—Google, 3M, and others—allow employees to spend a percentage of their time on personal projects. Some promote "hackathons" or sponsor innovation tournaments. Here are some recommendations that apply to any organization:

- **Identify and remove barriers to innovation**. This first recommendation is overarching and ongoing: find and remove (as possible) barriers that are getting in the way of innovation. There are many ways to identify barriers. You can, for example, include this question on surveys, work it into informal conversations, or conduct focus groups with employees. Common barriers include no time, not sure what to do with an idea, nothing happened with past ideas, and spending time and focus in this way could jeopardize other performance objectives. You may hear things that are appalling—but the bigger the barriers, the larger the opportunity.

- **Ensure managers see it and track it**. The innovation learning curve is steep—and it's common for managers, especially, to hold tightly to entrenched approaches and processes. You need an environment where new ideas are shared during team meetings, coaching sessions, and informal discussions (as well as through formal channels). You'll need managers to advocate for employees' great ideas, and coach them through the process, rather than passing the idea up through the chain with a perfunctory "thanks." The goal is to see innovation become an inherent part of the employee journey.

- **Establish an effective process for capturing, analyzing and implementing ideas**. You'll need a process and supporting tools for gathering, consolidating, evaluating, and tracking ideas. Without a thoughtful approach, ideas will get lost, become separated from the contributor, or blocked from going further. Should that happen, employees will for a time ask, "What happened to my idea?" They'll then quickly give up: "Why bother?" On the other hand, where employees see ideas firing everywhere, they understand innovation isn't just a "program." It's a critical and expected part of the culture.

- **Tie recognition to strategic opportunities.** If new product innovation is the key to revising an aging product line, be sure to make that connection when acknowledging those contributions. If customer service innovation is a strategic focus, recognize employees who contribute ideas that impact the service channels. Of course, don't limit the generation of ideas across any area. But concentrate brainpower in critical areas and communicate priorities through recognition. This is how programs like 2020's Earthshot Prize, a UK climate change initiative, are so effective— they incentivize and reward innovation, while drawing broad attention to the initiative itself.[4]
- **Tie innovation contributions to the impact they have on customers.** As you capture and tell stories, include the germination of ideas, details about the employees who developed them, and (as possible) examples of customers impacted by the idea. An insurance organization created life-size cut-outs of their quarterly innovation prize winners, along with a summary of the employee's innovative idea or project. After being displayed in the lobby each quarter, they were moved to the main hallways, where they lined the walkways of the organization. This created a visual reminder of the company's priorities.

Innovative organizations work at it. They make innovation a priority. They make removing fear and barriers a priority. If you say you value innovation, employees will notice whether products and services are fresh and evolving. They'll look at practices and processes. They'll pick up on what gets recognized at town halls and team meetings. Are you focusing primarily on productivity targets or the numbers "the street" (investors) is looking for this quarter? Or is innovation getting attention?

INNOVATION SELF-ASSESSMENT

- You routinely identify and remove barriers to innovation.
- Supervisors and managers effectively support innovation.
- You have a process for capturing, analyzing and implementing ideas.
- You provide sufficient time and autonomy for employees to develop ideas.
- You recognize and reward innovation; it is seen as a key part of your culture.
- You share and celebrate innovation stories—and tie them to how customers are impacted.

Ignore the critics and market (when you must)

You know the stories about companies that were successful—until they weren't. Kodak. Blockbuster. Gateway. These were solid companies with high-quality products, operating under established business rules. Then competitors offered something different. Their fates weren't written in the stars. We do, after all, still take pictures, watch movies and use computers.

Establishing clear market differentiation is an important part of driving distinctive customer experiences. And in some cases, it may be a matter of survival. Many times, this means you'll need to go your own way. The alter-

> 66 *Establishing clear market differentiation is an important part of driving distinctive customer experiences. And in some cases, it may be a matter of survival.*

native is to stay in a crowded market where your products are nominally better than your peers, your pricing is just inside the same ballpark, and your service promise is strong but indistinct. It's a crowded, messy and difficult place to be.

The quest to create effortless and different experiences means diverging from the pack and, often, ignoring conventional wisdom. As your competitors and industry head in one direction—toward the new technology, a hot new approach, a better mousetrap—that may be the time to move in a different direction.

Consider the last mattress you purchased. If it was anything like my experience, it was just… fine. We went to a local mattress store and tried five or six mattresses that seemed mostly the same. The salesperson was helpful enough, though she used technical terms like coils, polyfoam, and innerspring. We put the decision off and left feeling confused.

When we returned home, an online search yielded a long list of mattress companies we hadn't known about. Companies like Caspar, Tuft and Needle, Purple, Avocado and Eight had, while we slept, roared into the market with a laser-like focus on a frictionless buying and delivery experience. Their pitch: sleep quality versus mattresses' technical aspects.

These innovators have earned a sizeable share of the mattress market in a relatively short period. Eight mattresses promise to "unlock the best sleep of your life" with personalized cooling systems, automated tools to track your sleep, and a focus on health and wellness. As this was all happening, traditional mattress retailer Mattress Firm was making incremental improvements, but struggling. The company filed for Chapter 11 bankruptcy in 2018 and closed more than 200 stores.

This is the reality of customer experience today. A "safe" strategy is to make existing products and services better based on customer feedback—better discounts, faster delivery, online customization, a "choose your mattress personality" app. The problem is, your competitors are doing those things, too. What some consider safe can be the fastest route to the dustbin of business history.

When you're doing well, your competitors are testing the fences, looking for weakness. Differentiation doesn't necessarily require you to abandon your current products and move your company in an entirely

> ❝ What some consider safe can be the fastest route to the dustbin of business history.

new direction (although you may). It does mean that you will probably have to radically change your and your team's mindset toward innovation and customers.

There are many helpful books and other resources on innovation—a quick search will pull up many of them. But there's no cookie-cutter formula. One thing is for sure, though: organizations that begin with the customer in mind have the best chance of getting it right. This is where customer experience leadership shines. You and your team know what customers want because you are always listening, always learning (Chapter 3). You understand the issues that come up as you deliver service (Chapter 4). You know what goes well in their journeys with your organization and where there are pain points (Chapter 5). You are close to brand advocates and influencers, who help you see into the future (Chapter 7).

In other words, you know it's not a sink and tub customers are after—they want a luxury bathroom that is an escape. They are not enamored of a new computer system—but they're VERY excited about producing compliance reports in a third of the time. They don't want a high-tech medical device—they want worry-free time with their grandkids. Understanding these deeper layers of why (see Figure 8.2) leads to better marketing, product and service innovation and, sometimes, entirely new markets.

FIGURE 8.2   Examples: the deeper "whys" (top to bottom) behind customer needs

Mattress	Sink and bathtub	Computer system
☐ Good night's sleep	☐ Would like a bright, updated bathroom	☐ Improve our reporting system
☐ Need the energy to tackle tasks at work and home	☐ Place to escape-enjoy the jacuzzi tub and listen to music	☐ Producing reports is slow and laborious
☐ I have a child with special needs	☐ I'm taking steps to protect my health from stress	☐ Time to focus on strategic responsibilities

In 2009, the Cleveland Clinic, a respected healthcare provider, was at the top of its game. They were financially secure and nationally ranked for excellent patient outcomes. But the new CEO, Delos "Toby" Cosgrove, sensed a problem when he reviewed the hospital's mid-tier patient and employee satisfaction scores. They were mixed, with many that were just "okay." The good news—the hospital was hitting performance targets. The bad news? Medicare reimbursements were to become increasingly contingent on patient satisfaction scores.

Cosgrove created an "Office of Patient Experience" with C-level support. That core team then began implementing many of the principles we've covered in the book.[5] Customer feedback began highlighting service gaps. Collaborative training sessions brought together team members ranging from the janitorial staff to physicians to administrators. Together, they shaped a plan going forward and began addressing customer friction sources—dirty rooms, unclear caregiver communication, insufficient cross-team collaboration, long wait times, and others. They developed dashboards, feedback mechanisms, and rewards.

In the early days of these efforts, there were naysayers. But Cosgrove flipped the script. He asked his executive team, "What will be the cost [for patients and the organization] of not proceeding?" This dozen-year journey (so far) has earned the Cleveland Clinic a spot in the top quartile of patient satisfaction scores, improved employee engagement scores, and delivered strong boosts to cost performance and productivity.

> ❝ Organizations that begin with the customer in mind have the best chance of getting it right. This is where customer experience leadership shines.

Here's what I find most exciting. They have become so committed and inspired that they launched an event to codify and share what they learn—the annual Patient Experience Empathy & Innovation Summit.[6] The much-anticipated conference provides several major benefits: 1) it holds the Cleveland Clinic accountable to stay on the leading edge; 2) it's a way they give back (and therefore help improve the experiences of millions of additional patients of other organizations); and 3) it is a powerful source of input on leading practices.

Cosgrove is now retired, but the question he leaves us with is key: what do you risk by *not* innovating, not pushing the envelope? The age of safety and stability is over. The new normal in global business is risk and reward, renewal and reinvention.

> **❝ What do you risk by not innovating, not pushing the envelope?**

Turn products into services—and services into products

I'm writing and collaborating on software that is the latest and greatest, made available through subscriptions. It sure beats paying for the bloated packages of the past, which so quickly became obsolete. Some of my collaborators on this book prefer Google, others Office 365. I can jump on Zoom, Teams, Skype, or Google Hangouts. And tools such as Dictionary.com and Grammarly make writing easier than ever (okay, it's still hard for most of us—but easier than it used to be).

In industry after industry, selling products isn't the business model it once was. A colleague stopped by her carrier's store to check out the latest phone. She left with a new phone that will be upgraded annually through a lease program (appearing as a modest addition to her monthly bill). She also went with the protection plan, having paid out of pocket last year for a broken screen.

A young friend who's just getting started in his career excitedly showed me the app that manages his new car (a mid-range model Toyota). He can lock the doors or start the engine from across the globe. There's instant, automatic notifications to emergency services in the event of a serious crash.

Maintenance modules show satisfying green check marks next to brakes, belts, tires and other components; they'll turn yellow in a few thousand miles. Should someone try to take it—good luck, they'll be in a moving tracking device. And if that all seems impressive, computers, phones, handbags, briefcases, and dog tags all provide various combinations of similar services. They are products turned into services.

Consumers are embracing subscriptions. The product-to-service trend is a global force that is changing industries. Services drive a larger share of the world economy today—an estimated 61 percent of the global GDP—than ever before.[7] Many companies are wisely moving from the question, "How can we sell more product?" to "What do our customers really want? How will they use tools such as smartwatches and voice commands? What does the best customer experience look like over the next three, five, or 25 years they use this product?"

EXAMPLES OF PRODUCT/SERVICE COMBINATIONS

- Computer technology company Dell helped turned its once-waning fortunes around through enhanced training, consulting, integration, and other services.

- Luxury retailer Burberry offers the ability to interact with their products using augmented reality tools in Google Search; no special app is required. Want to know how that Burberry bag will look with your winter coat? Shoppers can view a 3D model of select products, projected onto any image or background.[8]

- It used to be a challenge to find help at Home Depot—a wayward cost-cutting initiative that about sank their ship. Today, they offer in-store classes, home renovation services, equipment rentals—and are enjoying record revenue and profits.

- Medical device manufacturer Medtronic and others are creating pacemakers that transmit results (and alerts) directly to physicians. These devices—and the services that are bundled with them—are saving thousands of lives annually.[9]

Furniture juggernaut IKEA purchased startup TaskRabbit in 2017. If you haven't heard of them yet, TaskRabbit (www.taskrabbit.com) is an online marketplace that matches consumers with "Taskers" who can help them move furniture, accept a delivery, mount a TV, or put together that new dresser you bought. This strategic partnership is more than just a marriage of convenience. Yes, it makes it easier to get a dresser home and set up, but IKEA also gains TaskRabbit's insight into how customers live in and use their home spaces. This informs innovation. And a better experience means customers are less likely to be drawn to a lookalike dresser on Instagram.

Services are becoming products, too. I recently had the privilege of introducing Duncan Wardle at an ICMI conference. I enjoyed learning more about his former longtime role as head of innovation and creativity at Disney.[10] Among their many creations, Duncan and his team were behind the Disney MagicBand, which eliminated the need for check-ins and waits in hotels and rides across the park. Okay, it's really a service—an ecosystem of queuing, scheduling and information services. But to customers, it's a cool little wearable product—available in a color of your choice. Use it to hurdle a line, pay for lunch or find your lost kid.

REINVENTING THE DOUBLE RAFTER RANCH

Kirsten and I recently had dinner with our friends Kristen and Bob. They had just returned from an unusual vacation—six days on a cattle drive at the Double Rafter Ranch in Sheridan County, Wyoming. Double Rafter is a 600-head working cattle ranch. Multiple times each summer, the cattle are moved to new pastures as part of the ranch's system of "rotational grazing" (which allows for the recovery and growth of pasture plants).

The ranch owners, Dana and Alice Kerns, have taken this opportunity to offer adventurers a genuine Western experience: gathering and moving cattle in the Bighorn Mountains, eating as American cowboys did more than a century ago, and sleeping under the stars.[11] We were fascinated by the authenticity of the experience Kristen and Bob described. It was no frills, the real deal: hard, dirty, and in the end, thoroughly gratifying work. (I couldn't quite shake the image of Curly in the movie *City Slickers*; if you've seen it, you know what I mean.)

I began to think about the experience they provide in the context of innovation. Making the transition took courage and planning—permits, pricing, marketing, insurance, safety courses—lots of big and small details. In the end, they've turned a product (livestock) into an innovative service and are thriving.

Make eliminating waste a never-ending pursuit

One of the themes driving innovation in customer experience is effort reduction—making things as simple and easy for customers as possible. Increased work-from-home employment options have accelerated customers' hunger for seamless, easy experiences. Many juggle responsibilities at home, work and school. Conveniences that have improved buying, pickup and delivery have forever changed expectations and behavior. As you consider how to reduce effort as part of your customer experience strategy, there are three themes that can point you in the right direction: convenience design, knowledge management, and automation.

Convenience design

I was once part of a large project for Amtrak, which was at the time consolidating service operations. I used my mom, Annie, as a persona in examples. They loved it—and I had a good visual of a real customer as I worked through processes. If only I had been as astute as Jeanne Bliss and used the idea for a book title. Jeanne's brilliant barometer for CX design is the title of her fun and creative book, *Would You Do That to Your Mother?* Long waits, cumbersome processes, stuffy communication, four-hour windows for service? Would you do that to your mother? No way.

Digital experiences aren't always more convenient. A colleague recently moved with his family into a new home. He rented a large truck to help, and sent me this note:

> I was thinking about our conversation on digital and convenience. Just last week I picked up a large truck required for our move. The store had significantly reduced their in-person hours, giving people the 'convenient option' of checking themselves out digitally. First of all, it's not really an option when you require it. Secondly, if you force this path, it better be done well. In this case it was not. The mobile app we were told to download failed miserably, not even showing our order. The web interface was hardly better, forcing us to jump through hoop after hoop. The result was wasted time and great feelings of frustration for myself and my family.

It's usually pretty obvious when organizations change an experience to reduce cost rather than improve the journey. This truck rental company is an example. When you think about effort reduction, digital transformation should play an important role. Consider which parts of the journey might be enhanced if they could be done on a mobile device or similar self-service alternative. Don't cut out other service options simply because an enhanced self-service alternative is introduced. Give your customers choice in how they interact. Then use the powerful tools and processes that are part of your CX initiative to gauge how things are going and where changes are needed.

Poor processes create costs and hassles that are passed on to customers. In *The LEAN Turnaround*, author Art Byrne makes a simple plea: "Reduce waste to maximize customer value."[12] He's right. When you run an efficient and effective organization, your customers win.

Knowledge management

So often the road to reducing effort begins with knowledge. It's surprising to me how few organizations have robust knowledge management processes in place. In many cases, critical pockets of knowledge are bottled up in inflexible systems or as "institutional knowledge" carried around as know-how and memories of employees.

Knowledge that is available and accessible enables smart automation. Self-service systems limited to a departmental or transactional view of the customer are frustrating and ineffective. Those based on comprehensive real-time information consolidated from across functions can be satisfying and very powerful.

Do you have someone who is responsible for the collection and curation of knowledge? Is there a process by which you audit the effectiveness of knowledge and its accessibility? These are important questions as you look for ways to reduce customer effort.

Automation and AI

Let's turn to automation, and the hottest new development since the internet itself—artificial intelligence (AI). Fast-evolving AI technologies are eliciting strong reactions, as did the marquee developments in prior decades—the internet becoming widely accessible through browsers in the 1990s, and the emergence of social media and smart phones in the 2000s. The opportunity to harness AI and other capabilities to bring improvements to customer experience is unprecedented.

Dr. Raj Ramesh (a friend I met through the National Speakers Association) is one of the clearest voices I know on AI and machine learning. He's the author of *AI and You*, a book he originally wrote for his children so they would understand how AI will impact their opportunities and careers.[13] (He also has some terrific tutorial videos, easy to find by searching his name.)

Raj makes a bold prediction about AI and machine learning: "Every aspect of business and every business will be impacted." But he also reminds us that AI is light years away from doing things that humans can do. For example, he says that in the near future:

- AI will drive cars, but won't be able to comfort your daughter after a romantic break-up.
- AI will find answers to customer questions, but won't be able to empathize with a customer who just lost their house in a tornado.
- AI will crunch a lot of data to identify underlying patterns, but won't be able to figure out what kind of data to crunch.

The human brain is infinitely complex. As Raj points out, the real breakthroughs in AI began to emerge when scientists realized they could not replicate human capabilities in one algorithm or system. They instead focused on specific, individual capabilities of the brain—recognizing objects, understanding language, and so forth.

FIGURE 8.3   The subdisciplines of artificial intelligence

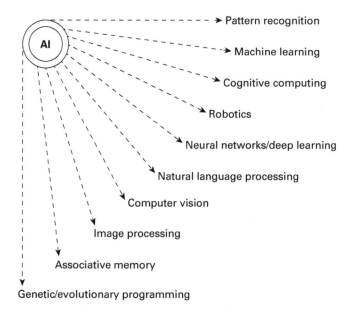

AI has since evolved into an umbrella term with many subdisciplines. They include (in no particular order):

pattern recognition: Being able to recognize patterns in data (e.g., object recognition, pattern analysis in data, and handwritten character recognition)

machine learning: Teaching a computer to learn so that it can respond to similar or new situations—e.g., face recognition, playing games, or predicting the weather

cognitive computing: Problem solving, which considers many facts to come to logical conclusions

robotics: Controlling mechanical objects in a nondeterministic environment through software

neural networks/deep learning: Replicating the neural structure of the human brain—e.g., being able to recognize objects and faces, learn new concepts, and make decisions

natural language processing: Understanding and responding to human language (e.g., automated phone responses and voice-driven commands)

computer vision: Replicating human vision to recognize objects, see color, and identify visual patterns

image processing: Processing digital images (e.g., for object and face recognition)

associative memory: Replicating human memory through association (e.g., recognizing the fragrance of a flower and making an association to the place where it's grown, or to an event that featured flower centerpieces)

genetic/evolutionary programming: Finding improvements through many iterative stages

These subdisciplines are not siloed—they borrow algorithms and techniques from each other. "For example, to train a machine to recognize a known object such as an aircraft, we would likely use algorithms and techniques from image processing, computer vision, pattern recognition, and neural networks," explains Raj. It's helpful to think of AI and its subdisciplines in this way, because you can then begin to find opportunities in the specific processes of customer experience. Examples might include:

- determining the customer's need
- authenticating existing customers

- pulling together relevant information and history
- getting the customer to the right place
- doing calculations and analysis
- capturing data on touchpoints
- sorting and analyzing customer feedback
- and others

As Scott McKain (who wrote the Foreword to this book) puts it, artificial intelligence is not artificial wisdom.[14] AI is real and powerful, but many of the effective applications I'm seeing are not grabbing headlines. They are instead quietly and significantly improving and transforming many aspects of the customer experience. They are helping with what were laborious, manual, or piecemeal processes. And most are working in tandem with employees, enabling technology to do what it does best—and humans to do what we do best.

Consider some examples. LinkedIn's powerful AI capabilities suggest relevant job opportunities and professional connections to users. Sterling National Bank (Yonkers, NY) uses conversational AI as the starting point to inbound interactions, authenticating and enabling many customers to self-serve while escalating the rest (along with relevant data) to agents.[15] Starbucks is developing menu boards customized to make suggestions based on the weather, time of day, popularity, customer's purchase history, and other factors.[16] In each of these cases, machine learning will deepen and expand capabilities over time. In fact, the experiences of many organizations suggest that the key to using AI successfully is to continually experiment, even if initial investments don't bring big returns.[17]

My recommendation is to think both big and small. Both will benefit from your customer journey maps (Chapter 5). Thinking big involves looking across the customer's journey and looking for entire processes that can benefit from AI and other automation capabilities. Checking in to a flight or hotel room, signing into a site or system, or checking out with a shopping cart of items, are examples of entire blocks of steps that can be dramatically simplified for customers.

Thinking small is just as exciting and powerful. I witnessed a team take a unique approach—they wrote specific automation capabilities on separate yellow sticky notes (see list of AI subdisciplines) and granular steps in customer experience processes on purple sticky notes. They then played around with combinations—an exercise that led to a handful of quick wins.

Use governance to propel innovation

The term governance may feel out of place in the context of CX innovation. In fact, creating a governance process may sound limiting, even stifling. I've found the opposite to be true. It's the department-spanning nature of customer experience that is precisely why governance is so important to innovation. Opportunities will impact budgets, the organization chart, and the status quo.

> 66 *The term governance may feel out of place in the context of CX innovation. In fact, creating a governance process may sound limiting, even stifling. I've found the opposite to be true.*

Here's an example. Let's say you provide business systems to corporate customers. Your customer feedback points to dissatisfaction in how you train new customers. You require them to fly their system engineers to your central "university" for a five-day training class. They must pass a grueling test at the end, timed perfectly to cause your visitors to just miss the early evening round of flights home. They do it—they don't have a choice—but lately, sales reps have been discounting travel and training costs because customers balk at the time and expense. And the engineers hate it. In a recent survey, one customer shared that their IT department has been pushing them to change vendors—just so they don't have to send engineers to your training!

Maybe it would be feasible to transition this training and testing to a virtual or self-paced format. The only problem? There's a whole department in the central office dedicated to training—a staff of trainers, beautiful training rooms, new technology, and a team to maintain it all. You could take a heavy-handed approach and force a change to remote alternatives. But how likely is it that the training lead will strongly push back? (My guess: 100 percent.)

Regardless of who "wins," how would a scenario like this contribute to an engaged environment? You can make the case for customer experience, but it's difficult to affect enterprise-wide culture and values when others are resistant to change. This is where governance is so necessary and helpful. A governing body is essential to innovation—it shifts the organization from siloed objectives to the customer journey perspective, and where that leads priorities and decisions.

Governance in practice

In practice, a governance team consists of cross-functional stakeholders who interpret data and ultimately determine priorities. You'll need a strong, influential senior leader to facilitate, influence, and drive action. This person should be both diplomatic and resolute in driving progress. You'll also need a team of senior leaders from across functions. While the group's make-up will vary, it should generally include the CX leader, the senior marketing executive who owns the organization's brand promise, the employee experience lead, the customer service lead, and a leader from IT.

I've seen various names for this group: customer advisory board, customer experience operating committee, CX change coalition, and others. Go with something that fits. Your goal is to create a group with the fortitude to address the deep, systemic cultural divides. To look ahead, to push for and facilitate innovation. In the next chapter, we'll look at a critical enabler to innovation—investments.

KEY RECOMMENDATIONS

- Strive for universal participation in product and service innovation.
- Ignore the critics and market (when you must).
- Turn products into services—and services into products.
- Make eliminating waste a never-ending pursuit.
- Use governance to propel innovation.

Notes

1 Deming, W E (1982) *Out of the Crisis*, MIT Press, United States

2 Drucker, P F (2002) *The Discipline of Innovation*, Harvard Business School Publishing, United States

3 Pink, D H (2009) *Drive: The surprising truth about what motivates us*, Riverhead Books, United States

4 Royal Foundation of the Duke and Duchess of Cambridge (2020) The Earthshot Prize, https://earthshotprize.org/ (archived at https://perma.cc/LQ6D-K87F)

5 Cleveland Clinic (2010) Focus on the Patient Experience, https://my.clevelandclinic.org/ccf/media/files/Patient-Experience/OPE-Newsletter-5-26-10 (archived at https://perma.cc/RF5E-HU6N)

6 Cleveland Clinic (2020) Patient Experience Empathy & Innovation Summit, https://my.clevelandclinic.org/departments/patient-experience/depts/office-patient-experience/summit (archived at https://perma.cc/7CE3-AX9A)

7 Plecher, H (2020) Share of economic sectors in the global gross domestic product from 2008 to 2018, *Statista*, 29 July, www.statista.com/statistics/256563/share-of-economic-sectors-in-the-global-gross-domestic-product/ (archived at https://perma.cc/FX58-CHDY)

8 Wong, E (2020) Burberry ups its marketing game with Augmented Reality, *Techwire Asia*, 10 March, https://techwireasia.com/2020/03/burberry-ups-its-marketing-game-with-augmented-reality/ (archived at https://perma.cc/MM4E-XKQW)

9 Burkhart, C (2020) Smartphones working with pacemakers are saving lives, *ABC12 News*, 18 August, www.abc12.com/2020/08/18/smartphones-working-with-pacemakers-are-saving-lives/ (archived at https://perma.cc/SHD3-LLZ3)

10 Beauford, M (2020) What did you miss at ICMI Contact Centre Expo 2020? *CX Today*, 23 October, www.cxtoday.com/contact-centre/what-did-you-miss-at-icmi-contact-centre-expo-2020/ (archived at https://perma.cc/Y5K9-SU99)

11 Double Rafter Cattle Drives (2020) https://doublerafter.com/ (archived at https://perma.cc/M6VP-7KVC)

12 Byrne, A and Womack, J (2012) *The Lean Turnaround: How business leaders use lean principles to create value and transform their company*, McGraw-Hill Education, United States

13 Ramesh, R (2019) *AI & You: How to think, transform, and thrive in an artificial intelligence future*, Wise Media Group, United States

14 Interview with Scott McKain, 26 October 2020.

15 Deloitte Insights (2020) Reshaping human-machine connections, Insights in Depth: Tech Trends 2020, 15 July 2020, www2.deloitte.com/us/en/insights/multimedia/podcasts/human-experience-platforms.html (archived at https://perma.cc/7XWR-FC4M)

16 La Roche, J (2020) How Starbucks is using AI to fuel its growth, deepen customer relationships, *Yahoo Finance*, 19 December, www.yahoo.com/lifestyle/starbucks-to-use-ai-at-the-drive-thru-151414041.html (archived at https://perma.cc/36GD-4NTC)

17 Knight, W (2020) Companies are rushing to use AI—but few see a payoff, *Wired*, 20 October, www.wired.com/story/companies-rushing-use-ai-few-see-payoff/ (archived at https://perma.cc/836T-NV7T)

PART FIVE

Build on the momentum

09

Rallying support for investments

I am fascinated by aviation. I have a pilot's license, which I earned soon out of college. Though I'm rated to fly only small, single-engine planes, I enjoy them all even if I'm just a passenger (as is most often the case).

I once flew on the Aérospatiale/BAC Concorde, the fastest passenger jet ever built. It was a stroke of luck. I was coming back from the UK and the airline I was scheduled on had a mechanical problem that canceled their flight. They offered to cover much of my fare on the only remaining flight back to the states that night—a Concorde operated by British Airways. The plane exceeds 1,350 mph (almost twice the speed of sound). We took off a couple of hours after dark, and it flies so fast that we caught up with the Sun, which was high in the afternoon sky when we landed in New York. It's the only day I've ever seen a sunrise in the west. (After about 30 years of operation, these planes were taken out of service.)

Before I learned to fly, I wondered how pilots kept track of all the variables involved in flight. I've since learned that there are six flight characteristics that are most important. Be it a biplane from the 1920s, a small modern plane such as those I fly, or the supersonic Concorde, six indicators reflecting each of these dynamics form the primary flight instruments. They are referred to as the "sixpack," and a quick scan of them provides the pilot with information on aircraft speed, altitude, climb/descent, attitude (angle), heading, and turning/banking.

The key—and this is essential—is to interpret them together. For example, the plane you're piloting might be flying very fast. That's generally a good thing. But if you're in a dive, that adds context to why you're moving along so quickly. Speed, turn, climb and the others—they make sense only as they are interpreted together.

FIGURE 9.1   Leadership Framework, Chapter 9: Rallying support for investments

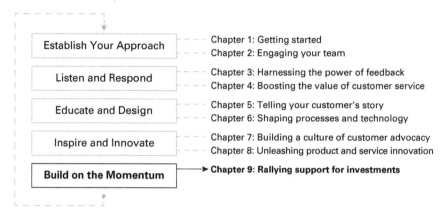

There is a similar principle at work in customer experience.[1] To really understand what is happening, it's important to follow key dynamics within your organization. How are these dynamics contributing to customer experience? Together, they shed light on the results you are seeing now, what's ahead, and areas that need attention.

In this chapter, we begin by identifying six dynamics that, as a leader, you'll want to keep your eye on. We'll then turn to making a case for investments, and look at what should be part of your cost-benefit toolkit. We'll summarize ways to effectively measure returns on the improvements you make to customer experience. Then we'll explore ways to measure the risks and costs of not taking action. Lastly, we'll outline the steps required to make your case for investments and operational budgets.

Keep an eye on six essential dynamics

Just as there are six flight characteristics essential to pilots, there are six dynamics essential to customer experience leaders—we can call them the "CX sixpack." While any one of them could be misleading in isolation, they make a lot of sense when interpreted together. They are: demand, supply, quality, employee engagement, customer satisfaction, and innovation.

You won't find—at least I haven't found—resources on customer experience that emphasize these dynamics (other than in piecemeal fashion). That puzzles me. Especially since these issues tend to force themselves on

FIGURE 9.2   Key dynamics—the "CX sixpack"

conversations during times of upheaval and change. My encouragement to you is to make a practice of following them whether the air is choppy or you're flying along smoothly. Let's summarize what each means.

Demand. What is the demand for your products and services? How is it evolving? For example, the onset of the global pandemic in 2020 significantly impacted the need for products and services. Some organizations—e.g., restaurants, commercial airlines and health clubs—saw demand rapidly decline. Others—e.g., shipping companies, cargo airlines, consumer technology providers and medical systems involved in Covid-19 testing or care—saw demand increase dramatically. Predictions on cases and hospitalization rates became front-page news. Every organization was forced to keep an eye on demand.

No one has a perfect read on the future. However, organizations that get good at forecasting customer demand make far better decisions on priorities and resources. You'll need to monitor demand at a level of detail appropriate for your role. For example, if you're CEO of a retail company, you don't need to track demand for every style of jeans. You do need an overall understanding of demand for your products. If you're, say, a contact center manager, or running a warehouse, you'll need to follow demand at more detailed levels.

Supply. What is the supply of products, services and support necessary to meet evolving customer demand? Again using the Covid-19 pandemic as an example, hospitals had to keep a close eye on the medical professionals, equipment and beds required to meet demand. This involved scaling down or pausing elective procedures and ramping up capacity to meet new demands.

Supply requirements always follow demand. The better a handle you have on demand, the more precise your estimates of supply requirements can be. And as with demand, you'll need information at the level of detail appropriate for your responsibilities.

Quality. The next key dynamic is quality—the quality of products and services being delivered. Quality cannot be assessed in isolation. It will always have some impact on supply and demand. For example, high-quality products and services can reduce demand. The quality of medical care can lead to rapid patient improvement and quicker discharge from the system. Service and support centers that handle issues to completion on first contact reduce repeat work (lessen demand) and free up capacity (improve supply).

In other cases, high-quality products and services stimulate demand. When Apple recently and finally released laptops with improved keyboards, they saw sales jump. A colleague was one of those buyers—she said she could hardly wait to get rid of her laptop with the obnoxious clickety-clackety keyboard. "I can now once again work in coffee shops without getting irritated sideways glances from other customers," she said. (Some improvements benefit your customers AND everyone around them.)

Employee engagement. Employee engagement is another dynamic to follow. Yes, metrics on employee engagement are already part of your dashboard (see Chapter 3). However, you'll also want a more immediate sense of how things are going as circumstances evolve. I worked closely with a number of organizations through the early months of Covid-19. Quick and frequent conversations with employees provided invaluable insight into how things were going. If you build on a strong foundation of employee engagement (see Chapter 2), you'll have more margin when the going gets tough—your employees will stick with you. But that comes with the expectations and responsibility to provide the resources and support they need as quickly as feasible.

Employee engagement impacts other categories—especially supply and quality. There's also a direct correlation between employee engagement and both customer satisfaction and innovation.

Customer satisfaction. Customer satisfaction, reflected in however you measure it—CSAT, NPS, CES or other—is one of the key performance indicators you established in Chapter 3. However, as with employee engagement, it is a dynamic you'll also want to follow more immediately. Especially so in times of significant change to products and services.

Customer satisfaction directly impacts demand. For example, as businesses and schools were forced online, many found Zoom easy to set up and use. They preferred it over alternatives. Zoom quickly became a go-to tool for many. That substantially contributed to demand (a good thing for Zoom), but also led to supply and quality issues as the company ramped up capacity (a challenging thing for Zoom). Security problems in particular dampened customer satisfaction, leading to some customer defections. The company wisely scrambled to fix quality problems—all the while keeping an eye on the other dynamics.

Innovation. Are your products and services evolving to meet needs? Your customers and especially your employees have a good sense of how innovation is going. And you'll see results in other dynamics, particularly customer satisfaction, demand, and employee engagement.

Canlis restaurant in Seattle, recognized as one of the best fine dining restaurants in the world, was forced to close its dining room during Covid-19 lockdowns. While many restaurants struggled to hang on, the Canlis team looked at ways they could innovate. For example, they simplified the menu and created an app enabling customers to schedule delivery of complete meals at convenient times. As they put it on their website, "Fine dining is not what Seattle needs right now. Instead, we're bringing the food to you. We've got this, Seattle." Business quickly bounced back under the new model.

Following these six dynamics will, I predict, become something of an addiction (a positive one). You'll learn to think holistically, to consider the overall impact of changes. Before you get a chance to try me on this, though, I can guess some of the questions you might be asking...

Wait, these aren't CX metrics. In fact, they aren't metrics at all. That's right. They represent major dynamics—categories of activities—involved in delivering products and services. I'm not asking you to measure them precisely, at least not for the purposes of leading customer experience. I am strongly suggesting that you be familiar at a general level with how things are going and how they work together to impact customer experience.

The responsibilities for some of these areas lie with others. Yep. The chief operating officer, those managing supply chains and others likely have direct responsibility for demand forecasts and product inventory. Marketing has a lot to do with creating demand and establishing expectations. The CEO or CFO sign off on investments and budgets. Again, I'm not asking you to manage these areas. But be that voice around the table that helps connect the dots to customer experience.

You left out the most important dynamic—money. Good catch. We'll go there. In flying, there are indicators beyond the sixpack that are also critical. For example, is the engine running? Do you have the fuel you need? Similarly, financial decisions are an important part of the picture and tend to be woven into every major decision. But get fluent with following these six dynamics and you'll begin seeing "ahas." You'll be better informed to make sound decisions.

When working on this chapter, I ran these six dynamics by a friend who is a passionate and knowledgeable advocate for all things customer experience. "I plan to cover them in the chapter on rallying support for investments," I explained. "What are your thoughts?"

He pushed back. "Employee experience and customer satisfaction, sure, but I just don't hear the others discussed often in the context of CX metrics," he said. "And I don't see the tie-in for someone leading CX."

"Try me," I challenged. "Name a company—any company."

He agreed and thought for a moment. He mentioned one of his favorite delis, Jersey Mike's subs (I'm with him on that!). I then prodded for problems that might impact customer experience. Here are some of the possibilities he mentioned (in bold) and how the six dynamics tie-in:

Long waits. Demand and supply. Or maybe innovation (faster payment system, ability to take pre-orders, etc.).

Wrong orders. Quality and/or employee engagement. And maybe long waits and a hurried environment contribute.

Rude employees. Can't say I've ever encountered one at Jersey Mike's. But you'd want to investigate areas such as employee engagement, pressures from demand and supply mismatches, and others.

Subpar quality. Dry bread, limp lettuce... whatever. And you guessed it, look at quality, supply, and other areas.

These are simple examples, but you get the idea. My friend is on board—even saying he'd buy the Jersey Mike's next time we have lunch. The vast majority of customer experience problems stem from one or more of these dynamics. My advice: keep an eye on them and watch your effectiveness as a customer experience leader grow.

The six dynamics we discussed form a powerful backdrop—really *the* backdrop—to interpreting customer experience metrics and investments (see Chapter 3 and Chapter 6 for discussions on metrics and dashboards). There have been so many times I've seen leadership teams go round and round on this or that metric. In many of those cases, thinking about these six dynamics would have quickly pointed to diagnosis and solutions.

Build a cost-benefit toolkit with returns on improvements

Let's turn to cost-benefit considerations that support customer experience. My main recommendation here is to build a "toolkit" (*repertoire* if you prefer) of methods you can use to quantify returns and costs. There are two categories you'll want to include in your financial analysis toolkit: the returns you realize when making improvements to customer experience, and the risk and costs of doing nothing. (I encourage you to read through the calculations—but skimming is fine; they'll be here when you need them.)

FIGURE 9.3   Returns on customer experience improvements

Returns on improvements	Costs of inaction
• Customer loyalty • Brand promotion • Operational improvements • Product and service innovation • Employee engagement	

Let's begin with the good stuff. These are five potential returns that come back to you as you make improvements to customer experience.

Customer loyalty

Loyal customers bring enormous benefits to organizations. There are many ways to measure loyalty: customer lifetime value, wallet share, repurchase ratio, retention rate, customer sentiment, and others. Each has advantages and disadvantages.

Customer lifetime value (CLV) is a common approach. It measures how valuable a customer is to your organization over time rather than just one purchase. CLV can be used in any organization that sells products or services, and in non-profits supported by donors. I like it, especially for its educational value.

This is how I walk teams through CLV. Let's use a relatively simple example—say, you run a small chain of several delis. The first step is to calculate the amount of an average sale. With 300,000 transactions and $4.5 million in annual revenue, you determine your average sale to be $15 (4,500,000/300,000).

Average sale amounts vary widely from one organization to the next. It might be $38,000 for a car, or $4 for ice cream. In large organizations, you may have to work with colleagues to piece together a customer's transactions with different divisions. But the underlying approach is the same.

Second, you determine the frequency of customer purchases by dividing the number of purchases by the number of unique customers. Let's say your deli chain had 10,000 unique customers (this number can come from data on accounts, payment methods, or point of sale information). The purchase frequency would be 30 (300,000/10,000) per year. If you sell big ticket products or services, sales may happen once every few years. And that's fine, you'll still want to look at them over a customer's lifetime of business with you.

Third, estimate customer life expectancy (CLE). Some healthcare providers have members most of their lives. A daycare center might have customers for a few years. Some executives push back here, predicting the business might not even exist in 20 or 30 years. That's fine, make an estimate that's comfortable. Let's go with 10 years for your deli. So, your customer spends an average of $15, she comes in 30 times per year, and she'll be with you an estimated 10 years. Put these figures together to determine Customer Lifetime Revenue. And, wow, over a lifetime, she spends $4,500 ($15 × 30 × 10) with you!

Customer lifetime value subtracts your average direct costs for serving the customer over those years. Let's say they are estimated to be $1,000. That would leave you with a CLV of $3,500 ($4,500 − $1,000).

Most employees are pretty amazed at these numbers. I heard one comment, "Just look at how much is at stake if a customer has a bad experience. Not $15. $3,500 in gross profits!" Yep, that's the thing to remember. I encourage you to use your own numbers. Then, ensure your employees understand the principle at work.

Brand promotion (word of mouth)

The better the customer experience you provide, the more likely you are to create brand advocates who promote for you. Brand advocates drive business to your organization, through word-of-mouth referrals to friends and family, and through posts and reviews.

So, how do you quantify brand promotion? First, you need to know how new customers find you. There are many technology options that can help, from customer management systems to point-of-sale terminals. Get your employees (and systems) in the habit of asking, "Have you shopped here before? How did you hear about us?" Explore ways you can capture that insight, and begin as soon as possible. If you don't have a reliable tracking system, samples of customers can be a good start.

Next, calculate the value of brand promotion by multiplying the number of customers generated through brand promotion by customer lifetime value (CLV—see discussion in prior section). Let's say you estimate that 400 new customers last year came from brand promotion. If CLV is $3,500, the value of brand promotion is $1.4 million (400 × $3,500). The value doesn't stop there. You now have an additional 400 customers who may also promote your brand and create even more customers.

Now, a common objection here is that some of those customers may have found you without a referral. That's a reasonable assumption, so you can discount that number to a level that is comfortable. I encourage you to show where your numbers come from, so your team can make adjustments as you get better data and estimates.

The final step is to estimate the role that good customer experience plays in brand promotion. You might broadly and reasonably assume that any referral is due to customer experience. However, if your product is completely unique, it's possible customers refer others even if other aspects of the experience are just okay. In that case, let's say you attribute half of the value of brand promotion to efforts you're making to improve customer experiences beyond the product itself. That would still be $700,000.

Your brand advocates are generating business for you. Ask your customers to provide reviews. Share this insight with colleagues. And ensure that your organization understands the impact of customer experience on brand promotion.

Operational improvements

Improvements in customer experience often involve improvements to operations—customer service, inventory, shipping, technical support, or others. The range of possibilities is endless. So, let's look here at two different examples, one for a retailer and one for a government agency.

Shoppers with an online retailer were unhappy with the amount of time it took to receive products. The customer service team identified that

25 percent of potential orders were canceled just after shoppers learned the estimated delivery date. With 15,000 abandoned carts and an average purchase amount of $100, the service director estimated that $1.5 million (15,000 × $100) in potential sales were being abandoned annually.

The problem, she discovered, wasn't shipping time, but the time it took to customize products. She and her team worked with others in the organization to simplify and streamline customization options. This work was based on what they were hearing customers really wanted (see how to harness feedback, Chapter 3). They ended up cutting delivery time by two-thirds and, as a result, retaining 70 percent of abandons. By multiplying lost revenue by 70 percent, they found that this added over a million dollars in annual revenue ($1,500,000 × 70% = $1,050,000).

Here's another example of an operational improvement. A governmental agency learned from frontline service employees that constituents (customers) were sharing information in a different way than the system was capturing it. Constituents were also complaining about the need to repeat information. The customer service team worked with IT to redesign the screens and data fields used during interactions. This cut the average time to handle interactions by 3 percent. At an average contact cost of $9, that 3 percent amounted to 27 cents per contact—that sure didn't sound like much. But their perspective changed when they put a pencil to the overall impact. They estimated their savings by multiplying the efficiency percent, by cost per contact, by contact volume. With 620,000 annual contacts, the value of this improvement was $167,400 (3% × $9 × 620,000) per year. That saving of 27 cents exceeded $1 million in less than six years.

Product and service innovation

Product and service innovation is another valuation approach you'll want to have in your toolkit. Here, think about a range of questions: How many non-value-added customer contacts are avoided? How are customer reviews and referrals influenced by improvements? What is the financial impact of new or improved products?

In Chapter 2, I mentioned the consumer products company that discovered problems with the child-proof cap on a line of cleaning products. As customers forced the hard-to-turn cap, they would often damage the spray nozzle. Upon learning this, the customer service team worked with their packaging supplier to redesign the cap. That eliminated those interactions and prevented problems for many future customers. Assume there were

5,900 contacts prevented annually, at $7 each. That's an annual savings of $41,300 (5,900 × $7), without even considering a better product and happier customers.

In a more dramatic example, that same team later prompted the organization to launch a new line of products. Customers had been asking if they had cleaning options for use on materials that were highly valuable—the upholstery and surfaces of antique cars, and others. The customer service team saw the opportunity for a new niche product. That new line eventually contributed over $2 million annually to gross profit.

There's no one report for these benefits. You'll want to focus on specific examples of improvements, and estimates of their value. As you develop this area, you'll be taking the conversation around the value of customer experience to a whole new level.

Employee engagement

Improvements to customer experience almost always boost employee engagement (and vice versa). Three important components to consider when calculating the value of employee engagement are attendance, retention and productivity. Attendance rates can be tracked through your workforce management or payroll systems. Divide the number of hours worked by the number of hours scheduled. If you scheduled employees for 2,000 hours, and they worked 1,900 hours, then your attendance rate would be 95 percent (1,900 / 2,000).

The value of increased attendance can be calculated by multiplying the difference in attendance rates by your scheduled hours and by your average pay rate. Let's say you have a new knowledge management system that has noticeably improved both customer and employee satisfaction. So much so that your annual attendance rate has improved from 83 percent to 87 percent. Assuming 100,000 scheduled hours at an hourly rate of $20, that four-point increase has a value of $80,000 (4% × 100,000 × $20).

Let's look also at retention. Say you had five fewer employees leave this year. Multiply the number of additional positions retained by your staff replacement costs. For example, if your cost to replace an employee is $20,000, then the value of increased engagement is $100,000 (5 × $20,000).

Productivity is another consideration when you improve customer experience. Let's say engaged employees are now spending 30 hours more each year with customers. Multiply these additional hours by the number of employees and their average hourly rate. In this case, 30 hours times 100 employees at $20 is $60,000 (30 × 100 × $20).

Some go further, and put a value on the better and more creative work engaged employees produce. If you have data that demonstrates this, use it. Now, no employee is going to say, "Hey, I'm going to show up more and be more productive if you make improvements." But the research is without dispute: the more engaged employees are, the stronger their contributions will be.

Add risks and costs of inaction to your cost-benefit toolkit

Let's now explore the second category in your cost-benefit toolkit: the risks and costs of inaction. Laura Grimes, co-founder of Harrington Consulting Group, Inc., is a financial aficionado who has worked with me on a number of CX projects. She often reminds leaders: "Use the cost of inaction to spur others in your organization to action. This is particularly important when the benefits of an initiative do not increase revenue."

FIGURE 9.4   Costs of inaction

Returns on improvements	Costs of inaction
	• Customer defection • Brand damage • Recurring problems • Compliance, safety, legal • Employee dissatisfaction

This is the bad stuff. These are five potential costs that you'll incur if you don't make needed improvements.

Customer defection

While attracting customers is important, retaining them is imperative. Fred Reichheld (creator of the Net Promoter Score) finds that increasing customer retention rates by 5 percent increases profits anywhere from 25 to 95 percent. What's the cost of customer attrition?

You may know how many customers you lose; it may even be a report that is readily available. Alternatively, you may have surveys, point of sale data, a loyalty program, or subscription-based services. If no data is available from these or other sources, you can calculate customer attrition this way. First, take the number of customers you have at the end of the year. Subtract from it the number of customers you had at the beginning and new customers. Let's say your credit union ended the year with 160,000 members. You began with 150,000 members and added 20,000 new customers during the year. This shows you lost 10,000 (160,000 – 150,000 – 20,000) customers during the year.

You can then multiply the number of lost customers by customer lifetime value to see the longer-term impact. If the average CLV is $500 then the combined value lost over the lifetime of those customers is $5 million (–10,000 × $500). To get your customer attrition rate, divide the number of lost customers by the beginning number of customers. Here, it's 6.7 percent (10,000/150,000).

Not all customer defections are due to poor customer experiences. Your customers may, for example, move away from the area you serve. You will want to analyze a sample of customer feedback to identify the reasons. Get hard data if at all possible. You can then estimate the portion of defections that you have the opportunity to impact through better customer experiences.

Brand damage

Customers who speak poorly about your products, services or organization represent a considerable business risk. But how do you estimate the cost of bad reviews? After all, rarely will someone reach out and say, "Hey, I thought about buying your product but I heard negative things and went elsewhere."

Google, Yelp, Tripadvisor and other sources can often provide these analytics on reviews. And if you enable customers to leave reviews on your own site, you can track insight yourself as well. Estimate the average number of lost customers from a bad review and multiply it by customer lifetime value. So if CLV is $2,000 and your research estimates you lose 30 customers for each bad review, then your loss from a bad review is $60,000 (30 × $2,000). Use your estimates to discuss how customer experience is important to preventing brand damage.

Recurring problems

I recently traveled to several countries in Asia, with different airlines involved. Somehow, the travel agency that helped me had my passport expiration date wrong by one digit. It resulted in hours of explanations to airlines and immigration officials. And it required lots of additional help from the agency. All from one simple mistake that would have taken 15 seconds to prevent.

Poor service or even simple product glitches cost time and money. Let's look at two examples of how you might quantify these issues. One common problem is with process or technology shortcomings. I recently observed customer service interactions with a government agency. One part of the process required a laborious effort to gather information from multiple systems and then do manual calculations—this routine added two minutes to the average time needed to support those customers. The organization handles around 30,000 interactions per month, and their cost to serve customers is $1 per minute. This routine in question was required about a third (33 percent) of the time. The formula they used is interactions per month × minutes used on the issue × frequency × cost per minute. That revealed the cost of the problem. So, 30,000 monthly contacts × 2 minutes × 33% × $1 per minute amounted to a monthly cost of $20,000 (30,000 × 2 × 33% × $1). That's an annual cost of $240,000 (20,000 × 12). The IT department had done some research and estimated the cost of automating this process (essentially removing the need for that time) would approach a quarter million dollars, $250,000. Too expensive, they assumed. But by looking at the costs of not fixing, they realized they would break even in about a year. Then, the savings would be ongoing.

Another common opportunity is in communication with customers. An organization that provides travel insurance was able to prevent thousands of customer questions per month—often occurring within several weeks of a claim—by better communicating that payments happen within 30 days. An investment company is preventing unnecessary inquiries by better communicating when tax documents will be ready. While these opportunities can seem obvious in hindsight, too many go unaddressed because the cost to handle and cost to fix them come out of different budgets.

> ❝ While these opportunities can seem obvious in hindsight, too many go unaddressed because the cost to handle and cost to fix them come out of different budgets.

Compliance, safety and legal costs

When I think of the role of customer experience in safety and legal issues, several cases come to mind. In one, a food company once distributed a product in Europe that was tainted and making people sick. The problem began at the start of a weekend, and customer inquiries to the company sat unanswered because the customer service department was closed. The problem quickly escalated through the weekend. The company later estimated that the direct legal costs, payouts, and damage to their brand could have funded weekend hours in customer service for over 100 years.

In a more positive example, a utility I'm familiar with has made robust investments that enable them to more quickly detect and address potential risks in their grid—power lines that pose fire risks and other things. They

> ❝ The company later estimated that the direct legal costs, payouts, and damage to their brand could have funded weekend hours in customer service for over 100 years.

estimate that problems avoided have saved them millions of dollars over other utilities that have struggled with tragedies that were unnecessary or became far worse because they went undetected.

Effective customer service in particular is an early warning system for potential regulatory, compliance, safety and legal troubles caused by product defects, security weaknesses, inaccuracies in communication, and dangers to people or property. To calculate risks, you'll need to identify possible scenarios. Consider:

- fines
- lawsuits
- suspensions
- brand damage
- bankruptcy

A provider of baby food products worked with authorities to quickly find and catch a person making counterfeit labels; their first clue was a call from a concerned mother. Something just didn't look right. They later estimated the cost of what could have happened had they not acted quickly, a minimum of $7 million. A life is priceless. But in dollars, that was two and a half times the annual budget of their customer service operations. Talk about a great case for maintaining good customer access.

General Motors has often been cited as a negative business case—but GM is making great strides. Some years ago, the ignition switch in some small cars interfered with airbags. GM's slow response in fixing the problem led to 124 deaths; and while you can't put a value on a life, the direct costs alone exceeded $2.5 billion. Here's the rest of the story. Under new leadership, GM is today harnessing customer service for early detection. These efforts have reduced risk, caught problems early, and helped to create loyal brand advocates.

You can explore the likelihood and magnitude of these costs by looking at what has happened to other organizations and especially by working with your colleagues in finance and marketing to think through possible scenarios. Assessing risks and defining the role of customer experience in detecting and avoiding those risks will save you time, grief and money.

Employee dissatisfaction

Many organizations are unaware of the extent to which poor customer experience contributes to employee dissatisfaction. When I ask employees what gets in the way of great customer experiences, they often cite the following:

- policies
- lack of authority to complete the job
- constant unanticipated change
- conflicting goals
- technology that doesn't work well
- process or communication barriers

Dissatisfied employees over time become increasingly disengaged. Good employees will eventually leave your organization. Apathetic employees may stay but not provide results that are as good. Studies also show they are more likely to avoid work, come in late and not work as effectively.

One of the things I encourage you to calculate is the cost of attrition due to disengagement. When employees leave, ask them why. Those that are leaving because they felt they didn't have growth opportunities are often really telling you they felt limited in improving customer experiences. Multiply new hire cost by the number of employees leaving the organization per year and the disengagement percentage. Let's assume that the cost to hire and train a new employee is $25,000, you replace 100 employees each year and your exit interviews show that 35 percent left due to disengagement. Your disengagement turnover cost is $875,000 ($25,000 × 100 × 35%). That is a lot of money that could be used to keep employees engaged!

Another cost to consider is disengagement while on the clock. McLean & Company, an HR research firm, estimates that a disengaged employee costs $3,400 for every $10,000 in annual wages. Let's use that assumption here. If your employees earn $60,000 annually, then the cost of a disengaged employee is $20,400 (($60,000/$10,000) × $3,400). If you have 100 FTEs, and learn that 14 percent of them are disengaged, the total cost of disengagement exceeds $285,600 ($20,400 × 100 FTEs × 14%). This is money you are already spending. Wouldn't it be much more satisfying to get value from it?

FIGURE 9.5   Complete cost-benefit toolkit

Returns on improvements	Costs of inaction
• Customer loyalty	• Customer defection
• Brand promotion	• Brand damage
• Operational improvements	• Recurring problems
• Product and service innovation	• Compliance, safety, legal
• Employee engagement	• Employee dissatisfaction

You've now rounded out your toolkit. You now have a full complement of tools to assess both the returns on improvements and the costs of inaction.

Make a case for sound investments

Your organization will need to make decisions around both one-off investments and funding for ongoing operations. Let's take a look at each.

Projects and one-off investments

How should you assess potential projects? Say, new technologies that can help you deliver services more effectively or efficiently? Or process improvement efforts? Or maybe a training program that will bring considerable value? Let's look at how to examine the costs and benefits of an initiative so that you can build a business case. These principles apply whether you're a project lead making a case for a specific improvement, or a CEO/CFO assessing potential returns and priorities.

Project phases

There are three phases to projects, and each will have costs you'll need to identify.

FIGURE 9.6   The three primary phases of projects

For the **Evaluation and Acquisition** phase, include all activities required to conduct the assessment and acquisition. For example, if you're considering a new knowledge management (KM) system, you will probably evaluate systems by assessing potential vendors and appraising their solutions. So, research costs should be included, along with other procurement costs.

The **Implementation** phase includes both internal and external costs. Internal costs would summarize the costs to prepare the project, acquire technology, test assumptions, pilot and train employees. External costs include implementation support you expect to need from consultants and solutions providers. For example, the implementation phase of a KM system would include acquiring technology, ensuring change readiness, transitioning information from the old to the new system, and the costs of training your employees.

The **Operation and Maintenance** phase reflects all of the costs required after the project is fully implemented. Increased personnel time should be included along with licensing fees and maintenance. These costs recur every year and may increase annually. The operation and maintenance costs of a knowledge management project include administration time, annual license fees, and maintenance costs.

As you identify costs, I recommend collaborating with your finance team. Sync with their rules or preferences. For example, do they want a three- or five-year business case? This check-in builds support early on. There's nothing quite like having the CFO nodding in agreement while you are making a case.

The costs of inaction (COI) and return on investment (ROI) are two distinct methods for explaining the impact of customer experience. But ROI is usually what is used to assess new projects. So I recommend viewing any impact you can from a positive perspective. For example, instead of computing the cost of employee turnover, calculate the value of increased retention. Being able to state the positive impact supports its inclusion in your ROI assessment. Some high-impact values to review (covered above) include increased customer lifetime value, increased brand promotion, increased customer referral value, savings from operational improvements, and savings from addressing recurring problems.

Let's walk through the three steps necessary to calculate return on investment, again using a knowledge management project as an example. This initiative will provide employees with quick, effective access to the information they need to resolve customer issues quickly, accurately and consistently.

The first step is to calculate the anticipated costs of the project. Year 0 is your investment phase. It includes everything incurred to implement the project. The following years include ongoing operational, labor and maintenance costs. Let's say your knowledge management project requires an initial investment of $135,000. To maintain the knowledge management system, an annual maintenance fee is required which you include on the investment line. You also plan for labor costs expected to support the technology. Both of these costs will increase over time, as shown.

FIGURE 9.7   Anticipated costs

	Year			
Investment	0	1	2	3
Investment	$135,000	$13,500	$14,000	$14,500
Labor	$0	$60,000	$62,000	$64,000
Annual costs	$135,000	$73,500	$76,000	$78,500

The second step is to summarize project benefits. Here, include customer lifetime value, customer referral value, and brand promotion calculations to project the expected increase in gross margin. (Remember that the total revenue growth resulting from improved customer experience is not pure profit. Your finance team can provide a gross margin percentage that you can use to adjust for costs. If it's 70 percent, every dollar of revenue will be reduced to 70 cents to cover the direct costs.) In our example, our first-year gross margin is $154,500 and increases annually.

FIGURE 9.8   Project benefits

Benefits	Year			
	0	1	2	3
Gross margin from additional revenue		$154,500	$159,135	$163,909
Increased productivity		$20,311	$20,819	$21,339
Increased efficiency		$18,109	$18,562	$19,026
Annual contribution		$192,920	$198,516	$204,274
Cumulative contribution	$0	$192,920	$391,436	$595,710

Next, include additional expected benefits. The knowledge management project eliminates some non-productive time, enabling employees to spend more time with customers. Plus, they can complete the same tasks during interactions in less time, which makes them more efficient. I've shown both benefits in the next two lines. (By the way, these benefits will be ongoing and should be included in future budget justifications.) You can then add up the annual value contribution to calculate your cumulative contribution.

In step three, the final step, you compare the cost of the project to the value contributions of the project over time. In this example, the project doesn't contribute value until the technology is implemented. In year two,

FIGURE 9.9   Cumulative benefits

Discounted flow (NPV)	Year			
	0	1	2	3
Discounted costs	$135,000	$71,707	$73,290	$75,681
Discounted contributions	$0	$188,215	$188,950	$189,689
Cumulative flow	– $135,000	– $18,492	$97,168	$211,176

you've recovered your costs and after three years, the project has saved just over $200,000.

Assembling an ROI is a matter of adding costs and contributions line by line, so take one step at a time. Your finance department may have an ROI calculator to help you structure and develop your business case. If not, there are a number of templates you can find through search. By thinking through the costs and benefits of a project, you can make smart decisions about which projects effectively support and advance great customer experiences.

Here are tips for overcoming objections and ensuring your ROI is credible:

- **Avoid numbers that others immediately discount as "inaccurate."** If you don't have access to all of the financial data, pull in someone from finance to help. Realistic values help earn credibility.

- **Don't present returns that sound "too good to be true."** Make sure that you haven't double-counted benefits. If you are looking at incremental revenue generation, you may want to present either customer lifetime value or the value of referred customers, but not both (even though both could realistically occur). If your return on investment starts to feel overly rosy, dial back your assumptions. It's better to have others say, "Hey, I believe we can out-perform those numbers."

- **Be realistic in your costs.** If you think there is a 20 percent chance that you will need consultants to help implement the project, build those costs into the equation. If you come in under budget, all the better.

- **Be realistic about timelines.** Many CX initiatives are not once-and-done projects—they are built out over time with an increasingly powerful impact on customer experience. Be sure to set realistic expectations.

- **Avoid calculation errors.** It is easy to miscalculate and even easier to create an inaccurate formula. It is also difficult to spot your own errors. Ask a colleague to look over your business case and make sure the math works.

- **Be ready to explain where the numbers come from.** Document your assumptions and the logic behind them. You don't need to present them all, nor do you need to walk through every formula. You do need to be able to explain anything that comes up in the discussions.

Secure the operational budgets you need

Let's now summarize important aspects of justifying operational budgets—the funding you'll need quarter after quarter, year after year. Here again, you'll want to use your toolkit. You might use any of the five ways to value returns on good customer experiences, and any of the five types of costs that result from poor experiences. Again, these principles apply whether you're assembling the case or the CEO/CFO approving it.

Which of the 10 methods should you choose? I think of it as a bit like planning a trip—you might use a taxi or rideshare service to meet friends for dinner. A train might be best to get across a region. And a flight will get you to a distant city. Some trips require a combination of methods. In budgeting, it's up to you to choose the methods that "get you there", those that best present your case.

First, facilitate a discussion around the costs of inaction. Let me be very direct: you want your colleagues to be uncomfortable with the costs of inaction. You want them to understand the risks and downside of poor customer experiences. To do this:

- Quantify how brand damage and customer defection decrease revenue, referrals and customer lifetime value.
- Explain the financial impact of ongoing problems, and highlight why those problems exist.
- Remind reviewers that subpar customer experience can lead to disengaged employees, with costs in attendance, turnover and poor customer experiences.
- Quantify the risks of non-compliance, safety and legal problems and estimate the potential costs.

You can then turn to a much brighter topic—the value of effective customer experience. I recommend reviewing the prior year, and the value contributions and cost savings that came out of it. I like to start this part of the discussion with some specific examples of how positive customer experience

> ❝ You want your colleagues to be uncomfortable with the costs of inaction. You want them to understand the risks and downside of poor customer experiences.

contributed to product improvements and more efficient operations. You can then highlight the impact of customer experience on:

- customer lifetime value
- brand promotion
- referred customers
- improved efficiency and productivity
- employee engagement

Be reasonable and conservative in calculating value. Projected values look at the future and often span multiple years (CLV is an example). When comparing these values to a budget, be sure to only include one year of value against the one year of expenditures. If your analysis looks too good to be true, make sure your assumptions make sense. I will usually show in some detail the top one or two projected value contributions, and then mention others more generally.

Finally, remember to keep your eye on the prize. You're not a lawyer trying to win one side of a case. Instead, you want others to understand the true impact of customer experience. The implications of good and bad experiences speak for themselves. You just have to make sure you're including them in the conversation.

Effective budgeting

A budget is simply a summary of proposed or agreed-upon expenditures for a given period of time, for specified purposes. That sounds tame enough. But many leaders see budgeting as tedious, time-consuming and distracting from more important responsibilities. Don't forget: the outcome of this process is the funding you will have to meet your customer experience goals. Here are some insider tips:

- **View budgeting as an opportunity!** Those who picture rows and columns of figures when they think "budget" miss the point. It's really a great opportunity to take a look at your organization's priorities and make decisions that are a win for everyone.

- **Remember that funding supports (NOT drives) your strategy.** In other words, budgeting should happen after you establish a vision and goals, determine the resources you require, and so forth. It's only then that you'll have an understanding of funding requirements. JetBlue built a brand around services and perks that flyers appreciate, like free Wi-Fi. Spirit Airlines is a low-cost competitor that offers bare-bones ticket prices, and then adds fees for everything from bags to seat selection. It's not that one is right and the other wrong; both are differentiating on their customer experience vision. Don't try to determine funding before you know what you want to accomplish.

- **Look for ways to maximize cross-functional resources.** Often, an organization's overall results can be improved by investing more in one area, to the benefit of others. For example, product development functions sometimes provide funding to customer service for improved analysis of customer experiences and input.

- **Ensure that operational budgets are an extension of resource planning.** Planning activities, such as forecasting workload, scheduling and cost analysis, are ongoing. They should take much of the work out of the budget process, because the budget should ultimately be based on the same workload predictions. My recommendation is to not create two disparate sets of planning activities.

- **Highlight investment opportunities.** Identify potential high-leverage investments in sensible areas, such as promising technologies, training and coaching initiatives, and others. The key is to focus on those areas that will yield a healthy return on investment and keep you ahead of customer expectations.

- **Stay focused on results that matter.** Serving 3 million customers or keeping shipments within targets are only the means to an end. Great customer experiences have real impact on business results, including customer satisfaction, profitability, market share, and word of mouth.

- **Ensure the budgeting process is completely honest.** Be realistic and candid about where customer experience has been meeting objectives and where you're missing the mark. Masking resource deficiencies can mask the true picture of the resources you need.

- **Make it human.** Sprinkle the conversation with real examples. "Sara Johnson, a small-business owner in Seattle and a four-year client, is one of our customers. She is concerned that..." And so forth. These examples can help bring discussions to life (see Chapter 5).

The budgeting process is a great opportunity to better understand the value of customer experience. You might even turn an obligation that few enjoy into a positive and enlightening conversation that you and others in your organization look forward to!

KEY RECOMMENDATIONS

- Keep an eye on six essential dynamics.
- Build a cost-benefit toolkit with returns on improvements.
- Add risks and costs of inaction to your cost-benefit toolkit.
- Make a case for sound investments.
- Secure the operational budgets you need.

Notes

1 Cleveland, B (2020) Six dynamics that drive customer experience and your business, *Forbes*, 22 December, www.forbes.com/sites/forbesbusinesscouncil/2020/12/22/six-dynamics-that-drive-customer-experience-and-your-business/?sh=61ac82de77ad (archived at https://perma.cc/5RVA-2K8E)

10

Going from strength to strength

For several years, I facilitated an assessment and management seminar for a financial services company. The training occurred annually, over the course of a week, for new managers. This gave me a view into the organization that was like time-lapse photography. The vice president of the division that initially brought me in was charismatic, with a big personality. The organization produced good results, and he was highly regarded as an effective leader.

When he left for another opportunity, however, the organization struggled. It was a tough season. Eventually, the new vice president who assumed his role found her footing. She had a quiet, understated leadership style. But I could see strength begin to return in the organization under her oversight. She, too, eventually moved to a different position, but the organization's successes continued.

The first VP was an effective leader. He set clear goals, created an engaged environment and enabled the team to achieve high levels of performance. But when he moved on, the organization began to decline. It felt rudderless. The VP who took his place established a culture and practices that enabled the company to continue to thrive without her. That's the difference between good leadership and great leadership.

This chapter is short and (hopefully!) sweet. Our discussion here is more personal and I'll end by asking some questions that only you can answer. I hope you find them helpful. I realize every day how much more there is to learn about leadership. Consider this a safe discussion, but a real one. There's a lot riding on customer experience leaders right now. Our organizations, our customers, our employees are counting on us.

FIGURE 10.1   Leadership Framework, Chapter 10: Going from strength to strength

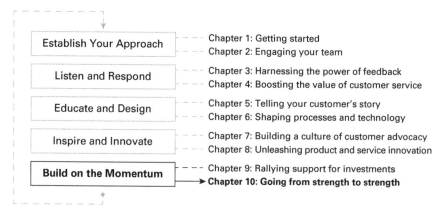

Aspire to the highest level of leadership

A few years ago, I had the opportunity to play golf with four NFL quarterbacks: Drew Brees, Carson Palmer, Chase Daniel and Drew Stanton. It was a charity auction item that included a dozen lucky bidders. I rarely play golf and when I found out I'd won a spot, I had to be talked into going. As it turned out, it was low pressure and a lot of fun (if you know golf, we played scramble).

I was one of the designated cart drivers. My objective was to not tip over and make the evening news. Beyond that, I was fascinated to hear these quarterbacks' inside perspectives. There's all the drama, politics, and pressure of so many other jobs. Some people see their role as trivial because, well, it's just a game—and look at those astronomical salaries! But I see it as the purest form of leadership. Out of millions of us kids who grew up dreaming of someday playing professional quarterback, only 32 get to start each week. If they don't perform, or don't get their teams to perform, they are out.

Drew Brees is a Super Bowl MVP. He holds about as many collegiate and NFL awards and records as it takes me shots to get through a golf game (a lot). But he is hardwired to give others, like staff, receivers, or offensive linesmen, credit for all that goes well, and takes responsibility when things don't go as hoped. That's what Professor Jim Collins refers to as "level 5" leadership.

Jim Collins and his team identified five levels of leadership in the book, *Good to Great*.[1] Though two decades old, it remains among the most influential business books of all time. The top two levels of leaders are both effective. A level 4 leader catalyzes commitment to a vision and rallies support to achieve high levels of performance. Level 5 is a leader who possesses the combination of humility and a ferocious will for the organization to be remarkable; their focus is on leaving the organization stronger. The level 5 leader ensures the organization can sustain success, even without them.

How can you lead an organization strong enough to thrive beyond your time? I believe there are several overarching parts to the answer.

One is to create a focus within your organization that goes beyond what customers need and expect today. Where are those expectations going? What do you need to do now to meet and exceed them? Customer feedback (Chapter 3) is important. But building a culture of customer advocacy (Chapter 7) is, I believe, the secret to staying ahead of the game.

Another part of the answer is to give your employees every opportunity to grow and contribute to their potential. The most influential leaders in your life over the years—teachers, coaches, other leaders—were probably like mine. They believed in you. They most certainly weren't easy on you. They saw your potential, gave you the chance to learn from mistakes and thrive. That's life changing. One of my strong beliefs, which I mentioned in the introduction, is that customer experience must be inviting and inclusive. To make a lasting difference, you'll need everyone's best talents at work. And you have to discover their capabilities, which even they might not know they have.

You'll also need to build strong systems and processes. The enduring successes of companies such as Toyota, Apple, L'Oréal, Amazon and Disney are due in no small part to the systems and processes they put in place. Technology changes rapidly. But an intense focus on keeping things simple for customers has helped guide the investments these organizations make. Many of the same capabilities used by global behemoths are available to the accounting firm of 10 employees, or the dentist's office of five down the street. The secret to powerful technology platforms isn't just in the technology itself—it's the commitment to tame it, the processes required to shape it.

Lastly, I believe the most important part of the answer is humility. Not lack of confidence, but the humility to know you can't do it alone—you need the insight, engagement and contributions of everyone. Collins refers to the mirror and window. Leaders who haven't reached level 5 tend to look through the window to find factors for failure and look in the mirror to take credit when things go well. Level 5 leaders look out of the window to credit others for success and look in the mirror to take responsibility when things don't go as planned.

Use your strategy to guide decisions

I define customer experience strategy as a plan of action designed to support your customer experience vision and achieve your long-term goals. It is my hope that the topics and recommendations we've covered throughout the book have helped you and your team shape an overall approach—a customer experience strategy. I encourage you to create a high-level illustration and description of your strategy. Yours will be unique to you and your organization, but it should include the essential building blocks we've covered.

> **" Customer experience strategy:** *A plan of action designed to support your customer experience vision and achieve your long-term goals.*

Generally speaking, organizations that achieve great results have well-established strategies that are understood and used. Organizations that struggle usually lack clear direction. But there are exceptions. Sometimes I find what seem to be solid customer experience plans in organizations that struggle. They never quite have the impact they should. Is there a secret to ensuring that your customer experience strategy is effective? Here are some practices that can help.

Routinely refer to your strategy. I once worked with an insurance company that was struggling with direction and trying to tackle a multitude of initiatives. I encouraged them to get in the habit of using their customer experience strategy to guide priorities. One leader asked, "Do we pull it out and reference it before each meeting?" As a matter of fact, yes. For a while anyway, you should begin every meeting, every major message to your team with a brief reminder of your vision and strategy.

Do you have to review your strategy in every meeting forever? Of course not. Eventually it becomes so familiar that it organically guides decisions. (In the case of this company, their strategy was too detailed, too cumbersome, to explain easily. Once they streamlined it, it became more usable and inspiring.) You don't have to go into every detail of every step in your approach to customer experience when getting others on board. It's impossible and deflating.

Consider making your strategy widely available. Post it prominently on your intranet or where you'd find internal communication and documentation. Some organizations make their strategies accessible to customers or anybody by posting them prominently. Southwest Airlines, Moo.com, the Cleveland Clinic, Ritz-Carlton, FedEx and others provide significant details of their customer experience strategies—right on their websites. Some (Ritz, Cleveland Clinic, Disney) provide public training programs and conferences that teach the principles they use to outsiders.

Some leaders view strategy as a competitive secret. This is your call, and you can consider what's appropriate given the detail in which your plans cover financial, competitive, or other specifics. But at least make sure your strategy is not a mystery to employees (and frankly, the strategies of the most successful organizations become pretty obvious anyway).

Introduce your strategy to new employees. For many years, Dan Gilbert, founder and chairman of Quicken Loans, helped to personally facilitate an eight-hour orientation for new employees. His goal: ensure that every employee understands the company's values and direction, and how much they matter to its success. His approach helped grow the company into the largest mortgage provider in the United States. Some organizations present strategy to prospective employees as part of the hiring process. This gives them a sense of what they will be part of, and is helpful to both parties in determining whether there's a good fit.

Use your strategy to focus. No organization can be or do all things. There will be trade-offs with time and resources. And this is one of the most important uses of strategy—it can help identify those initiatives and priorities that are most important. When good ideas come along that don't fit into your strategy, you have a choice. You might decide they are not a fit, or you can revisit your strategy. But don't let your customer experience strategy and specific decisions remain in conflict.

Celebrate—often!

Would you go to a game and wait until your team won to cheer? Building an organization (or division, function, or team) that consistently delivers great customer experiences takes focus, work and unwavering commitment. Celebrating progress along the way is essential (and it sure makes things a lot more fun!). Whether the wins are big or small, celebration provides some significant benefits:

- First, it leads to a "mindset of success." Acknowledging the achievement of even small milestones puts success front and center. Success in moving things forward becomes both familiar and a foundation to build on.

- It helps all see the big picture. When you celebrate achievements, it gives you an opportunity to take stock of how your initiative is helping customers, employees and your organization. It's an opportunity to emphasize the overall mission.

- It is a motivator. Employees of all generations want to do work that's worthwhile. Celebrating milestones, especially when done in light of the bigger picture, reinforces the value of their contributions.

- And, celebrating builds team spirit. Having your team take a breather from work to celebrate progress is a great way to build *esprit de corps*, which leads to unity of purpose.

The most successful leaders don't fall prey to the most-cited reasons why celebration doesn't happen. One of them: "I'm sure people know that we're on target." However, your employees are likely working on different aspects of your customer experience initiative. They may not have insight into whether you're on target or not.

Another misconception is, "People will get complacent if they think things are going well." Actually, celebrating wins motivates, and prevents complacency. It's dead wrong to assume you have to achieve a large goal in order to celebrate.

And the biggest (and most understandable) excuse, of course: "There's not enough time." But there's always enough time to do the things that matter most. A central responsibility of leadership is to keep your team engaged and working towards the right goals. There's tremendous power in celebration, especially when it is focused on the positive impact you are

> ❝ There's tremendous power in celebration, especially when it is focused on the positive impact you are having on customers.

having on customers. Remember the game—don't wait for the elusive closing buzzer (does it even exist?). Find ways to celebrate now!

Ask yourself these three questions

As we approach the end of our journey, let me suggest a few questions to ponder:

- What's your drive—deep down and more personally—for your interest in leading customer experience? A strong resonance to the benefits you'll be helping to create is essential to effective leadership.

- What level of commitment can you give this effort? Customer experience doesn't happen overnight and it's not all easy. My encouragement is to take stock of time and priorities before you begin the journey.

- What's the legacy you'd like to leave? One of the most rewarding aspects of leading customer experience is to set your organization on a course that is sustainable, that continues to produce great results. This is a perspective to keep in mind as you work through these recommendations.

Customer experience is big, multifaceted and ongoing. You'll navigate personalities, agendas, setbacks and successes. It demands—and, in turn, heartily rewards—effective leadership.

Determine your next steps

Let me make a few final suggestions on next steps. First, start with some bold thinking around what you *really* want to accomplish. For example, how can a focus on customer experience bring out the best in your organization and employees? How can you position your organization to adapt and thrive in the months and years ahead?

Next, take inventory of gaps in any of the key areas we covered: establishing your vision, engaging your team, harnessing feedback, building a culture of customer advocacy, and others. The complete list of recommendations follows this chapter. You can use it to inventory where you are and areas to develop.

As you think through your approach, you'll want to pull in others. I've found that in many cases—even in organizations that feel they are far behind—there are pockets of activity going really well. There are strengths to build on and things already in motion. Don't scrap what's established and working. Bring them into a bigger, more cohesive approach.

Finally, use the book as an outline for a process that is ongoing. Start with vision, and work through each of the 10 topics covered by the chapters. As you establish your approach, you'll gain traction and be building on wins. Going through all 10 topics (chapters) should then take you back to your vision. A new cycle. You'll be going from strength to strength.

I recently visited the demilitarized zone (DMZ) that separates South and North Korea. The DMZ is accessible only through carefully managed tours, and it was the last place on Earth I expected to get inspiration from on customer experience. Others in our group that day included a KLM pilot from Holland, an endocrinologist from Shanghai, a group of students from France, and a family from Louisiana. We shared a common interest in wanting to better understand a conflict that never officially ended.

Our first stop was the Dora Observatory. From our vista, good weather enabled us to gaze far past a massive North Korean flag in the distance, to a smattering of roads, villages and industrial areas on the horizon. It was heartbreaking to contemplate the poverty, oppression and fear of those to the north. It was impossible not to draw a contrast with the dynamism of high-tech South Korea.

Dorasan Station was the last stop on our tour. It's a railway station that initially opened in 1906, and once linked Seoul and Pyongyang. It was destroyed in the Korean Conflict of the 1950s, but restored in 2013 with help from thousands of private donors. No trains are allowed to pass through; the rebuilding was a labor of love, with hopes that the rail line would once again reunite the North and the South. Some see the eerily empty station as a symbolic reminder of an intractable separation between North Korea and its neighbors.

On a wall inside, there is a map that illustrates a powerful vision. It shows a rail route that connects South Korea to Pyongyang, passing through North Korea to China, Russia, Mongolia, and beyond. Our young Korean guide was matter of fact: "Someday, this station will be part of a system that connects North Korea, China, Russia, and Europe." She added with a smile, "It will open up so much opportunity for so many."

I looked around at the beautiful empty station. With my customer experience hat on, I imagined throngs of people passing through someday, experiencing new connections, opportunities and freedoms. Regardless of your industry or organization, your efforts to improve customer experience will impact the lives of others in ways no one can quite imagine. Ultimately, customer experience goes to the heart of the things we all long for.

While it's been my privilege to be your tour guide, the fact remains that this is *your* journey. It is my hope that this book continues to be a resource as you travel towards your customer experience destination.

KEY RECOMMENDATIONS

- Aspire to the highest level of leadership.
- Use your strategy to guide decisions.
- Celebrate—often!
- Ask yourself these three questions.
- Determine your next steps.

Notes

1 Collins, J (2001) *Good to Great*, Harper Business, United States

WHERE TO NEXT?

There are so many exciting things happening in customer experience! Books, research, statistics, examples—more than would fit comfortably in a book. Keep up to date online at www.bradcleveland.com/resources

RECOMMENDATIONS AT A GLANCE

Establish Your Approach	Getting Started (Chapter 1)	• Establish a broad and accurate understanding of customer experience
		• Use a proven framework to guide your leadership approach
		• Build your core leadership team
		• Define and communicate your vision and goals
		• Avoid common pitfalls
	Engaging Your Team (Chapter 2)	• Build on a foundation of employee engagement
		• Strengthen individual purpose across your organization
		• Ensure your culture supports customer experience objectives
		• Align quality standards with your customer experience vision
		• Initiate and encourage voice of the employee
Listen and Respond	Harnessing the Power of Feedback (Chapter 3)	• Practice seeing things from your customer's perspective
		• Implement an effective tactical approach to managing feedback
		• Execute a voice of the customer strategy that fully leverages feedback
		• Establish and track key performance indicators
		• Assess and improve your feedback initiative
	Boosting the Value of Customer Service (Chapter 4)	• Assess the current value of your organization's customer service
		• Develop services around evolving customer expectations
		• Eliminate the most damaging customer service frustrations
		• Shape a cohesive customer access strategy
		• Build the strategic value of customer service

(continued)

Educate and Design	Telling Your Customer's Story (Chapter 5)	• Develop the art of telling your customer's story • Become a proficient educator • Harness the power of journey mapping • Identify and leverage complementary tools • Keep your eyes on the prize—an engaged organization
	Shaping Processes and Technology (Chapter 6)	• Build your dashboards • Design processes that support customer experience • Leverage the potential of technology • Establish essential customer experience tools • Excel in managing change and improvements
Inspire and Innovate	Building a Culture of Customer Advocacy (Chapter 7)	• Establish a holistic definition of customer advocacy • Empower all employees to be customer advocates • Develop customer advocacy within and across functions • Acknowledge and empower brand advocates • Build brand reputation and momentum
	Unleashing Product and Service Innovation (Chapter 8)	• Strive for universal participation in product and service innovation • Ignore the critics and market (when you must) • Turn products into services—and services into products • Make eliminating waste a never-ending pursuit • Use governance to propel innovation
Build on the Momentum	Rallying Support for Investments (Chapter 9)	• Keep an eye on six essential dynamics • Build a cost-benefit toolkit with returns on improvements • Add risks and costs of inaction to your cost-benefit toolkit • Make a case for sound investments • Secure the operational budgets you need
	Going from Strength to Strength (Chapter 10)	• Aspire to the highest level of leadership • Use your strategy to guide decisions • Celebrate—often! • Ask yourself these three questions • Determine your next steps

LIST OF FIGURES

GLOSSARY

Acronyms and abbreviations

AI	artificial intelligence
CCO	Chief Customer Officer
CEM	customer experience management
CES	customer effort score
CIO	Chief Information Officer
CLE	customer life expectancy
CLV	customer lifetime value
COI	cost of inaction
CRM	customer relationship management
CSAT	customer satisfaction or customer satisfaction score
CX	customer experience
CXO	Chief Experience Officer
ERP	enterprise resource planning
EX	employee experience
FCR	first call resolution or first contact resolution
FTE	full-time equivalent
HR	human resources
IM	instant messaging
IoT	Internet of Things
IP	intellectual property or internet protocol
IT	information technology
IVA	intelligent virtual assistant
IVR	interactive voice response
KM	knowledge management
KPI	key performance indicator
LBS	location-based services
ML	machine learning
MM	multimedia
NPS	net promoter score
QA	quality analysis or quality assurance
ROI	return on investment
RPA	robotic process automation
SaaS	software as a service
SLA	service level agreement
SMS	short messaging service

TTS	text-to-speech
UX	user experience
VoC	voice of the customer
VoE	voice of the employee
VR	virtual reality

Glossary

24/7   Refers to operations that are always open for business (24 hours a day, seven days a week)

analytics   Broadly refers to data analysis and reporting tools that enable the organization to analyze disparate data to uncover correlations and better understand customer trends and business activities. Related terms: speech analytics, text analytics

application service provider (ASP)   An outsourcing business that enables other organizations to access and use technologies or services for a fee

architecture   The basic design of a system. Determines how the components work together, system capacity, ability to upgrade and ability to integrate with other systems

artificial intelligence (AI)   Refers to computer systems simulating human intelligence, i.e., in decision making, speech recognition and translation, and others

attrition (employees)   See turnover

attrition rate (customers)   Also referred to as churn; the percentage of customers lost in a given period of time

augmented reality   See virtual reality

authentication   Verifying the identity of a customer, user, or process

back office   Business applications and functions that are "behind the scenes" to a customer, e.g., accounting, finance, inventory control, fulfillment, productions and human resources. See front office

balanced scorecard   An approach to metrics and management that aims to gives managers a "balanced" view of performance by establishing key performance indicators (KPIs) in different categories. Common categories include customer, employee, financial, and process or organizational maturity.

best practice   Practices or procedures that have been proven across a large number of organizations or situations to be correct or most effective

big data   Large sets of data that can be analyzed using software tools to identify trends, associations, or insight on specific issues or variables. See analytics

brand advocate   See customer advocacy

brick and mortar   The physical facilities in which an organization does business (versus online)

business rules   A phrase used to refer to various software (or manual) controls that manage customer routing, handling and follow-up. At a basic level, business rules are a sequence of "if-then" statements. More advanced business rules can harness AI technologies. Often used interchangeably with workflow

business-to-business (B2B)   Business or interactions between businesses. See business-to-consumer

business-to-consumer (B2C)   Business or interactions between a business and consumers. See business-to-business

C-level   Refers to top-level leadership roles: chief executive officer (CEO), chief financial officer (CFO), chief operating officer (COO), and others. Where the role is established, the chief customer officer (CCO) oversees customer experience management.

career path   Career paths guide individual employee development through structured advancement opportunities within a department or organization. See skill path

change management   Refers to guiding the organization through complex change; generally refers to the people aspect of change. (In technology settings, change management can refer to rolling out new versions of software.)

chatbot   A chat robot that can converse with a human user through text or voice commands. Related term: intelligent virtual assistant (IVA)

chief customer officer (CCO)   Also referred to as chief experience officer (CXO). The senior executive responsible for the design and coordination of all customer-related activities across the organization (CX Accelerator)

chief experience officer (CXO)   See chief customer officer

chief information officer (CIO)   A typical title for the highest-ranking executive responsible for an organization's information systems

cloud-based services   Software or services delivered "on demand" through shared services, over a network

co-browsing   A term that refers to the capability of both an agent and a customer to see web pages simultaneously and share navigation and data entry

coaching model   A structured approach to providing ongoing feedback to individuals on their performance, which helps set the expectations of agents, coaches and managers, and holds coaches accountable

collaboration tools   Broadly refers to technology capabilities that enable a group of users to easily communicate and share information

contact history   The history of a customer's interactions with an organization, generally recorded and stored in a customer information system

control chart   A quality tool that provides information on variation in a process

core values   A set of principles that determine how an organization does business with its employees, customers and vendors (CX Accelerator)

cost/benefit analysis   A term used to describe the process of comparing the value of a potential project with the cost associated with implementing the project

cost center   An accounting term that refers to a department or function in the organization that does not generate profit. Related term: profit center

cost of inaction (COI)   The costs of not moving forward with a project or not making CX improvements. These can include customer defection, brand damage, the costs of recurring problems, employee dissatisfaction and others. See return on investment

cross-sell   A suggestive selling technique that offers additional products or services to current customers. Related term: upsell

customer access strategy   The overall strategy that defines how customers will interact with the organization. According to ICMI, it is "a set of standards, guidelines and processes describing the means by which customers and the organization can interact and are enabled to access the information, services and expertise needed."

customer advocacy   Refers to the actions the organization takes to do what is best for customers, which, in turn, rewards the organization with loyal customers who become advocates (brand advocates) for the organization's products and services

customer effort score (CES)   A customer satisfaction metric based on surveys that ask customers to rate how easy it was to resolve their issues. Typically based on a 7-point scale from "very difficult" to "very easy"

customer engagement   Organizational stakeholders from different functions work together to understand a customer's needs and enhance the business relationship. (CX Accelerator)

customer experience (CX)   Refers to all of the experiences customers have with an organization, including products, services, processes, policies, expectations, and other factors. More specifically, customer experience is: everything a prospect or customer hears about your organization; every interaction they have with your organization and its products and services; and, ultimately, how they feel about your organization. Related terms: customer advocacy, voice of the customer

customer experience management   The overall approach and specific steps involved in managing customer experience

customer experience management (CXM) platform   A technology platform designed to perform core customer experience management tasks, such as funnel voice of the customer data into one system, organize, tag, show trends, establish scores, generate dashboards, illustrate return on investment (ROI), and provide suggestions on CX improvement

customer journey   All interactions and touchpoints a customer has with an organization

customer life expectancy (CLE)   Also called average customer lifespan. The average time (in days, months and years) that a customer is engaged or active with your organization

customer lifetime value (CLV)   Expresses the value of a customer to the organization over the entire probable time period in which the customer will interact with the organization

customer loyalty   Typically defined in terms of the customer's repurchase behavior, intent to purchase again or intent to recommend the organization. See customer advocacy

customer persona   Written and/or graphical representation of the different customer segments a business is serving or targeting (CX Accelerator)

customer relationship management (CRM)   The process of holistically developing the customer's relationship with the organization. It takes into account their history as a customer, the depth and breadth of their business with the organization, and other factors.

customer satisfaction   The level of satisfaction customers have with the organization and the organization's products and services. See customer loyalty

customer satisfaction score (CSAT)   A metric that gauges customer satisfaction, based on variations of the question, "How would you rate your experience?"

customer segmentation   The process of grouping customers based on what you know about them, in order to apply differentiated marketing, relationship and service strategies

customer sentiment   A reflection of how your customers feel about your products, services and organization; analysis of many types of feedback produces a customer sentiment metric you can track

customer success   The methods or approach for ensuring that customers are successful in using a supplier's products or services to achieve their objectives. Often used interchangeably with customer experience; however, the term is typically used in cases where customers are using technology-related products and services. See customer experience

dashboards   Easy-to-comprehend graphical reporting of critical KPIs and supporting metrics

data mining   Generally refers to the use of analytics capabilities to analyze data, e.g., to identify trends and causal factors. Related terms: big data, analytics

digital transformation   Broadly refers to harnessing digital technologies to improve efficiencies and create new or better experiences for customers and employees

employee advocate   An employee who promotes and defends the company they work for, similar to customers who are brand advocates. Related term: customer advocacy

employee engagement   Quantitative representation of the enthusiasm or emotional commitment an employee has to the organization and the work they do

employee experience (EX)   Similar to customer experience, but for employees. How employees perceive their total interactions with an organization. See employee engagement

empowerment   The authority and means provided to employees or customers to make decisions and take action

engagement rate   The percentage of users who see a social media post and take action (e.g., share, reply or click to contact the organization)

escalation   The process by which a customer is transferred to a specialist or a more senior representative (such as a supervisor or manager) to handle or resolve an issue

exit interviews   Interviews with employees who are leaving the company or department, to gain candid and honest insight into why they are leaving, and ways the organization might improve to minimize turnover in the future. Can also refer to exit interviews with customers who have decided to no longer do business with the organization. See stay interviews

finesse standards   Quality standards that measure how something was done. Performance can happen in degrees, and so finesse standards are usually measured on scales (often three- or five-point scales). Related terms: foundation standards, quality standards

first contact resolution (FCR)   The percentage of contacts that are handled to completion in the initial interaction. The customer does not need to contact the organization again, nor does anyone within the organization need to follow up.

focus group   A group of customers or prospects that participate in a discussion to provide candid feedback on the organization and/or its products and services

forecast accuracy   Formulas that measure the accuracy of a forecast against what actually happened

foundation standards   Quality standards that measure whether something was done. Performance can be objectively measured by a yes or no—the employee either did it or did not do it. Related terms: finesse standards, quality standards

freytag's pyramid   The components of an effective story, as identified by Gustav Freytag: exposition, inciting incident, rising action, climax, falling action, and resolution

front office   Generally refers to customer-facing services and technologies. Related term: back office

full-time equivalent (FTE)   A term used in scheduling and budgeting, whereby the number of scheduled hours is divided by the hours in a full work week. The hours of several part-time agents may add up to one FTE.

geotagging   Technology that adds information on location to a photo, video, or social media message. With GPS-enabled smartphones, geotagging has become a core aspect of social media, search, photographs and location-based marketing and customer service.

governance   The framework and team responsible for overseeing customer experience objectives, standards, policies and priorities

hashtag   In social media, a word or phrase preceded by the hash symbol (#), which enables users to find, sort or identify groups or topics (e.g., #customerexperience)

histogram   A type of graph that illustrates the underlying frequency distribution (shape) of a set of continuous data

information technology (IT)   A generic term that refers either to computer and/or communications systems and technologies, or to the profession that develops and manages these systems

intelligent virtual assistant (IVA)   Bots that emulate human conversations, and used in customer service, technical support, marketing and other applications. The term is often used to describe advanced chatbot applications. Related terms: chatbot, robotic process automation

interactive voice response (IVR)   An IVR system responds to caller-entered digits or speech recognition in much the same way that a conventional computer responds to keystrokes or clicks of a mouse. When the IVR is integrated with database applications, customers can interact with databases to check current information (e.g., account balances) and complete transactions (e.g., make transfers between accounts).

Internet of Things (IoT)   Extending internet connectivity to everyday objects such as washing machines, doorbells and refrigerators

job description   An outline of the functions, responsibilities and requirements of a specific job

job role   The function or responsibilities related to a specific position in an organization

journey mapping   A visual tool used by organizations to tell the story of a particular type of customer's experience (CX Accelerator)

key performance indicator (KPI)   A high-level measure of performance. Some interpret KPI as the single most important measure in a department or unit; however, in common usage, most organizations have multiple KPIs. See performance objective

knowledge management (KM)   Developing and leveraging an organization's knowledge resources to prevent the need for employees to "reinvent the wheel"

Lean Six Sigma   A disciplined variation of Six Sigma that focuses on the elimination of different kinds of waste in production and service delivery. Related terms: system of causes, process, Six Sigma

location-based services (LBS)   Services that are appropriate for or customized for specific locations. See geotagging

machine learning (ML)   Technology that enables programs to access and use data on their own, learn for themselves, and improve as they learn

managing customer feedback   The process by which an organization collects, analyzes and acts on customer feedback. This can be tactical (acting on feedback as it happens to solve problems or deliver personalized service) or strategic (collecting and analyzing feedback from many customers over time to look for recurring problems and opportunities).

measure   A fundamental, quantifiable unit, such as length, amount or size. Examples include the time it took to process a claim, and number of customers served. See metric

mention   In social media, tagging a user's or an organization's account name or handle in a message. See sentiment analysis

metric   A quantifiable value that is often composed of more than one measure. For example, average cost of a service interaction incorporates both costs and the number of interactions. See measure

moments of truth   The points in a customer relationship in which a business has the largest opportunity to either increase or decrease customer loyalty (CX Accelerator)

multichannel attribution   In marketing, analytics that aim to understand how customers discover, evaluate, purchase, and use products or services. (Example: seeing a product in a social post, doing a search, visiting the website, making an inquiry through chat or call, and then making a purchase online or in a retail store)

multimedia (MM)   Combining multiple forms of media in the communication of information (e.g., a traditional phone call is "monomedia," and a video call is "multimedia")

natural language processing (NLP)   Enables computers to interpret, analyze and process human language

net present value   A method of determining the attractiveness of investments. The value of future cash flows over the life of an investment, discounted to the present.

net promoter score (NPS)   A specific methodology of gauging customer experience, based on the survey question, "How likely is it that you will recommend us to others?"

omnichannel   Systems and methodologies that integrate multiple channels to create a seamless customer experience regardless of channel. Customers may start out in one channel (e.g., a social platform or website) and move to another (e.g., phone, text, or chat); regardless, an omnichannel approach enables the organization and customers to interact seamlessly across channels.

onboarding   The process of integrating a new employee into an organization and its culture (e.g., through orientation, training, nesting, etc.). May also refer to familiarizing new customers or clients with the organization's products and services

performance objective   Usually stated as a quantifiable goal that must be accomplished within a given set of constraints, a specified period of time, or by a given date (e.g., reduce turnover by 20 percent within one year)

performance standards   See quality standards

performance target   An interim improvement point at a specific point in time, when striving to attain a new level of performance. Related terms: key performance indicator, performance objective

personalization   Customizing services for the needs and characteristics of individual customers, e.g., an IVR greeting that recognizes customersby name, or web pages tailored to individuals

process   A system of causes. See system of causes

process improvement   Methods that guide ongoing diagnosis and improvements to processes

process mapping   A technique used to visually depict how work is done. Shows how events, resources, timelines and other variables interact to achieve a predictable outcome (CX Accelerator)

products or services per customer   A performance measure—a simpler variation of sales per customer—products or services per customer can be a measure of cross-selling effectiveness

profit center   An accounting term that refers to a department or function in the organization that generates profit. Related term: cost center

project management   An approach that keeps projects on track and within budget

propensity to contact   The likelihood or number of times customers contact the organization, typically on an annual basis. Typically, a numerical correlation between total contacts and total customers—for example, 4 would mean customers contact the organization an average of four times per year.

pulse survey   A survey that consists of a short set of questions provided on a recurring basis (e.g., every one or two weeks)

qualitative analysis   Analysis that interprets descriptive data and is usually expressed as text. Related term: quantitative analysis

quality   The attributes or characteristics of a product or service. See quality standards

quality management system   Can refer to either the technologies that enable quality management or, more often, the totality of the technologies, tools and methods an organization uses to manage and improve quality

quality standards   Also referred to as performance standards. The requirements, specifications, guidelines or characteristics established for customer service and customer experience

quantitative analysis   Analysis that focuses on numerical, mathematical or statistical data. Related term: qualitative analysis

relationship survey   Also referred to as enterprise survey, a comprehensive survey that generates feedback on all key elements that can impact customer satisfaction. Questions on a relationship survey are broad and cover issues such as product quality, ease of use, price, service, and others. They are sent at random to a small percentage of customers on a regular basis. See transaction survey

retention   The opposite of turnover; keeping employees in the organization. See turnover

return on investment (ROI)   Strictly speaking, this is the net income or savings divided by the amount invested for a specific initiative. In customer experience, ROI has come to define an overall method of estimating the value of an investment. See cost of inaction (COI)

robotic process automation (RPA)   Software robots that automate tasks previously requiring humans—finding and maintaining information, calculations, transactions, and others. Related term: intelligent virtual assistant (IVA)

root cause   A primary cause of a problem or outcome. Can be identified through root cause analysis. See system of causes

self-service system   Systems that enable customers to access the information or services they need without the help of an employee

sentiment analysis   Tools and methodologies used to assess the nature of a customer's views and feelings about an organization's products, services and brand

service level agreement (SLA)   An agreement—between departments within an organization or between a client organization and an outsourcer—that defines performance objectives and expectations

short messaging service (SMS)   The communications protocol that mobile carriers employ to enable users to send and receive text messages

Six Sigma   A disciplined process that focuses on developing and delivering near-perfect products and services. Sigma is a statistical term that measures process variation. Lean Six Sigma is a variation of Six Sigma that focuses on the elimination of waste. See system of causes

skill path   Skill paths focus on the development of specific skills rather than the progression of positions through the organization. See career path

social listening   The process of finding and assessing what is being said and written in social media about an organization, product, service, person or other topic

social media management   The technologies and processes for managing social media, engaging audiences and measuring results

span of control   The number of individuals a manager supervises. A large span of control means that the manager supervises many people. A small span of control means that he or she supervises fewer people.

speech analytics   Broadly refers to analytics applied to speech content, e.g., to call recordings. Related terms: analytics, text analytics

standard   When related to customer service, standards refer to the requirements, specifications, guidelines or characteristics you establish for customer service and the experiences you want to create.

stay interviews   Intentional conversations with employees on why they stay—what they like about their jobs, the organization's culture and benefits, career development opportunities that could further engage them, etc. See exit interviews

structured feedback Feedback that comes in an organized manner, the result of directly soliciting input from customers or employees. Surveys are a common example. See unstructured feedback

system of causes The variables that are part of a process. Customer experience management is a process or system of causes, made of many processes. See process improvement

text analytics Broadly refers to analytics applied to text content, e.g., email or calls that have been converted into text documents. Related terms: analytics, speech analytics

text messaging Composing and sending short electronic messages between two or more users on mobile or other devices. See short messaging service (SMS)

text-to-speech (TTS) Enables a voice processing system to speak the words in a text field using synthesized—not recorded—speech

thread A string of messages that make up a conversation, common in most forms of online communication

threshold The point at which an action, change or process takes place

time to proficiency The time needed or taken by an individual to acquire the skills and knowledge needed to meet a specified level of performance

touchpoints The different points in which a customer interacts with a business. Touchpoints are commonly used as part of the journey mapping process and typically include three phases—before purchase, during purchase, and after purchase. (CX Accelerator)

transaction survey A survey that is specific to an interaction or service. Designed to tie satisfaction to specific touchpoints. See relationship survey

trend analysis Analysis that examines past and current activity to predict the future

trending A topic that is popular on social media at a given moment

turnover Also referred to as attrition. When a person leaves a job or department. Turnover can be categorized as voluntary (when the employee decides to leave) or involuntary (when management makes the decision for the employee to leave). It can also be categorized as internal (the employee leaves for another position within the organization) or external (the employee leaves for another organization).

unstructured feedback Feedback from customers that is not organized into predefined categories or responses—for example, a social media post. It comes in many forms and tends to be impromptu. See structured feedback

user-generated content Content that is created and published online by the users of a social or collaboration platform

virtual interviewing Systems that ask candidates interview questions and record their answers for viewing at the organization's convenience

virtual reality (VR)   An immersive, interactive, computer-generated experience. It can be similar to the real world—walking through an existing city or visiting a virtual store. Or VR can be otherworldly, e.g., with imaginary landscapes and very different living creatures. With augmented reality (AR), elements of the real world are "augmented" by computer-generated information (for example, virtually trying on different outfits).

voice of the customer (VoC)   Broadly refers to tools, methods and collaboration that capture customers' input and perceptions, seek to understand customer needs and wants, and use captured data to improve products, services and processes. See customer experience, managing customer feedback

voice of the employee (VoE)   Broadly refers to tools, methods and collaboration that capture employees' input and perceptions, seek to understand the employee journey, and use captured data and input to improve the employee experience. See voice of the customer (VoC)

voicebot   A voice-activated chatbot. See chatbot

wallet share   The portion of a customer's total spending in a product category that goes to a company or product. See market share

word of mouth   Refers to customers telling others about their experiences

INDEX

CPSIA information can be obtained
at www.ICGtesting.com
Printed in the USA
JSHW011439201021
19715JS00002B/34

9 781789 666878